# MAYA

## I BOW TO THEE, YOU CANNOT BE OVERCOME

# MAYA

## I BOW TO THEE, YOU CANNOT BE OVERCOME

ACHARYA
PRASHANT

JAICO PUBLISHING HOUSE
Ahmedabad Bangalore Chennai
Delhi Hyderabad Kolkata Mumbai

Published by Jaico Publishing House
A-2 Jash Chambers, 7-A Sir Phirozshah Mehta Road
Fort, Mumbai - 400 001
jaicopub@jaicobooks.com
www.jaicobooks.com



MAYA
ISBN 978-93-93559-41-8

Jaico Print-on-Demand Edition: 2025



Page design and layout by Inosoft Systems, Delhi

Cover design by Gavin Morris

Printed by
Repro India Limited, Mumbai

# Contents

## Only She Can Lead You Into Reality

# About the Author

The Vedas are the oldest religious documents known to man. And Vedanta is the crown jewel, the absolute peak, of the Vedic essence.

The world today finds itself grappling with problems unseen in history. The problems of the past were mostly related to poverty, disease, hunger, illiteracy, lack of knowledge, and lack of technology. In short, the challenge was external, the enemy—whether in the form of a microbe or lack of resources—was outside. It was about man struggling against the tyranny of his external circumstances.

The last hundred years, however, have been different. The spectre of man's conflicts has risen to a very different and difficult theater in this century. The secrets of the atom and the universe have more or less yielded to man's relentless investigation. Poverty, illiteracy, and disease are no more the invincible monsters they used to be. Today, matter is at man's beck and call, and there is ambition to colonize the universe, and even beat death.

It should then sound like the best of times. The current period should be the best one in the history of our species. Far from that, we find ourselves staring at, as we said, a very different dimension of challenge in the inner theater. Having conquered almost everything in the external world, man finds he is a bigger slave to himself today than he ever was. And it's an ignominious slavery—to rule all, only to find that inwardly one is a huge slave of an unknown oppressor.

Man has immense power over his environment today, but is himself controlled by his inner destructive center he has very little knowledge about. Together, these two mean that man's tendency and ability to wreak havoc over his ecosystem is unlimited and unquestioned. Man has only one inner ruler—desire, the ever-sprawling desire to consume and experience more and more happiness. Happiness, that is experienced only to find that it evades all experience.

In this context, Vedanta, as the pure essence of spirituality, becomes more important today than it probably ever was. Vedanta asks the questions: Who is the inner one? What is his nature? What does he desire? Will fulfilment of his desires give him contentment?

As a response to the situations mankind today finds itself in, Acharya Prashant has taken on the solemn project of bringing the essence of Vedanta to the world today. His calling is to bring the pure essence of Vedantic spirituality to all, and apply it to solve today's problems. These problems of today are born out of man's ignorance towards himself, and therefore they can be solved only by sincere self-knowledge.

Acharya Prashant has approached the matter of bringing Vedanta to the public in a two-pronged way. One, he has spoken on scores of Upanishads and Gitas and his comprehensive commentaries are available in the form of video courses and books (solutions.acharyaprashant.org). Two, he addresses the daily mundane problems of people and demonstrates how to solve them in the light of Vedanta. His social media channels are dedicated to hosting tens of thousands of such open QnA sessions.

## A BRIEF BIOGRAPHY

Prashant Tripathi, now popularly known as Acharya Prashant, was born on the auspicious day of Mahashivratri in 1978 at Agra, India. Eldest of three siblings, his father was a bureaucrat and mother a homemaker. His childhood was spent mostly in the state of Uttar Pradesh.

Parents and teachers found him to be a child who could often be quite mischievous, on occasions, and then suddenly, deeply contemplative. Friends too recall him as having an unfathomable temperament, often not really sure whether he was joking or serious. A brilliant student, he consistently topped his class and received the highest commendations and prizes possible to a student. His mother fondly remembers how she was honored several times as 'Mother Queen' for the academic performance of her child. Teachers would say that never before had they seen a student who was as brilliant in Science as in Humanities, as adept in Mathematics as in languages, and as proficient in English as in Hindi. The then Governor of the state felicitated him in a public function for setting a new benchmark in the Board examinations, and for being an NTSE scholar.

The prodigy was a voracious reader since he was five years old. His father's extensive home library consisted of some of the world's best literature, including spiritual texts like the Upanishads. For long hours, the child would be tucked away in the most silent corners of the house, immersed in stuff that was meant to be understood only by men of advanced age and maturity. Lost in reading, he would skip meals and sleep. Before he had turned ten, Prashant had read almost everything in the father's collection and was asking for more. The first signs of the mystical appeared when he started composing poetry at the age of eleven. His poems were imbued with shades of the mysterious and were asking questions that most grown-ups could not grasp.

At the age of fifteen, after being in the city of Lucknow for many years, he found himself in Ghaziabad near Delhi, owing to his father's transferable job. The particular age and the change of city accelerated the process that had already taken deep roots. He took to waking at night, and besides studying, would often be staring silently at the night sky. His poems grew in depth, a lot of them devoted to the night and the moon. Rather than academics, his attention started flowing increasingly towards the mystical.

He nevertheless continued to do well academically and gained admission to the prestigious Indian Institute of Technology, Delhi. His years at IIT were full of exploration of the world, deep involvement in student politics, and shining as a debater and an actor in nationwide events and competitions. He was a vibrant figure on the campus, a dependable student leader, and a soulful performer on the stage. He would consistently win debate and extempore speech competitions in which participants from across the country would compete, and would also win prizes for directing and acting in meaningful plays. In one of the plays, he got the 'Best Actor Award' for a performance in which he did not utter a word and moved not a single step.

He had been sensing since long that there was something fundamentally amiss in the way most people perceive the world, the way our minds are conditioned to operate, and hence something is distorted in the way the relationships between people are, the way the worldly institutions are designed, the way our societies function—basically the very way we live. He had started seeing that incomplete perception was at the root of human suffering. He was deeply disturbed by man's ignorance and cultivated inferiority, the evils of poverty, the evils of consumption, violence towards man, animals, and environment, and exploitation based on narrow ideology and self-interest. His entire being was raring to challenge the all-pervasive suffering, and as a young man, he guessed that the Indian Civil Services or the Management route might be an apt one to take.

He gained admission to the Indian Civil Services and the Indian Institute of Management (IIM), Ahmedabad in the same year. However, because the service allotted to him based on his rank was not the Indian Administrative Services—the service that he had wanted, and because he could already see that the government was not the best place where revolutionary changes could be brought about, he opted to go to IIM.

The two years at IIM were obviously rich in the academic content he absorbed. But he was not the one who would confine himself to slogging for grades and placements, as is the norm in these coveted institutions. He would regularly spend time teaching kids at an NGO that operated in a slum close to Gandhi Ashram, and would also teach Mathematics to graduates to earn to spend at the NGO. Besides, his angst at human ignorance expressed itself through theater. He took up plays like 'Khamosh, adalat jaari hai', 'Rhinoceros', 'Pagla Ghoda', and 'The Night of January 16th' and directed them, besides acting in them. At one point, he was directing two parallel plays. The plays were performed in the IIM auditorium to packed audiences from within and outside the city. In the profit-centered and self-interest driven atmosphere of the campus, he had found himself an outsider. These existentialist and rebellious plays helped him vent out his anguish, and also prepared him for the bigger stage ahead.

The next few years were spent, as he puts it, in the wilderness. He describes this period as one of particular sorrow, longing and search. Looking for a piece of sanity in the corporate world, he kept switching jobs and industries. To gain composure, he would take time off and be away from the city and work. It was increasingly becoming clear to him that what he wanted to do, and what was crying out to be expressed through him, could not happen through any traditional route. His reading and resolve intensified, and he designed a leadership course for post-graduates and experienced professionals, based on wisdom and spiritual literature. The course was floated at some reputed institutions, and he would sometimes be teaching students elder than himself in age. The course was a success, and the way started becoming clearer to him.

At the age of twenty-eight, he bid goodbye to corporate life and founded Advait Life-Education for 'creation of a new humanity through intelligent spirituality'. The method was to bring a deep transformation in human consciousness. The initial audience chosen was college students who were offered self-development courses. Wisdom from ancient literature was taken to students in the form of simplified texts and engaging activities.

While the work of Advait was great and gained appreciation from all and sundry, there were great challenges as well. The social and academic system had conditioned students to study to just clear examinations and to have a degree to secure jobs. The self-development education, the education of the Beyond, the life-education that Advait was attempting to bring to the students was so new and so different from everything that they had ever read or experienced that it would often lead to indifference towards Advait's courses, and sometimes even hostility from the system. Often, even the management body of the colleges and the parents of the students would totally fail to grasp the utter importance and immensity of what Advait was courageously trying to do. However, amidst all these difficulties, Advait continued to do well. The mission continued to expand and is touching and transforming thousands of students.

Around the age of 30, Acharya Prashant started speaking in his Samvaad, or clarity sessions. These were in the form of open discussions on critical life-issues. Soon it started becoming clear that these sessions were deeply meditative, brought the mind to a strange peace, and had a miraculously curative effect upon the psyche. Acharya Prashant's voice and videos would be recorded and uploaded on the internet. And soon a website too was developed to publish his writings and the transcriptions of his talks.

Around the same time, he started organizing self-awareness camps. He would take true seekers with him to the Himalayas, in groups of around 30 each, for periods of around a week. These camps turned out to be deeply transformational events and the frequency of the camps increased. Hundreds of camps have been organized so far, providing immense clarity and peace in relatively short spans of time.

Acharya Prashant's unique spiritual literature is at par with the highest words that mankind has ever known. His genius is founded on Vedanta. With his broad Vedantic foundation, he is seen as the coming together of the various spiritual streams of the past, yet is someone not confined by any tradition. He attacks the mind vigorously and simultaneously calms it with love and compassion. There is a clarity that radiates from his presence and a soothing effect from his being. His style is forthright, clear, mystical, and compassionate. The ego and the falseness of the mind do not find a place to hide while facing his innocent and simple questions. He plays with his audiences—taking them to the very depths of meditative silence, laughing, joking, attacking, and explaining. On one hand, he appears to be somebody very close and approachable, and on the other hand, it is obvious that the words coming through him are from somewhere beyond.

Over 10,000 videos and articles uploaded by him on the internet are freely available to all and make the world's single biggest repository of spiritual content on the internet, of which more than 20 million minutes are watched daily (as of May 2022). He has been regular speaker at IITs, IIMs, many other prestigious institutions, as well as platforms like TED. In print media, his articles get regularly published in national dailies. His discourses and interviews have been broadcasted via national TV channels too. Today, his movement has touched the lives of tens of millions of individuals. Through his direct contact with people, and through various internet-based channels, he continues to bring clarity to all.

# Introduction

This book was spoken first, and written later.

As a Vedanta philosopher and teacher, Acharya Prashant has been interacting with diverse audiences for over a decade. Though the questioners come from varying backgrounds, each of these interactions is usually in the form of a question that the teacher responds to. The length of each such interaction varies from ten minutes to as much as an hour. Every chapter of this book is essentially based on one such interaction. This means that each chapter, though coming from a single center, exhibits the response of the speaker to very different people and their peculiar life-queries. The questioners are spaced apart across years, continents, genders, and everything else that makes a human being distinct from the other. As a result, the readers get an enriching kaleidoscopic perspective as they go through the range of human conditions, confusion, and questions—all related to a certain desire for inner clarity, which is what brings us to Maya.

Maya is a commonly used yet most misunderstood spiritual concept. Be it the common man who finds Maya synonymous with materialism, or the spiritual man who accords Maya some esoteric imagery, all fail to comprehend her. This failure translates into mankind's unmitigated suffering, thus making it necessary for every conscious person to investigate Maya deeply.

Is Maya a sly antagonist determined to keep us shackled in our own inner chains? Or is she another name for the game of life, in which we could be a master player or a hapless pawn?

The reader of this book should understand Maya in the most scientific terms—anything that occupies our consciousness is Maya, anything that compulsively pervades our mind-space is Maya.

At a time when a lot of neo-spirituality is just about tools for an alternate kind of entertainment, Acharya Prashant takes us towards a genuine understanding of Maya as she plays out in our daily lives. He draws his essence from Vedantic seers and philosophers from all ages. Timeless wisdom in a contemporary context and vernacular metaphor is what makes this work unique. When you really see how all mind stuff is Maya, how Maya is never going to quit chasing you as long as you are tied to the body—the matter, the seeing itself brings peace. One stops the chase and relishes the drama.

A word of advice: Because of the vast differences among seekers and their queries, the responses of the teacher too are customized. At some places, therefore, the responses in one chapter may appear to be apparently contradictory to the responses in another chapter. We hope our discreet readers will be able to appreciate the differences as various roads leading to the same core.

# So Real She Looks

# 1

# Who Is She?

*Life has no regards for your opinions or fancies. If you live in imaginations, you will keep struggling and hitting against events, and you will stumble and fall many times in many places.*

**Listener (L):** The concept of Maya, the idea that the whole world is an illusion, is at the core of Advaita Vedanta. However, Maya as a concept is unfathomable to many of us. How can someone who doesn't have a deep knowledge of Vedanta understand this concept?

**Acharya Prashant (AP):** You said Maya is the concept that the universe is an illusion. The concept actually is that there is nothing called *the* universe. This universe that you and I perceive is a purely subjective entity. The subjectivity exists at two levels: at the level of meaning, and at the level of the fact.

Take for example a building that you perceive. This building can be taken as symbolizing the universe. The universe consists of objects; let the building represent them. Now, nobody looks at a building without assigning meaning to the building, and the meanings that we assign to anything that we see, experience, think of, or imagine are purely subjective. There is nothing absolute about them, and that much is obviously very easy to see.

Then comes the more austere part: Even the fact that the building is, is actually subjective. The three-dimensional shape that the building appears as—the height, the width, the entire spatial geometry—all that is a function of the way your brain is configured to look at things. So, it is not as if the building exists objectively or absolutely by itself independent of the perceiving subject. Not at all. If your own personal configuration changes, the building would no more remain the same.

Even among the different subjects that perceive the same object we find a great difference in perception. There are sentient beings that are able to hear particular wavelengths that you and I just cannot experience, beyond 20,000 Hz, let's say, or subsonic, less than the 20 Hz threshold. We just wouldn't know. For us there would be nothing to perceive, whereas for them there would exist a reality, and that reality they would call as objective.

That is ego: to think of one's own projections and perceptions as absolute.

So, when you look at the building, first of all you attribute a meaning. Nobody looks at a building—I have said and I am repeating—without assigning it a meaning. Someone is looking at a building out of jealousy, somebody out of curiosity; somebody wants to study the building; somebody wants to steal the building; somebody wants to own the building; somebody wants to rent the building; somebody has some kind of a memory associated with that building; somebody else might just be scared of buildings.

So, there is that meaning part and that meaning, obviously, is purely subjective. Because there is such a heavy component of subjectivity—in fact, because there is hundred percent subjectivity—therefore, what Acharya Shankara said was that the world is not how you perceive it to be. 'Mithya' does not mean non-existent. When he said jagat (world) is mithya, he didn't mean that the world or the universe does not exist at all. What he meant was that it does not exist in the way you think it does. What is the reality of the universe? He called that as Brahm. And Brahm you cannot think of; Brahm is truly unfathomable. Therefore, the solution lies in just negating the subjective part. And that subjectivity, we said, is ego. Maya is another name for that.

So, the more you get rid of Maya, the more you dissolve, and the more of what remains is the Absolute. You can call that as the Atma or Brahm or Truth. It is an absence of the personal self, the subjective experiencer.

So, there is not much complication in the concept of Maya, because we all know that things are not as they appear to be. And the proof of that is our daily frustrations. Have things in your life or my life turned out as they promised to be? Why do we often feel deceived, then? Why do we get setbacks? Why do we then say that "Oh, I misinterpreted"? The thing is, it is only sometimes that we admit that we misinterpreted. Misinterpretation is happening all the time because the interpreter itself is illusory. The interpreter is called the ego. "I am the interpreter, I am the ego. And because I am interpreting, so I am bound to misinterpret." This is Maya.

So, Maya really does not principally or primarily have to do with the world as such. Before we set out to enquire and negate the external world, it is more important to investigate why we are first of all in illusion with respect to the external world. It is because Maya resides within. The experiencer himself is subject to greed, desire, fear, and many other such tendencies, due to which his entire perception is skewed, biased, distorted. He sees things where none exists, and that which exists he definitely fails to see. This is Maya.

Maya is said to have two aspects: āvaraṇa and vikṣepa. The first one is about your failure to see the reality, and the latter is about seeing, projecting, imagining stuff that does not really exist. It should be obvious by now that this Maya which resides within, fundamentally, is at the root of all human misery. Because if you do not see a pothole where it exists, you will receive a rude jolt, won't you? At the same time, if you are driving down a highway and you start imagining that a deer has suddenly leaped in front of your car, then again you will receive a huge jolt. You might actually slam the breaks so hard that you hit your head against the windscreen. You don't require an object outside the car to hit you; you will hit the car from the inside and suffer. That's how we usually suffer: hurting and hitting ourselves from the inside, when actually there is nothing outside to hurt us. That is Maya.

**L:** Recently I read a quote of yours where you said that the madman is the last to admit that he is mad. I think the quote resonates with what we are currently speaking about—the ego and its projections. The madman, the mad person is very close to his ego, which is why he is not admitting that he is mad.

My question about this is on two levels. Firstly, how can we, as human beings, remove the biases and prejudices that we have and maybe become less mad, less close to the ego? And secondly, how should we deal with people who are very biased, prejudiced, and very stubborn about their perceptions and opinions?

**AP:** The answer to the second part is contained in the first part. In the second part you asked how do we deal with people who are prejudiced, biased, and pretty stubborn about their perceptions or opinions. If you can deal with yourself first, you will know how to deal with all such people. Because every single person, including the questioner and this speaker, is bound to be biased and prejudiced. So, if we can know how to figure out our own biases and prejudices, it will become very easy to spot the same things in others and help them out of these.

We have a stake in living in fancies and imaginations, and that stake offers us comforts. That's the reason most people prefer imaginations over the reality.

We are born deluded. The newborn has no faculty for clear perception. Yet the newborn is taken care of in several ways, and the newborn has prakritik—by 'prakritik' I mean physical nature, biology—systems in place to help her navigate through the initial months and years. And that works. Without any deep understanding or consciousness, kids of all species manage to live through their initial years in a healthy way. That tendency continues. In animals, the continuation of that tendency is not a problem because their consciousness anyway has no urge towards liberation. But in human beings, there does exist that urge.

But if you have to be liberated of your tendencies—the same tendencies that I referred to as internal bondages, the same internal bondages that result in several external bondages—

then you have to pay the price for it. Paying the price is a tough choice; most people do not want to make that choice.

So, you ask me, "How?" I say, choose.

You ask me, "How to do it?" I say, choose to do it.

The answer is so simple. The answer is frustratingly simple! How to drop your biases? Choose to drop your biases! Because it's not that you do not know that you are biased.

I'll tell you why it is impossible to not know that you are biased. Life has no regards for your opinions or fancies. If you live in imaginations, you will keep struggling and hitting against events, and you will stumble and fall many times in many places. So, life has an inbuilt mechanism to communicate to you that you are not living in facts, let alone the Truth.

So, we know. We are being delivered the message again and again. The diagnosis of our condition is not a secret; it is being displayed to us almost daily. Even when external situations do not display that, our internal climate is ample proof. If one were living rightly, why would one be so scared? Why would one be jealous or insecure or temperamental? There would be no need, right?

So, all these things clearly tell you that you are not living in a real world, you are living in your head. But then, as we said, one has to make efforts to break out of the jail, and one has to pay the price. The thing with our biological condition is that we are luxury-loving people. Inertia applies not only to insentient objects but much more to human beings. If you have been living in a certain way and you are used to it, then you grow a thousand inner arguments against challenging the status quo. We just don't want to pay the price.

Ignorance is actually nothing. Let nobody say that he or she is not making the right choices in life because he or she does not know. We all know. We prefer to suppress the inner knowledge. It's an inner conspiracy against ourselves, just because we want to continue enjoying certain privileges in life—certain physical privileges, material privileges, monetary privileges.

And if you want to just test whether people are living in ignorance or self-deception, there is a simple test: Go and declare something to them that takes them towards the Truth. Declare loudly. Had they just been ignorant, they would have at least shown curiosity, if not been welcoming of it. But you will find that the moment you show the mirror to people, the moment you want to bring the Truth to people, they actually actively balk away; they might even feel offended. What does that tell? They knew very well in advance that they were living in the false. They knew. That's the reason why the moment the Truth was shown they became scared and defensive.

So, ignorance is just an ugly ploy against oneself. Nobody is really ignorant; we just don't choose to live rightly, to know the Truth, to drop our biases. We have a stake there. We keep getting some small, petty benefits, and those petty benefits are enough to keep making us side with the false. Very unfortunate!

---

"The more you get rid of Maya, the more you dissolve, and the more of what remains is the Absolute. You can call that as the Atma or Brahm or Truth. It is an absence of the personal self, the subjective experiencer."

---

*IIT Bombay, 2021*

# 2

# She Exists, or Does She?

*You are living Maya, you are eating Maya, you are running Maya, you are breathing Maya, you are seeing Maya, you are thinking Maya. You are nothing but Maya personified.*

**Listener (L):** We have been on the spiritual path for a while now. We feel convinced that we are Atma—never threatened and never disturbed. Ego, Maya, and ignorance are merely concepts of the mind. Is there any need to really make such a big deal of Maya?

**Acharya Prashant (AP):** A lazy son is sleeping even as the Sun is overhead. He has become accustomed to the boundaries, and his laziness does not let him get up and move out. So, the father comes in and says:

"Son, there is a divine metaphysical mango outside. You have never seen anything like it, let alone tasted something like it, and that mango gives joy that cannot be described, has a color that cannot be seen, a fragrance that is beyond experience."

It is probably the only way remaining for the father to somehow make the lazy, clumsy son get up and move out, the only way left to make him somehow quit the bed—a great flowery, tempting description.

So, the son gets up, goes out, comes back in a while and says, "Thanks, dad! I have eaten the mango, and it is indeed juicy and divinely delicious." Saying so, the son crashes on the bed again. Now, he's not only asleep, but he is confidently asleep as the divine eater of the blessed and rare mango.

In another scenario, a little girl, being agitated, won't go to sleep. The mother comes in and puts the restless child in her lap, and starts singing a sweet lullaby that talks of great fairies and demons and beautiful lands far away, and events such as never happened. And having sung for an hour, she finds the child even more restless. The mother is befuddled and asks, "What's the matter, girl?" She says, "Now I am preparing to travel to those divine lands, for now I see that I really belong there. I realize my home is in the transcendental heavens."

Stupid boys and girls have been defeating well-meaning helpers since long.

Will we ever gain some sense? Will we ever be honest enough to look at our lives?

Our lives are nothing but a sorry tale of someone who has always been disturbed, displaced, vacillating and suffering. And that has been happening continuously. Not for a moment have we been restful. Even if we have found a little peace, it has only been relative to one's otherwise deeply restive state. When disturbance drops a little, we celebrate it as calmness; but we take not one moment to quickly proclaim, "I am the untouched seer; I am the absolute Self."

To the lazy boy, a great description beyond imagination was made so that he may come out of the room. The father wanted to rid the son of his current state of inertia. The father says, "Come out, son. There is a divine mango outside." But the son goes out, somehow dishonestly dreams of eating the mango, comes back, and says, "Now I am the eater of the divine mango," and horror! He goes back to sleep, more self-assured, more self-deluded.

Will we ever look at how we are living? It's not very surprising that we deceive ourselves. It requires great intelligence to admit one's madness. The mad one is usually going to be the last to admit that he is mad. The mad one is much more likely to say, "I am the divine blissful Atma."

Spirituality is not the art of cramming knowledge from here and there. It is first of all a deep cry to not remain as one currently is or has become. You say, "Maya is just a concept, ego is just a concept." I do not know whether they are just abstract concepts. What I know is that your face is the face of Maya. Maybe you too are a concept. Maybe Ravi, Ramesh, Suresh (common first names) are all just concepts.

What is Maya? Your unmitigated suffering is Maya. Do you want to deny that you live in total anarchy, disorder, chaos, and psychological imbalance? If you do and you call yourself real, then Maya is very much real. How do you call Maya a mere concept?

There is no proof here except one's own inner honesty. If you come and make a loud claim that you are contented, never disturbed, never threatened—fine! Your claim will be accepted; to each his own. If you come and say that you need not be cautious of Prakriti (physical nature), avidyā (nescience), Maya because you are the great Sākṣī—witness beyond any disturbance, temptation, threat, greed and fear—then wonderful. There is nothing like it—you have already arrived! Only you know where. Nobody would dispute your claims. But why do you want to deceive yourself? Why do you want to live in atma-pravañcana (gross self-deception)? You say there is no Maya for you and there is no disturbance in your mind. Is that coming from your life? Is that how you are living?

Do you know what Maya is? All that is gross and subtle is Maya. All that you can think of or experience or speak of is Maya. Does the world not stir you up? Does it not cast its bewildering shadow upon you? You are in a spell, bewitched, and you are talking as if you are untouched, uncorrupted.

Keep the relation between Maya and mind aside. You tell me, what is the relation between you and money, between you and sex, between you and greed, between you and food, between you and knowledge, and you and ignorance? That would be a more useful discussion. Useful because it will come straight from your life, from your honesty.

And you will see that the markets do tempt and distract you; that disease, old age, and young age are indeed meaningful to you; that you do not like being scolded and that you are pleased when you are praised; that there exists a significant word called insult or humiliation in your vocabulary; that things hurt you. And then you will know whether or not Maya disturbs the mind.

Look at your life and answer honestly. And as long as you are the one who gets hurt, tempted, disappointed, elated, happy and sad, and call yourself sometimes healthy and sometimes diseased, you better admit that which has been defined as Maya is indeed a great force upon you.

And that is the reason why saints, seers and teachers through the ages have advised caution—great caution. They have said, "Do not take her as feeble, do not take her ever as defeated, and never think of her as imaginary. Her very name is Maya—that which is not but surely appears to be is Maya." And it is not to the Buddhas alone that she appears to be. She appears real to us, the commoners too.

Yes, absolutely speaking, Maya is a concept. But then, by the same yardstick, you too are a concept. Take your name and tell me, what is it? Is that not a concept? You will say, "No, I am a fact because I can touch myself, experience myself." If you are a fact when you are running towards the market, glory or sexual gratification, then you are also Maya. Now isn't Maya a fact too?

If you say that "I," let's say your name is Ramesh, "am *not* a concept, rather I am a fact," then this same Ramesh is also the proof of Maya. Ramesh running blindly towards his objects is the proof of Maya. The face of Ramesh blinded by the promise of gratification is the face of Maya. Now tell me, is Maya a living fact or not?

The face of a woman when she knows nothing but attachment to her child is the face of Maya. Now tell me, is Maya merely a concept, or is the woman's face, in the moment of physical attachment, the very face of Maya?

Words like Maya are just pointers, but they direct us to something very, very definite and important. Ignore the pointer at your own peril. If you want to say that Maya is just a product of imagination, a mere academic concept of sorts, then tell me which word in the dictionary is not a concept. No word in itself is ever a living thing, or is it? You say camera, but is a camera not a concept? You say grass, but is grass not a concept? Is greenness contained in the word 'grass'—G.R.A.S.S.? Nevertheless, grass, the word, is a pointer towards something that is indeed green: not something merely conceptual, but a living thing to be experienced.

Sorrow, too, is a concept. So what? Aren't you living in sorrow? The day you can call your sorrow just a concept, you have earned the right to call Maya a concept too. You get swept away by sorrow. Do you ever say that sorrow does not exist? No, but see how boldly you are asserting that Maya is not a real thing. To you Maya is just a play of words, but sorrow, suffering, humiliation, greed and arousal—these you would not call a play of words. You live in them, and it's not possible to live in a house of words, is it?

Somebody waves a big check at you, and you start running after him. Somebody humiliates you a little, and you show the middle finger to him. In those moments, you do not say that all those things are just unreal.

It is our great subconscious ploy to call Maya unreal so that we can continue wallowing in Maya. When we are totally consumed by her, we start denying her very existence. Accepting her existence as the most important driver in our life would entail a big responsibility. The responsibility would be to break free of her. Such responsibility is effort and courage, and we shy away from both. We take a dirty shortcut—we simply say Maya does not exist.

Never must we call ourselves as the untouched, unblemished, eternal, infinite Atma because as we are, we are none of that. We are the ones greatly enslaved by Maya. We are the ones greatly identified with our body, clothes, conditioning, girlfriend, society, and profession, aren't we?

How then do you muster the ignorance to call yourself the Atma or Sākṣī, the witness? Are you really, really a Sākṣī? The Sākṣī to you is the mango. The great fathers talked of the mango to you so that you may leave your bed and your sordid sleep, come out of your enclosure, and breathe in the open skies. The mango is not there to be eaten. The mango really does not exist at all. The Atma has no existence—in the way we use the word 'existence'—and that is why it is classically said to be beyond existence, or metaphysical.

The son is indeed wonderful. He manages to eat a mango that can't ever be eaten. The mango has been digested, and he is back to his sombre sleep. Just as the boy managed to eat a non-existent mango and continued sleeping, you manage to become a non-existent Atma and continue sleeping.

Given how our lives are, we must rather say, "Atma does not exist; only Maya exists." That would be an honest description of our condition. No Atma exists for us; only Maya does. But we upend the whole thing and say, "Only the Atma exists and I am the Atma. Maya? Oh, that's merely a concept."

*You are living Maya, you are eating Maya, you are running Maya, you are breathing Maya, you are seeing Maya, you are thinking Maya. You are nothing but Maya personified. And then you have the gall to say Maya is just a concept?*

You ask, "What is the proof of Maya?" You are the proof of Maya. Look at your face in the mirror. That face is the proof of Maya—the sorry face that stares back at you. You are quick to label that as your face, and that's the proof that Maya has ensnared you. Your face is just material and you are identified with that material. Why do you call that face as your face? Such identification itself is proof enough that Maya is now all over the mind, that Prakriti has totally entrapped the Puruṣa.

Otherwise, why would you call that face your face? Does Atma have a face? If you say you are Atma, how do you still manage to have a face? Divine distant lands and holy mangoes!

The fathers are totally bewildered. The mango trick has returned to haunt them. In fact, they are now confused. They have begun to suspect that such a mango really exists! The deeply assured ones have been put into doubt by the son—the mendacious, dumb, and assertive son.

The ego loves to talk of Maya as something distant and Truth as something intimate. I repeat to you, Maya is intimate, and the word 'Truth' is just a concept. You cannot talk of Truth, for the moment you talk of Truth, you have reduced it to a concept. So, if there is something that is indeed a concept, it is the word 'Truth'. You better not call yourself the Truth or Brahm or Atma or the pure Self.

The moment you talk of Atma, your talking has reduced Atma to a concept. Maya you can surely talk of because it is always Maya doing the talking. Maya is real. Maya is what you are living as and living in. Kindly do not deny her existence; the proof of her existence is your confusion, your sorrow, your conflicts. Come and claim that you are not experiencing any conflicts, that you don't have nightmares, that you are not addicted to this or that, would you? Your addictions are Maya, your obsessions are Maya. When we walk, she walks. She walks and says, "I am not."

And it is a great fad; people come and say that they want to experience being the witness; they want to achieve the Atma.

This same son from the earlier example, the snoring enthusiast, at another hour is found crawling on the ground. The father, in his compassion, comes again to him. The mango trick has failed, but the father is indefatigable and redoubtable. His compassion is unending. He comes to his crawling son and says, "Son, up in the skies is a great sky lotus. If you can have it, then you will have everlasting bliss."

The father wants the son to get up and at least stretch his limbs. There is no sky lotus, nor any possibility to attain the sky lotus. But when he talks of the sky lotus, the father hopes that at least the temptation to have the sky lotus will make the son stand up on his two legs and jump a little. He hopes the son will not only leave his pitiable crawling state but also get a little exercise when he tries to jump and touch the metaphorical sky lotus. That is why the scriptures talk so much of the great Atma—the sky lotus.

The scriptures say Atma is the only liberator from suffering. The father says the sky lotus is the only liberator from the crawling state. The father's intention is not that the son attains the sky lotus but that he stands up on his legs and starts walking on the earth like a man, not like a reptile, a crawler, a rodent. Instead, the son gets up, takes one lazy leap and says, "Here, the sky lotus is in my hand, and now I am again lying down to crawl."

Please understand. Your suffering is real, at least to you. Had your suffering not been real to you, you wouldn't have suffered at all. This suffering is Maya. We are in her spell. The sky lotuses that you keep talking of—enlightenment, liberation, Puruṣa, Atma—they are beyond reach but are useful tricks. They help you grow up.

Now the question arises: is Atma nonexistent? Even that is not right to say. Why? Because, though the sky lotus is unattainable, without it you wouldn't rise up at all. The Absolute cannot be attained, but without the presence of the Absolute, how did relative progress happen? Even your relative progress is a strong proof of the abstract existence of the Absolute. That, however, does not mean that one day you will be able to rise to the Absolute and capture it. The Absolute, though itself unattainable, helps you attain all that is worthy of being attained in life. I leave it to your subtle intelligence to appreciate whether the Atma exists or not.

The way you and I exist, the way this chair exists, the way these rain droplets are falling upon us *(at the time of the discussion it was raining)*, Atma does not quite exist in the same way. Atma and Maya are vastly different dimensions. In our context, Maya exists and Atma does not because we do not exist in any dimension other than that of Maya. In our dimension, there is no Atma, there is only Maya. That same Maya is making us claim that Maya does not exist.

Be a little humble and honest. Live in the constant acknowledgment that you are being fooled and fooled again—by the body, by the mind, by this apparent universe. When you admit that you are being fooled, then you will have to admit that you are not the Atma, because the Atma cannot be fooled. The power, fearlessness and the honesty to ruthlessly acknowledge your sorry situation can come only from a source beyond you, the enslaved one. That source is called Atma.

Does Atma exist? Depends on you. If you can live in humility and honesty, Atma exists for you. If you live in denial, deception, and delusion, then Atma does not exist for you. Your life—you decide.

**L:** Won't life be lifeless if we eliminate Maya? What would be left to achieve then? Nobody knows Atma, one can't even talk of Atma, so Atma is anyway not useful. So why not simply do one's duty, eat, relax, and live peacefully with Maya?

**AP:** The question must be turned back upon the questioner, otherwise there can be no solution. I can give an answer but that won't solve the situation.

You are asking, why not live peacefully with Maya? Maya, by definition, is your lack of peace. First, you have to be loving and sensitive enough towards yourself, and honest enough to acknowledge that you are living in a great lack of peace. And if you have still not come to the point where you can acknowledge that life is hell, then spirituality has not yet begun for you, and you do not need any spiritual sessions.

Spirituality is only for those who have, first of all, realized that they are stuck and fed up. They want to break away, and then spirituality begins. If you are saying you want to live peacefully with Maya, please go ahead. It's like saying, "Why can't I live peacefully with a self-imposed headache?" It's like saying, "Why can't I peacefully torture myself?" Go ahead, if that is your definition of peace.

You ask me, why not do one's duty, eat and relax? But you anyway aren't doing your duty; you are just doing Maya's bidding. You are her servant. Your so-called duties are her commands. Were you born with your duties? How do you know what is your duty? How do you know what you are really responsible for? Who told you all that? You do not care to inquire within to see how you have come to accept those so-called duties. How did you start identifying with particular roles and responsibilities? You will not inquire. Instead, you just want to keep toiling.

You have been tutored to take some specific actions as your duty. In the *Bhagavad Gita*, Krishna teaches Arjuna, "Sarva-dharmān parityajya mām ekaṃ śaraṇaṃ vraja: O Arjuna, leave all your duties and come straight to Me." That is the very basis of surrender. That is the very basis of wisdom, and that is where liberation begins—when one is prepared to leave these bogus duties.

Krishna asks you to leave all your duties and responsibilities because they are fake and false. And you are asking, "Why not do one's duty, eat, and relax?" The answer is: because you won't be able to really relax with these so-called duties.

Relaxation is not possible unless you start moving towards the Truth. You are demanding the impossible: you want to live peacefully with Maya. You want to relax in the middle of your servitude. Unless you are doing Krishna's bidding, you won't experience the relaxed state. Unless you have done away with Maya, you won't experience peace.

You ask, "Won't it be lifeless if we eliminate Maya? What will we achieve then?" Who told you that you must achieve this or that? Who indoctrinated you into believing that life is sheer waste without achievement? Even if something must be achieved, how do you know what is the right goal? Who sets your targets? You don't want to inquire into that because inquiry would be painful, and it demands courage, conviction, and rebellion from you.

You want to take the easy way out. You want to deny the very fact that you are trapped. You want to decorate your prison. Within the prison, you want to eat, make merry, and relax. Self-deception at its worst. Avoid, please!

**L:** I am stuck. Parents keep insisting on my duty as a daughter and a woman. They keep telling me to get settled, get married, etc.

**AP**: Do get obediently married, and you too would become a parent very soon. Knowing fully well how you are, would you tell your kid to blindly follow you? If not, why do you listen to parental moonshine?

Would you listen to the wise ones, the compassionate ones, the Buddhas, Krishnas, Kabirs, and Ashtavakras? Or would you rather listen to your parents? Look at your parents' lives and ask them, "Do you want me to lead the same kind of life as you do?" If your parents really love you, they'll say, "Daughter, we let you go—fly free!"

---

"It is our great subconscious ploy to call Maya unreal so that we can continue wallowing in Maya. When we are totally consumed by her, we start denying her very existence. Accepting her existence as the most important driver in our life would entail a big responsibility—to break free of her."

---

*Advait Shivir, Uttarakhand, 2018*

# 3

# She Is Illusion, and Beyond

*Our world is full of knowledge that harms us. And when I say 'our world', I do not mean the Earth; I mean our personal world, our mind. The aim of spirituality is to rid the mind of false knowledge.*

**Listener:** Dear sir, I came to know you through your videos on YouTube. I am very grateful that I came to know about the *Ribhu Gita* from your session organized on Mahashivratri day.

Since then, I have read the full document more than five times, and it is difficult to accept that everything is just an illusion. I read about sadhana (spiritual discipline) affirming, "I am Brahm." Is this the only thought I must hold to come to the Truth?

**Acharya Prashant:** Please appreciate what is meant by 'everything is illusory'.

When you look at a tree at night and confuse it to be a man, that's an illusion, right? Does that mean that the tree does not exist? When it is said that the world is an illusion, it means you are so heavily conditioned that you are looking at things as they are not. It does not mean that the world does not exist.

I will insist that the world exists. And I will insist on it because I know that I am speaking to persons and their bodily ears. I know that I am responding to voices that are emanating from human throats.

As long as the material body exists, the material universe too exists. It is quite preposterous to claim, as a body, that the embodied universe is merely an illusion.

Look at the absurdity of a person saying that the universe is an illusion. He is saying that the sofa-set does not exist, but he, the one sitting on the sofa, exists to talk of the non-existence of the sofa. If the sofa does not exist, then what are you sitting on? Or, if the sofa doesn't exist, accept that you too do not exist. If you accept that you do not exist, then who is there to accept the non-existence of everything and everyone?

In the game of negation of everything, rarely do we play till the end. Because if you do not exist, then who is talking? So, you can just stop talking, but you find it difficult to do. Once you have stopped talking, then let's talk. But you still haven't stopped talking, you are talking a lot. And if you are talking, then remember that the talking is happening through the body, and also that the talk is vulnerable to a lot of your bodily tendencies.

The Buddha too talked through the body. But at least his words were free of the tendencies embedded in the body. You are not only talking through the mouth, but your words are also arising from the glands, hormones, and stuff contained in the body.

So, the body is a very definite thing for you. And if the body is a definite thing, the sofa too must be a definite thing. If you, the body-identified one, negate the universe as nonexistent, it would be duplicity.

The world is not an illusion. Why did the seers say 'jagat mithya' (the world is an illusion)? It is because there are a lot of people who do not consider a sofa as a mere sofa. The sofa is ten thousand things to you, and those ten thousand things keep changing depending upon your mood, your conditioning, and your upbringing. They don't stay, they deceive. You think of something as one thing, it is not that thing. And then there is sorrow, because no one likes to be betrayed.

Even when you look at a man, you are not merely looking at a man. Has it ever happened that you looked merely at a man? Even to call a man a man is to begin a lot of obfuscation and unnecessary extrapolation.

The whole game of language is to generalize. You cannot use language and be precise. These days people are annoyed when stereotypes are used, but if you look closely, you will find that it is impossible to use language and still not stereotype.

The very word 'man' refers to a stereotype. The very word 'tree' refers to a stereotype. Where there are concepts, there is stereotyping. Ask yourself: Is it even possible to conceptualize and yet not generalize? Aren't you preparing the ground for deception if you generalize? Yes, generalization helps to make things convenient and practical for us. But practicality is not the same as purity, is it?

You are asking: "Is the constant affirmation of 'I am Brahm' the only way to be in the Truth?"

Yes, of course. There can be a hundred kind of sadhanas (spiritual discipline), but all of them are just negations. No sadhana is affirmative. Even when you are constantly affirming to yourself 'I am Brahm', all that you are doing is negating that you are something other than Brahm.

*Brahm is that nothing which dissolves everything. Brahm is that deal where you give up everything for the sake of nothing. The scriptures are constantly encouraging you to take that deal.*

So, whether you say "I am Brahm" or "The world is an illusion" or "I am nobody" or "I am Saccidānanda (Existence-Consciousness-Bliss)", you are essentially saying the same thing. There is no difference.

Our world is full of knowledge that harms us. And when I say 'our world', I do not mean the Earth; I mean our personal world, our mind. The aim of spirituality is to rid the mind of false knowledge. The only true knowledge is that all knowledge is false, in the sense that it may be practical for a short while, but does not endure. It does not bring you to the last point.

You must understand knowledge. Knowledge is surely needed. Why is knowledge needed? Knowledge is needed because you are already knowledgeable. Had you been like the naked Adam and Eve, with no knowledge at all, you would have never been required to have knowledge in the first place. That was the instruction, right? "Don't eat the fruit of the tree of knowledge. Just don't begin the cycle."

But we are past that stage. We are in the cycle now.

You have a lot of knowledge. It is not merely knowledge that you acquire after birth; you are also born with knowledge. The infant, the one-day-old, is full of knowledge. If you want to measure in bits and bytes how much knowledge an infant has, you will be surprised at the amount of space his knowledge would consume.

*You require more knowledge in order to get rid of the limitations and falsities of the pre-existing knowledge.*

So, knowledge brings you to a point of relative betterment and then leaves you stranded. Betterment surely occurs with the help of knowledge, but that betterment is just relative to your previous state. You can say that you are less thirsty now, but you are still thirsty. And even the consolation that you are less thirsty exists only when you compare yourself to your previous state. On a binary scale, you are just thirsty, not less thirsty.

This is something delicate. Let's understand.

Knowledge can make you less thirsty, and you can get that consolation only when you compare yourself to your previous state. But if someone comes and asks you, "Are you free of thirst now?" you won't be able to say yes. And in that sense, your suffering is unending—not only unending but unmitigated too.

Even though it appears that with every step in knowledge, with every bit of progress, mankind's suffering is reducing, that is not really the case. Is the man of today any less in sorrow than the man three thousand years back? I am talking of psychic sorrow, not physical hardships or material accumulations.

Sorrow continues unmitigated. Man is still cunning, jealous, insecure, and very afraid.

That is why knowledge doesn't help beyond its own plane. The aim of the scriptures is to give you knowledge that will bring you out of the cycle of knowledge.

And why must the scriptures give you more knowledge when you are already loaded with knowledge? Because your constitution won't allow you to have anything except knowledge. But a true teacher can give you something else disguised as knowledge. When the true teacher speaks, you think that you are receiving mere words, but something else has also been silently, surreptitiously communicated to you without your consent, without your consciousness.

---

"If the mind just dissolves, where does it go? It goes to the same place it came from. Figure out where the mind came from. And if you can figure that out, you will know where the mind goes. It came from nowhere and goes nowhere. If you want to call that 'nowhereness' the Truth, you are not wrong."

---

*Advait Shivir, BodhSthal, 2018*

# 4

# She Owns Your Mind

*Had we not been told what to do, what would we have done? It is scary that we act only by imitation. Some of us try not to imitate. But it's even scarier when it turns out that even not imitating is an imitation.*

**Acharya Prashant (AP):** Our friend here *(referring to a listener)* notes that he starts feeling bored when there are bored or boring people around him. The topic is the infectiousness of states of mind.

Well, not only is boredom infectious, but the bored mind is also prone to being infected by almost everything it experiences.

The mind itself is an infection and acquisition—an import. There is nothing in the mind that arises on its own. On its own, the mind is nothing. The mind is dependent on the world. The mind operates in a duality where each extreme is dependent on the other.

So, what exists on its own? Does the world exist on its own? No, not really; the world is dependent on the mind.

Does the mind exist on its own? No, not really; the mind is dependent on the world.

Where do both come from? That will be answered when there is no mind to ask this question. That will be answered when there is no mind to receive the answer. And that's a pretty impossible thing for the mind to grasp.

Since morning you would have experienced shades of happiness, boredom, sadness, excitement, depression, frustration, ambition, hope, anxiety, and playfulness, right? Why are we unable to observe that it is not arising from within, that it is just a reaction to some external stimulus? Secondly, how are we able to perceive that these moods and states of mind are infectious?

You would have heard this story. The cuckoo keeps its eggs in the crow's nest. The crow is not watchful enough, not vigilant enough. She lacks discretion, viveka. The crow does not enquire, "Are these eggs my own?" It tends to protect and nurse those eggs as its own, only to be disappointed later. In the moment when she is caring for those objects, she is very sure that they have arisen from her own self. Just as we get attached to our thoughts, the crow remains attached to those eggs. Like the crow, we remain attached to our thoughts because we think that these thoughts are *ours.*

The cuckoo keeps singing her way to fame. The crow, on the other hand, works hard and still faces disappointment.

Do we know whether what we consider as our own is our own at all? I am talking of the mind, of our inclinations, attitudes, opinions, and ideologies. Do they really belong to us? The question is important because we invest a lot in them.

There is a woman ready to divorce her husband because he does not support a particular politician. A particular ideology is extremely important to her, and she believes it to be her own. She believes that her thoughts have arisen from within herself. So, she considers the ideology as more intimate to her than her husband.

We invest so much in our thoughts, but are we even sure that our thoughts are our own? In this case, a relationship is being disturbed because of ideology. How about all the families that have *started* based on an ideology? Is that not a greater tragedy? If disrupting a family based on ideology is tragic, is it not more tragic to begin a family based on an ideology? Are our relationships authentic then? We might have been unconsciously indoctrinated into so many ideologies that influence our decisions.

We invest so much of ourselves into everything that is born out of thought. To a vast majority of human beings, what is religion except an ideology? To a vast majority of human beings, is religion a relentless dive into the Truth? Or is it about pursuing ideals, myths, codes of conduct, stories, and thoughts? And don't we give ourselves up to religion?

I am not only talking about established religions. We also have prevalent beliefs that we do not commonly name as religious institutions, though they are every bit as dogmatic as organized religion: greed, career, progress, and knowledgeability—these are the religions of today.

Had we not been told what to do, what would we have done? Don't dismiss this question as naive or childish; it's extremely important. Because, like the crow, we might be investing our lives on something that is not our own.

It is scary that we act only by imitation. Some of us try not to imitate. But it's even more scary when it turns out that even not imitating is an imitation. Even the thought to not imitate is an external insertion. We are so deeply buried under the weight of these layers of conditioning that even the thought that these layers are loathsome is now superficial.

Had we realized that these are external, then we would have, by now, gotten rid of that which is external and yet sitting upon us. Had we really *known* that we imitate—the stress is on the word 'known'—would we still be imitating? The knowing that I am talking of is a different quality; it's real.

We keep imitating and say that we know we imitate. Surely, this realization that we imitate is not at all real. This is imported. Isn't that scary? Even the thought that we are conditioned is a conditioned thought. So, what are we left with?

**Listener (L):** We are inside the boundary, but we are talking of something outside the boundary.

**AP:** Of course, because a book and a great guru inside the boundary tell you fancy stories about the space outside the boundary. So, despite being caged, we act knowledgeable about freedom: "Oh, we know what heaven is like! Oh, we know what it means to transcend!"

**L:** Don't we have anything of our own?

**AP:** That is not a very relevant question. The relevant question is: Are even these words your own? It is not material whether or not we have lived a borrowed life so far. It is much more important to know whether even this realization right now is authentic.

I have spoken to thousands and thousands of people. At least a few hundreds of them have gone back 'realized'. It is this realization that I am apprehensive of. Ignorance comes to us from the outside because ignorance is not our internal nature. The bigger trouble is that even our realization is imported.

Don't be too quick to be realized. Don't be too sure of your realization. I am very wary of enlightenment. We have somebody here, his favorite line is, "Now I realize." He has been on a realizing spree since the last three years or so—a serial realizer!

Be cautious of your own confidence. The ego likes to conclude matters too soon. Wherever there is a conclusion, a settlement, an ending that the thought can grasp, it is a false ending, a false realization. I have no interest in talking about what true realization is like. We should rather be warned of that which is false.

Much as it likes to conclude quickly, the ego can never be restful with loose ends, uncertainty, and ambiguity. With things that don't begin or end, matters that seem absurd in a sequence of time, issues that apparently do not have a cause and actions that apparently do not result in anything, the ego will be restless. So, in its lazy helplessness, it tries to close matters, conclude, and assert knowledgeability.

The assertion cannot be, "I do not know." That is a very unstable assertion. If you accept that you do not know, then staying with this acceptance becomes difficult. Sooner or later, after passing through a series of 'I don't know' admissions, the ego would feel pressurized to come to 'I know'. Please be cautious of that. The ego can accept its ignorance a few times. But soon it would want to bridge its lack of knowledge by acquiring more knowledge, and knowledge is always imported.

**L**: Yes.

**AP**: Was the 'yes' yours? Remain attentive. Do not fall prey to the pressures of the environment.

Boredom was inflicted upon you by somebody. Watch out whether excitement too is inflicted by somebody. Does excitement ever arise from within? Can you be excited without stimulus? Don't easily conclude that, "We don't know." It is better to stay in a position of finding out. So, go and discover. See how the environment influences you in shopping malls, in front of the television, your mobile screens, your loved ones and your enemies.

You must watch the whole process. Watching the process is infinitely more important than coming to conclusions. General truths are hardly any help.

---

"We have prevalent beliefs that we do not commonly name as religious institutions, though they are every bit as dogmatic as organized religion: greed, career, progress, and knowledgeability—these are the religions of today."

---

*Advait Shivir, BodhSthal, 2016*

# 5

# She Is Not the Problem, She Is the Experiencer of the Problem

*How do you define a problem? The problem is the one who experiences the problem. If you don't experience the problem, will there be a problem?*

**Listener (L):** Sir, life seems to be a series of problems. The moment one problem is solved, another problem always crops up. What is the solution for a complete cessation of all problems?

**Acharya Prashant (AP):** Shouldn't we rather ask, *for whom* is the problem? A problem always exists for the consciousness that experiences the problem. In the physical world, there is essentially no problem. In the physical world, there is movement, life and death, but there is no real problem in the psychological sense.

Go to a jungle, and you will not find any problems there, provided man isn't meddling. Go to the depths of the Amazon, untouched by man, and you will see that there is no problem. Go to a hilly river or even to an uncharted desert, and you will find no problem. A problem arises when the 'I' gets entangled with happenings in the physical world. That is when complications arise. We don't let Prakriti (physical nature) function as it would, and we start energizing some small and favored part of Prakriti. In our bid to solve our problems, we further complicate matters. It is not something that we do consciously; we are born entangled.

When a child is born it is already entangled with Prakriti, and that is the problem. Because you are born with problems, you have an urge to solve them. But because you are a part of the problem now, rather you *are* the problem now, your efforts to solve will further complicate the problem.

Therefore, what is Mukti or liberation? Stop identifying with the problems, stop energizing the apparently problematic situation, and step away from it. See that the problem does not exist by itself; the problem exists only with reference to the consciousness that experiences the problem. The one who is experiencing the problem is part of the problem. In fact, he is the energizer of the problem. Therefore, he must disassociate himself from this tangle called the problem. That is liberation, disassociation, and disengagement.

Problems are not objective entities; they do not exist by themselves. In the objective world, there are no problems. For example, a black hole eats up a star and an entire star is gone—is that a problem to anybody? A star which is a million times the size of the Earth has been gobbled up by a black hole, it is a massive event—but why is it not a problem? Because you are not associated with the event.

*A problem is only to the consciousness that is associated with the problem. Otherwise, it is just another happening with nothing personal involved for you.*

If even a small teacup in your house breaks, it might be worse than the formation of a supernova somewhere in the universe because you are involved. The problem is not in the occurrence itself, but in your entangled state of consciousness. How can you solve it? You can stop giving it the energy of your association. Just observe, don't energize, and see the magic. Things will just be things, events will just be events, happenings will be happenings, and there will be no problems as such.

How do you define a problem? The problem is the one who experiences the problem. If you don't experience the problem, will there be a problem? Don't put a value on the experience you have of the problem. Don't secretly relish the high you get on feeling like a problem-solver. If you want to feel like a conqueror of problems, you will necessarily look around for problems, even create them.

Let us say you experience a dire physical event—there is an earthquake. Of course, there is a need for action. Must the action come from a disturbed state of mind? Must the earthquake enter your being for you to take necessary action? Must you declare it important to feel internally disturbed? In other words, a problem is a false value system—false and flawed. You are attributing importance to a needless state of mind. That which does not deserve much value is being accorded a lot of value, and that's a problem.

**L**: To say that nothing is particularly important feels a bit depressing. Life feels meaningless.

**AP**: Because you accord value to a state of mind that values problems highly, hence when a problem is shown as needless, the ego feels hurt.

You must value stuff, and when that stuff is threatened, you must feel troubled—that's our core value. You must find things so essential to your existence that their dislocation makes you lose your sleep—that's your mantra. People will casually ask you, "What is important to you?" And the strong assumption is that something must be important to you. Of course, there can be nobody who does not accord importance to anything. You must consider certain people, things or ideas as very important. But why are the things of importance to you so fragile and fleeting? Have you ever wondered about it? And if they are so undependable and ephemeral, do they deserve to be valued so highly?

We have internalized a value system in which the first priority is to have values. Our value system is a hierarchy: the most important thing is this, then this, then this. Out of all these things in the hierarchy, that which occupies the top position is: do have values.

When you are taught that nothing is of so great a value that it becomes a problem to you, then your first value gets offended:

"My life is so barren. There is nothing valuable in it! Oh my God, I am so poor. Everyone has rich things in life, and there is nothing in my life!"

This is a flawed value system at the very outset. Don't you see it is all so very materialistic? When you say, "I must have something valuable in life," to what are you referring? Aren't you referring to something very carnal and material? Are you referring to a formless peace, a nameless love, or a noiseless silence? No, you are not. When you say there must be something of value in life, the intention is to have something that you can hold in your hands.

Remember, what your hands can hold, your hands will drop as well.

**L**: What is the most important thing that needs to be done?

**AP**: See what is hurting you the most. We spoke about disassociation, disengagement, and de-energization. We used the negative to describe the things to do. We said, "Don't just keep doing. First see what troubles your excessive doing is causing you." That is what needs to be done: not something extra, rather a discontinuation of much that you are obsessed with doing.

**L**: How is a false value to be identified?

**AP**: Through the impact it has upon you. If you are holding a false value, the inevitable outcome is suffering. So, your suffering will tell you which of your values is false. Be sensitive to your suffering and be determined to be liberated from it.

**L**: Is my perception of suffering wrong?

**AP**: Yes, yes! It is quite possible. You need the right company, where you see an example of what real liberation, freedom from suffering or joy means. Then you will be reminded of something that is possible for you. We get so accustomed to suffering that suffering does not appear like suffering anymore; it becomes the default mode of life. When this happens, you need disruptive company; you need somebody who is quite unlike you. Only then will you be impelled to ask, "That quality of life which radiates through his being—why is it not available to me?"

---

"What is Mukti or liberation? Stop identifying with the problems, stop energizing the apparently problematic situation, and step away from it."

---

*Advait Shivir, Mumbai, 2019*

# 6

# She Is the Experiencer, She Is the Experience

*All experiencing depends on the experiencer and the experiencer predates the experience. Moreover, the experiencer is not only a product of experience: the experiencer exists first, then comes the experience. The experience has no validity or sanctity on its own.*

**Listener (L):** Sir, whatever we experience in a dream state is unreal. In general, we remain ignorant even in the waking state. So, are all experiences to be taken as unreal?

**Acharya Prashant (AP):** All experiencing depends on the experiencer and the experiencer predates the experience. Moreover, the experiencer is not only a product of experience: the experiencer exists first, then comes the experience. The experience has no validity or sanctity on its own.

You are programmed to experience certain things upon certain triggers. All experience is just your own fiction and pre-programmed, so it cannot be called real. You determine your experiences; they don't happen to you. The proof is that you know what you will experience if a particular event occurs. You know in advance that if you get a trillion rupees, you would be elated, don't you? You haven't yet experienced receiving the money—then how do you already know your response to it? You know because it is pre-scripted. The experiencer already knows what kind of event leads to what kind of experience. There is no newness. That is why the experiencer keeps living a very closed and circumscribed life.

How would my life be if I know in advance what would please or displease me? It would be well-programmed and circumscribed since I would only be trying for things that would please me and avoiding things that would displease me. We know our experiences in advance, so the new is never available. Do you want to feel good? You already know what would make you feel good. If a certain thing is happening and you know in advance that it's not pleasurable, you don't allow it to happen or you escape. Part of it is genetic, and part of it is social. Both can be done away with.

There are too many absolutes in our lives. For example, you are supposed to experience happiness when you get a new job. When you get a new job, the fellow you meet next won't even ask you how you are feeling; he will just congratulate you. After all, you are *supposed* to feel good. He doesn't even bother to crosscheck, "Are you okay with things? You like the job?" He just says, "Congratulations!" The experiencer is pre-programmed, and these events only reinforce the programming.

A similar scenario plays out when you get married or your baby is born. Does anybody come to first verify whether you like what is happening? They just go, "Wow!" Even that awe is pre- programmed; it is not as if they are experiencing it in reality. The newborn may look like all newborns do. A newborn is not particularly attractive to look at—that attractiveness comes after a few months—but your cousin would come shrieking and yelling at the two-day-old baby, "Wow, this is the most beautiful baby ever born!" You're *supposed* to experience happiness.

Newspapers and news sites know the experience in advance, and they don't even hide it. Very unabashedly, the headline runs, "You will fall in love with these pics" or "Ten things that you must know about pumpkins and ladyfingers" or "Where are these stars having their vacations—this you must know!" Have you not come across such titles? Look at their confidence and look at your predictability. They know in advance where our handles are and they are telling you, "We are turning your handle."

If you can just see the ways of the world, all the falseness falls apart.

We really don't have a heart; no experience arises from within. All experiences are things that you are supposed to go through. When you are watching a celebrity child, you are supposed to call him a cutie. If you don't, then you are ostracized. They don't ask you, "Do you find him cute?" They tell you, "See how cute he is." You get the difference? There is a great difference between these two.

Similarly, you are supposed to experience sadness when a particular kind of thing happens. If you don't experience sadness, then you are an outsider. If you don't experience what they want you to experience, then you must experience desolation.

People come to me and say, “We don’t feel happy.”

I ask, “Where?”

They reply, “In parties.”

“But which sane person can really feel happy in those stupid parties?”

They say, “Everybody seems to be feeling happy.”

“They are lying, they are cheating. They don’t even know what they are feeling. They don’t *exist*. How will they feel?”

The fellow wonders, “Only I seem to be unhappy at all these things people feel so happy about.”

I respond, “Your problem is not that you feel unhappy in parties. Your problem is that you are found in parties. Why are you found there at all?”

Yesterday someone said, “I don’t relate to my work. I can’t even answer questions. I don’t feel any happiness there.” I quipped, “But one thing is certain: you’d always be found there. What on earth are you doing there?”

Somebody with a loud mouth comes along and says, “These pictures are hot.” What if you find them gross or worth spitting at, or not even worth spitting at? He has determined in advance that you must be aroused by them. And you oblige, don’t you? Not only is it arousing, but you are also experiencing the arousal. Do you know what is unbelievable about it? You start believing that it is arousing. You do not find it arousing. You are *trained* to find it arousing. That’s how the world moves.

Many studies have been conducted on people across cultures, religions, and places. They have found that even the determinants of sexual arousal are greatly different from one demographic to another. If it was just about man in general, all men should have found broadly similar things to be hot or arousing. But there are great differences between what you find arousing depending on whether you are an American, a Filipino, or an Indian. Why? Is it genetic? No, it is not genetic—it is how you are trained. In India, if you wear a blouse and a sari, the exposed tummy, the midriff, is not arousing at all. Many women wear saris, but nobody considers it sexual. But if a bit of cleavage is exposed, then Indians find it hot. Go to the West. There people rarely expose the midriff, but they find it casual to expose part of the breasts. In India, such things are scandalous. Similarly, in the West, exposing the legs is commonplace. But in India, if you find legs uncovered, you go ballistic—"LEGS!"

We have been trained to find this or that arousing. We internalize the training. We start feeling physical stimulation too. We forget that it is part of the narrative, and we just soak it in. I'm very sure if you can somehow train a generation to think that the earlobes are arousing with proper training, all the poets and the shayars would be composing ballads and ghazals on earlobes: "These are not earlobes; these are petals of a heavenly lotus!"

Anything can become arousing; you just need to train the experiencer. That also tells us that freedom is a possibility. If you realize that you are trained to experience, then you do not remain captive to experience. The moment that emotional surge arises, you will realize that you have been trained to let it arise and dominate you.

The whole game of experience is a sham. If you have been trained, then you can also give up the training. The social aspect of the training is easier to give up, but the biological and hormonal training is a little more difficult to give up. Nevertheless, you can get rid of both. That's such a fantastic possibility of liberation—to be freed of these fraudulent experiences.

Don't you see that the world controls you through your experiences? They know how you can be made to experience happiness; then, they can control you.

If someone can make you happy, he can control you because your happiness now lies in his hands. He knows how to make you happy because the experiencer has been programmed in advance. He knows, "This is what makes him happy. So, use that to control him." Similarly, if he knows what arouses you or what disappoints you or makes you sad, that can be used to control you.

The man of Truth is very unpredictable. You cannot control him. You think you know him, but you will never know him. You cannot determine his experiences. You know what would make him sad, and you try that out; to an extent, you will succeed. Then, you'll suddenly find yourself failing because he is beyond experiences and experiencing. He can see through things; he will not let predictable experiences rule over him. He will know that sadness is not him, it is a programmed thing. He will not let it dominate his consciousness. Any emotion or personality trait will not be too important for him. He will say, "How can I let it dominate me? It's all a game of Prakriti (physical nature) and society. Part of it I was born with; the rest of it they gave to me. How can it be so meaningful for me? Right now, I'm going through a hot flash. Right now, it's a mood swing and a terrible wave of disappointment. But all this is alien to the real me—don't I know that?"

That's why the scriptures worship realization. Realize, and you are free. When experience is taking possession of you, realize what is happening. When you are being swept or carried away, realize what is happening and stop—and you are free.

**L**: So, aren't emotions just chemicals?

**AP**: Correct. Stand in front of a person trying to hijack your consciousness with physical charms. With one sway of your hand say, "Chemicals!" and turn around—you are free. At that moment, it might appear gross by common standards. But you are liberated.

Your phobias, manias, anxieties, obsessions and attachments are not yours. You were taught to experience them. Why should you accept that teaching? Be a little rebellious. "I was taught to experience phobia. Why should I accept and live by that teaching when it is just harming me?"

Take this example: an instrument has been tied to your arm. The instrument carries a blade. It can be remote controlled by anybody in the world. Somebody uses the remote there, and the blade starts cutting you here, on your arm. You start thinking that something within you is causing the suffering. You start thinking that the suffering is yours. What you don't see is that both the instrument and the operator of the instrument are not you; both are aliens. What do you do then? You don't fight him. Remember, the entire world is holding the controls. Would you fight the entire world? What would you rather do? You just take the instrument off your arm. "Now I am free. Now you have no control over me." The instrument is the ego—it is the experiencer that is actually a foreigner but remains strapped to your arm as if it is a part of your being. Just unstrap and keep the thing away.

**L**: What if it comes back?

**AP**: Not without your consent. Have great faith in your ability to choose. Nothing happens without your consent. Exercise your power well.

---

"If you realize that you are trained to experience, then you do not remain captive to experience. The moment that emotional surge arises, you will realize that you have been trained to let it arise and dominate you. The whole game of experience is a sham. If you have been trained, then you can also give up the training."

---

*Advait Shivir, BodhSthal, 2018*

# 7

# She Is Biology and Society

*There is not much difference between a human infant and a puppy. But if you look at a dog and you look at a man, there is a lot of difference. A dog is alright as a dog. Man is not alright just being a man. Man is restless.*

**Acharya Prashant (AP):** A small particle of snow falls from a hillside. As it rolls down the slope, what does it gather?

**Listener (L):** More snow.

**AP:** More snow. Ultimately, it becomes quite big. So, if you ask, "What is the fundamental unit that has become big?" it becomes interesting.

Has the first particle gained in size? No. Has the second particle become big? No. It is just an accumulation of influences. In fact, the entire snow on the slope of the mountain is now being represented in the form of the snowball. There is just the *tendency* to accumulate. That tendency continues in time and results in a significant mass.

So, who are you? You are a representation of the entire journey of mankind, the whole evolution. Travelling, travelling and travelling—you have picked up so much. And you are only that which you have picked up.

Is the snowball anything except that which it has picked up?

**L**: Sir, can you please elucidate?

**AP**: Don't go too far back, start from here. Some part of your genetic configuration comes from your father, some from your mother. Your father's genetic configuration comes from many other places, and your mother's comes from many other places. So, to whom does your genetic configuration belong? To everybody. It is everybody who finds an expression in you. But the expression is partial.

**L**: How?

**AP**: The snowball cannot represent all the snow. It will only represent that which it has experienced. So, the expression is partial in that sense, and that is why people differ. People differ because their evolutionary journeys have been different.

**L**: This is a gathering; that too is a gathering.

**AP**: You are a gathering, she is a gathering, I am a gathering.

**L**: What is this entire movement for?

**AP:** This movement has a purpose only in the case of human beings. The difference between man and animal has to be understood. Why have people continuously talked about the importance of human birth?

Man thinks, man is conscious, and man analyzes. Now, this analysis, this thought, this yearning to know and to be peaceful, to be relaxed in knowledge, can work two ways: Either it can make you follow your animal instincts, or it can make you understand your primal conditioning, which is your animal nature, and liberate you from it.

We are all born animals; we are all born like puppies and kittens who have no longing to be liberated. Liberated from what? From the cycle of birth and death, accumulation and dissolution of snow, wanting and not wanting, and from experiencing or suffering pain and pleasure. Animals are alright as they are—settled and contented. And that is not too bad a place to be in. They are alright with their limitations. A dog is alright as a dog. Man is not alright as man. Do you see this?

And as man's brain develops, as his age grows, he becomes even more restless. There is not much difference between a human infant and a puppy. But if you look at a dog and you look at a man, there is a lot of difference. Man is not alright just being man. Man is restless.

That restlessness can go in two different directions. The first way is that he starts depending on thought for liberation. Now thought will become another layer on the mind. You were already an animal; now you also become a social being, a thinking being. You started thinking so that you could be liberated from your animalistic instincts. You did not like that you were a prisoner of lust, fear or insecurity; aren't these things that even an animal experiences? You did not like all that. You turned towards the order of thought which manifests itself as civilization so that you may be liberated. But all those things, instead of liberating you from the animal within, just became another beast on your mind. You were already an animal, and now you are an animal plus the new beast. The new beast could be ideas, thoughts, social conditioning, concepts, books and knowledge.

This is man's predicament. This is what usually happens.

But there is an alternative.

The second way is that man, instead of depending on thoughts, depends on something else and then thought remains just an instrument, a tool. As evident from the first example, man is restless; he is bound to depend on something. He can depend on his own limited capacity, which is the capacity of the thinking mind—a capacity representing the very illness he is trying to cure. Alternately, he could refuse to be dependent on his little self—which is the courageous state of surrender. If man surrenders, then instead of thought becoming another bondage, it becomes liberating. The same thought can enable man to move not only into thoughtlessness but also into freedom from his primordial tendencies.

When thoughts originate from the right point and are surrendered to that which is beyond thought, they take you to that deep meditative point where not only are you free of vicāra (thought), but also free of vṛtti (insticts, tendencies). And now you are liberated from society as well as the animal.

Man is born as dog but gradually becomes worse than the dog—doubly conditioned. The dog is just physically conditioned, but man becomes both physically and socially conditioned. But it is possible for man to go beyond his dogness. The dog was born a dog, will remain a dog, and die a dog. Man is born as dog, but it is not necessary that he die a dog.

The liberated one dies fully before his body dies its usual death; he dies to his dogness. Others continue living as a dog. Their evolutionary journey continues. Their tendencies exhibit them as a dog, next they will be a cat, and then they will be born as a human being. When that happens, somebody will come and say, "Oh! It is such great fortune for them that they are now human beings." It's nothing. The dog became a parrot, the parrot became a river, the river became a bacterium, the bacterium became an elephant, and the elephant will someday become a man. You are not only the elephant; you are the elephant, the jackal, the whale, the dust from Jupiter, the amoeba and the plankton all rolled into one. But you can be freed from all that.

It is up to man to bring the dog life to an end. Else, the dog keeps rolling on until it dies to its doghood. For the dog being manifested as a man, it is a great opportunity to be liberated from animalistic tendencies. Only man has the capacity to bring the inner animal to a final death. But usually man will squander the chance. He will misuse the human form to feed and fatten the inner animal and reaffirm his doghood.

This birth as a human being is precious because it is an opportunity at the very least. It is mostly a squandered opportunity, but at least the chance exists. That is why sages have eulogized human birth so much.

**L**: The opportunity to be liberated—for whom is this opportunity?

**AP**: For you—the one who is asking the question, the one who is eager and restless to ask.

**L**: That is my mind.

**AP**: That is 'me'; not 'my mind'. That is you.

**L**: That is me, exactly. But that's again a gathering!

**AP**: A very active gathering. Soon, it will produce a baby. It has a way of continuing. It rolls on like a huge evolutionary snowball, has a great momentum, and doesn't want to stop.

To roll on is to have an influence on the future. You can have an influence on the future if you produce a baby. You can influence the future if you condition somebody. You can influence the future if you leave your marks and stains on the earth. You can influence the future if you create any ripples in the great ocean of consciousness. You are leaving something behind which will carry forward into the future. That is how the journey continues.

We do not allow the whole thing to die. We always leave something behind—a body, an idea, some effect or some influence. You know, like those idiots who go to temples and scribble their names on the walls.

Where there is nothing, we want to leave a trace. That's the whole mechanism—we are insecure and anxious to continue.

**L**: Sir, is only man privileged to be liberated?

**AP**: It is not so much a privilege; it is mostly a misfortune. Don't be proud of it. Remember, a dog never falls from its dog state. Have you ever seen a corrupt, vicious and scheming dog that attempts genocide?

To be born human is mostly a great misfortune. However, it must still be celebrated for the slim opportunity it offers. Only a Buddha takes up that opportunity, one in a million.

*For most people, to be born human is to be doubly conditioned. Only for the sage does it mean freedom from conditioning.*

We are just being optimistic when we sing praises of human birth. Potentially, yes—to be born a human baby is wonderful, but only potentially.

You must observe both—the social man and the physical animal. If you truly observe the social man, you will have freedom from social conditioning. And if you observe the physical animal closely, you will have freedom from physical conditioning.

If you observe a dog and a bitch mate, you will know what your sexual urges are mostly all about. Then, all that which is venal in your sexual movements will have to drop. When you look at the endeavors of the bitch and the desperation of the dog, you will not be able to avoid seeing that both the dog and the bitch exist in you and the other person. All your romantic notions will simply vanish.

You look at the bitch taking care of the puppies, and you see how caring and ferocious she is when guarding the puppies. You also see that it is cyclical. Some hormones rise within her, and she feels like becoming a mother—there is nothing more to it. The season passes; the urge passes too. The puppies grow up, and the bitch has nothing to do with the puppies. Haven't you seen that?

It is all so pre-scripted. The female animal will want to become a mother; the baby will be born and will have an attachment with the mother; then the season will pass, and then she will again want to become a mother. Now, how can you take your own urge to become a mother seriously?

Having clearly seen what urges you towards maternity, even if you do become a mother, you will be a mother of a very different quality. You would have gone beyond the dog and the bitch. Now you are really a mother. But that cannot happen unless you see that what you usually call sacred motherhood is just that—a very mechanical, biological game.

Observe animals; that will give you freedom from much that is animalistic within you. And observe society; that will give you freedom from that which is social within you. Observe truly, honestly—that is most important.

And if ever you have to choose between the social and the animal, what must you choose? The animal, because the social is doubly conditioned. The animal is just an animal at least. The best thing is to not choose at all or to choose only the Truth. But if ever you are faced with this choice for your bondage, then go for the animal bondage. The animal bondage will be easier to break.

If you choose a partner due to social constraints, you are doomed. If you choose a partner because he or she appears attractive to you, then this too is a curse but a relatively smaller one.

If your union with your partner is social—the social man meets the social woman—then it is a doubly doomed meeting. It is better that the wild man meets the wild woman without any social consideration. Wildness too has its own bondage, but that is a weaker, smaller bondage. It is better to meet your man or woman like a wild animal than meeting them socially. But only relatively better; some people start thinking of the wild as the ultimate and suffer.

The highest meeting is neither as a social being nor as an animal being, but as someone who understands. You are neither a social slave nor an animal. Let the understanding have its way.

---

"You must observe both—the social man and the physical animal. If you truly observe the social man, you will have freedom from social conditioning. And if you observe the physical animal closely, you will have freedom from physical conditioning."

---

*Myth Demolition Tour, Dharamshala, 2016*

# 8

# She Is All That You Like

*That which we call our 'own want' comes really from our body, the past, the conditioning and the influences. It is not ours at all.*

**Acharya Prashant**: There is no bigger slavery than doing what you want to do. There is no bigger slavery than that, and there is no deeper and more malicious slavery than that.

It is not the society that rules us anymore. We now live in a free world which is largely democratic. Nobody rules us from the outside, at least not by force. We are masters of our own choices.

We are ruled from the inside; we are ruled through the desires, wants that we call as our own: "I want this, I want that." And in the absence of an illuminated environment, nobody exists to tell us that that which we think of as our desires are completely external. That which we call our 'own want' comes really from our body, the past, the conditioning and the influences. It is not ours at all.

But in a world that does not acknowledge subtleties, slavery is only acknowledged in its gross form. So, if somebody has yoked you to his carriage and is whipping you from behind, it will be called slavery because it is a gross event available to be seen through the senses. The whole thing is materially evident, so it will be definitely classified as slavery.

See, if somebody is pressuring you and dominating you from the outside, the whiplashes are evident on your body. The entire thing is very bodily, very sensual, very material, and people will readily say, "Yes, yes, this is an incident of slavery."

This is because we live in a world that does not acknowledge anything subtle—it acknowledges only the material. Therefore, internal slavery is not really acknowledged. If you are being controlled from the inside, it is not called slavery at all.

*In fact, the 'inside' is considered the 'real you', while it is really the farthest that you can be from yourself.*

When you say that there is outside and there is inside, the outside is surely external. But that which you call as 'inside' is even more external. Still, we think of the so-called inside as our own.

"Oh, it is mine! My thoughts, my feelings, my desires and my wants!"

This is called the freedom to be a slave.

Long back, if you remember, I had written, "It is bad to be a slave to others and it is far worse to be a slave to yourself."

---

"There is no bigger slavery than doing what you want to do. There is no bigger slavery than that and there is no deeper and more malicious slavery than that."

---

*Advait Shivir, BodhSthal, 2019*

# 9

# She Appears Real and Veils the Reality

*To see the world as an expression of the Truth is one thing; to see the world as the Truth is an entirely different thing.*

**Listener**: Sir, Ramana Maharishi said, "Maya is used to signify the manifestations of the Reality." How can I come to the realization that the world around us is a manifestation of Reality? And if Maya is the only Reality, why is there a negative connotation associated with it?

**Acharya Prashant**: From where Maharishi is looking, there is no difference between Truth and the material-mental manifestation called Maya. He sees no difference, which means that he sees Truth in every aspect of Maya. Therefore, Maharishi can talk of Maya as something innocuous and harmless.

When Maharishi talks of Maya, Maya is no threat. To him, Maya is this entire manifestation called the world, the universe, the saṃsāra. Maya is things, people and our relationship with them.

Maya is mind and matter. When Maharishi looks at the mind, he penetrates the mind deep enough to go to the source of the mind. So, the mind is the Source, the Truth, to Maharishi.

Maharishi can penetrate Maya. Maya can do him no harm. But for you, Maya is distinct from the Truth, is an alternative against the Truth. Therefore, for you, Maya must necessarily have a negative connotation. Do you get the difference?

For Maharishi, the world sprouts from the Source. Maharishi looks at the world, and all he sees is the Truth. He is not held captive by the senses. He holds no expectations from the world. He holds no desires or aversions, so he can see right through the world. When you see right through the world, it is from the Source that you are seeing, and it is only the Source that you see.

So, to Maharishi, the world is an expression of the Truth. For us, the world is an alternative against the Truth. You see the stark difference? We have a choice. When we want to turn away from the Truth, we find refuge in the world. We start expecting from the world that which can only be expected from the Truth. We start considering the world as the Truth.

Get the difference straight. To see the world as an expression of the Truth is one thing; to see the world as the Truth is an entirely different thing. I will give you an analogy. Use it just as a pointer. When the Maharishi looks at a shadow, he smiles because the beloved is near. The shadow indicates the proximity of the beloved. Now the shadow is a beautiful thing as far as Maharishi is concerned. He looks at the shadow of the beloved, and he knows that it is the shadow of the beloved, so he smiles.

The way we operate is very different. We look at the shadow of the beloved and start hugging and kissing the shadow. We think that the shadow *is* the beloved. We think that the shadow can be used as a comfortable and convenient alternative to the beloved. We say, "Oh, the beloved is so demanding, but the shadow demands nothing. So why take the pains of going to the beloved? Since the shadow is available, let's make do with the shadow!"

You get the difference? Do you see how the saints have no problems with Maya or the world? They are the only ones who are very well adjusted to it. The common man is a victim of Maya. Is the difference clear?

Liberation is to see that really there is no alternative to that which you are seeking liberation from. As long as the material body exists, there will necessarily be material Maya all around. There is no escape from Maya. If you want liberation, even that will have to be attained in and through Maya. Liberation is being liberated of your ignorance of the real nature of Maya. If one believes that he is in bondage and seeks liberation, he must realize Maya in the true sense and know that Maya is an expression of Truth.

---

"Liberation is to see that really there is no alternative to that which you are seeking liberation from. As long as the material body exists, there will necessarily be material Maya all around. There is no escape from Maya."

---

*Advait Shivir, BodhSthal, 2019*

# 10

# She Is the Seen

*As far as we are concerned, Maya is real to us. We don't see through Maya; it obstructs our vision, and we do not see it as an obstruction. We call it the vision.*

यत्तदद्रेश्यमग्राह्यमगोत्रमवर्णमचक्षुःश्रोत्रं तदपाणिपादम् ।
नित्यं विभुं सर्वगतं सुसूक्ष्मं तदव्ययं यद्भूतयोनि परिपश्यन्ति धीराः ॥

That the invisible, That the unseizable, without connections, without hue, without eye or ear, that which is without hands or feet, eternal, pervading, which is in all things and impalpable, that which is imperishable, that which is the womb of creatures, sages behold everywhere.

~ Mundaka Upanishad, Verse 1.1.6

**Acharya Prashant (AP):** What do the sages behold everywhere? That which is not available to be seen. The invisible, the unseizable, without connections, without hue, color, without eye or ear, without hands or feet, eternal, pervading in all things, and impalpable, imperishable, the womb of creatures, the origin, the source. That is what the sages behold everywhere.

The sages behold That everywhere because there is nothing else left to be seen.

How do you see something? You see something only when it *blocks* your vision. You see something only when you take it as real, and the moment you see it, it is confirmed that it is real.

Would the sages ever behold Maya? Maya, firstly, cannot block their vision, Maya doesn't reflect anything back to them, and Maya is not real to them at all. So, they see through Maya. If you can see through something, can you see that thing? If you can perfectly see through something, does that thing even exist for you?

But as far as we are concerned, Maya is real to us. We don't see through Maya; it obstructs our vision, and we do not see it as an obstruction. We call it the vision.

It is like this: I want you to look at the sky; I say, "Please, look at the sky," and you shut these doors upon yourself, and then you start calling the blackness of these doors as the sky. What I am saying is, if the sky is real, then the doors have to be taken as something that obstructs the real. Instead, we start calling the doors themselves real. The doors aren't real, they are an obstruction.

Similarly, whatever we see from morning till evening is really an obstruction, not the reality.

*What you are seeing is preventing you from seeing because what you are seeing is not the sight but the screen.*

So, that's the sky *(pointing upwards)*. Now, put your hand in front of your eyes.

*(The listeners experiment)*

It is literal! It is as literal as the sky is to your eyes.

**Listener (L):** So, in this context, what is Maya? When I see you, does the person exist?

**AP:** No. All you are looking at is my skin. And that is not who I am.

**L:** Does that mean that the person does not exist or that my opinions, reverence, or whatever I have for him are not real?

**AP:** The person as *you* see him does not exist at all.

**L:** But the shape and the matter is there, right?

**AP:** You do not know about it. Why are you talking about it? All you know is this skin, and that too some particular parts of the skin. They will remain even when the person is gone.

**L:** But this fact is corroborated by everyone sitting here.

**AP:** How does that matter? Just as you do not know me, how are you so sure that you know anybody else here? Isn't it a vague evidence to cite?

It is like this: *(closes his eyes)* I cannot see anything. But so many other people around me say I can see a lot. If you cannot see anything, how do you even see that there are others here? How do you know anything? How are you so sure of anything?

**L:** But that is the only thing I have known for sure. I can question that, I do question that, but I don't find any other alternative.

**AP:** Just the absence of alternative is no justification to continue with things as they are.

**L:** If it is not a justification to continue with things as they are, it seems to imply that I have a choice.

**AP:** Of course you have.

**L:** I do not see that choice.

**AP:** You don't see that choice because you are very comfortable with the status quo. Why will you ever see a choice when you are happy as you are?

**L:** On the surface I might be happy, I might feel comfortable, but there is a discomfort in the subconscious.

**AP:** That discomfort has to grow, or a vague unspeakable love has to arise. Either you have to grow dissatisfied with how things are for you, or a very far-flung, remote, hazy love has to seize you.

**L:** Love I can't force, obviously.

**AP:** Then at least have that dissatisfaction.

I mean, is it something that *I* need to impress upon you? Don't you see how you get cheated by life frequently? Had things really been as you take them to be, why would you so often be cheated or deceived? Things have either already turned bad for you or are waiting to turn sour. There is stuff that has already deceived you, and there is stuff that is waiting to fall flat. Then how do you claim that you know anything?

Anything and everything that you have trusted has either already betrayed your trust or is vulnerable to betrayal. And that is the reason we remain so suspicious and insecure: because we know that vulnerability.

Your very insecurity is the proof that you do not see anything. Otherwise, why would you be insecure?

You buy a product. Does it really greatly surprise you if it doesn't function? It's almost as if something in you knew that the thing was waiting to fail.

You receive a breakup message. Does it really, really shock the wits out of you? No. Something in you somewhere knew that this was about to happen.

Then how do you propose that you see anything? Why this false and self-defeating confidence?

Humility will afford you a second look at everything in life. But we don't want to have that humility. We want to be cocksure of a lot of things, we want to assume certainty where it is not, and then we pretend to get shocked. "What happened? Oh no! He just got that pink slip and he is stupefied!" And he actually is. Come on, why pretend? Didn't you see it coming?

In a relationship, don't you know what feelings you have towards that other person you call your partner? Then why are you surprised when he reciprocates with the same feelings? Who over here has only goodness and piousness and piety towards his or her partner? Come on. You haven't ever been in a relationship if you haven't ever thought ill of your partner. Then why does it shock you when the same thing comes from the other side? It's just that the other one has made the first move.

All our life we are just somehow trying to come to terms with change. We are grappling with the way things change color. Why do we have to worry so much about change? It is because things just do not remain as they once were; they mutate into something very unpredictable, something unknown. No promise is ever kept.

Even a simple T-shirt doesn't remain the same once you pack it out of that store. A motorcar, the way it appears in the showroom, is it the same when you park it in your own garage? And you paid for the thing as it appeared in the showroom. Had it appeared to you as it appears to you in your own garage, would you have dished out the same sum? Come on.

**L:** No.

**AP:** And still we say we know!

All you know is the surface.

You could say, "But that is something we obviously know, that things change!" If you obviously know that things change, then why do you resist change? Why do you struggle with change? And why do you do so much to cope up with change? It's an entire discipline, no? Coping with change.

Had change really been so acceptable to us, had we really known about change in advance, then why would we be so frightened of change? What is all this future planning? What is all this anxiety and worry? Nothing but a result of our incapacity to see. That is Maya.

Maya is defined as that which is not. Yā mā sā Maya: that which is not is Maya.

Classically, they say Maya exhibits itself in two forms, it has two powers: prakṣepa and vikṣepa.

Prakṣepa implies seeing things where they are not—you see love where it is not, you see cause for concern where there is none—and vikṣepa implies not seeing things as they really are. Your sight is obstructed by a screen, that is vikṣepa. The Truth is not being seen because something nearer to the eyes is being termed as the Truth. And if you have an easy truth comfortably available, why will you go for the real thing?

The sages behold the Truth, the invisible Truth, everywhere because they do not behold anything else. We behold everything else, therefore we do not behold the Truth.

What does it mean to behold? Pay attention. That does not mean that the sages will not see a banana when they see a banana; it's just that the banana is not important enough to be seen. Or you could say, more accurately, that the banana is important enough only for the instrument that sees the banana. The sage is not the instrument, and therefore the sage does not see the banana. The banana is useful to the body, and therefore only the body sees the banana. The banana is not useful to the sage, and the sage is oblivious to the banana. That is what is meant by saying the sages behold only the Truth.

Why would the sage be interested in a banana? These eyeballs are interested in the banana because the energy from the banana would keep these things active, these balls of flesh. So, they may look at the banana. And the mind, for its own movement, requires energy; the mind too might try to figure out how to obtain the banana. What will the sage do with the banana?

In our case, that distinction does not exist. We coolly, confidently say, "I want the banana." If you want the banana, then you are the body. How else does one become the body? The body is entitled to crave for the banana. But when you start craving for the banana, then you are the body—the body and the mind both, remember. Body and mind are one entity. The body may crave for the banana, the mind may find means to get the banana, but all that is none of your business.

The sage does not behold the banana, therefore the sage beholds only the Truth. So, when he looks at the banana, what Truth exactly does he behold? Nothing. No Truth.

When I say, "Look at the sky," is there anything to be seen there? And I am not even talking of the clouds; the clouds too are a screen. When I say, "Look at the sky," am I referring to a tangible object? What is there to be seen in the sky? The sky is not a thing to be seen. But even as you look at the sky, there is so much else to look at.

The sage is not interested. Now you have come to a very simple and easy world. He is not interested in the clouds. Is he interested in the sky? The sky is not a thing to be interested in, so he has no interest. Because he has no interest, therefore he has joy. That joy is another name for Truth—a pure happiness sans interests, sans reasons, sans objects; a pure, simple, innocent happiness requiring nothing.

This has to be very carefully understood, else you will hallucinate that the sages are seeing deities everywhere as they show you in your TV serials. And then they say, "Don't the Vedas say that the sages see God everywhere?" So, the sage is looking this way and there appears some figure here, and then...

The highest and the most sublime thing is brought down to the most gross and grotesque level by our ugly imagination. And the gods do not merely appear—they appear with a bang! And you go: *(joins his hands in a prayerful fashion with eyes wide open)* "The sages behold Truth everywhere!"

So, that is the reason I said don't be so interested in the sky. You already have ample interests. Why do you want to add another one to the list? It is about reducing the length of that list, not doing a plus one to it. So, your Facebook or some other status will read: interested in pizza, skirts, toothpaste, men—and Paramātmā (Supreme Self)!

Like sometimes those Hollywood chaps come up and say, "You know, these days I am into spirituality." How exactly? "I visited that meditation resort in India and did some cool yoga for two months!" That is actually a new brand of yoga. We already have had hot yoga—and now we have cool yoga as well! Plus one, plus one, plus one, plus one... That is how the list has become endless now.

So, don't do a plus one. Instead, do Neti-Neti (not this, not this). Negate, negate, negate. Refute, refute, refute. That is the method of the Upanishads. Say no. Say no, no, no, no!

The Upanishads are like a war cry. They are like a rebellion anthem. They are like an inner uprising. "No! Enough!" That is what the Upanishads cry out.

**L:** Going back to the example about the banana. So, one way to look at a banana would be to see it as a source of energy, and the other way, for example, would be to fantasize about it: "This banana is from Mexico. If I have it, I will feel a certain way. I am a rich person, I can afford an imported banana."

So, these are two different ways of looking at that yellow object. When we say that the banana is just food for the body, or a car is just a way to get from A to B, or a job is just a way to earn enough money to survive, is that kind of a way of looking at things better than thinking that this job will give me prestige, this car gives me a certain status, this food gives me a certain gratification, etc.?

**AP:** It is subtler than the subtlest. What you are talking of is a progressive sublimation of concepts. But nevertheless, you remain within a conceptual frame. So, this kind of ascension is good but not sufficient.

Yes, when you move from a place where you say, "Having a Mexican banana enriches my identity," to a place where you say, "A banana is just a banana," obviously you have made progress. But there is a vast sky beyond. Because, after all, a concept is a concept. Though we agree that there are some concepts more suited to us than others—there are subtler concepts, there are useful concepts—nevertheless, concepts are concepts.

So, the state of the sage really cannot be described. If you are asking what happens in him when he looks at a banana, that is beyond description. At the centermost point, actually nothing happens; no vibrations occur, nothing moves, nothing responds. You could even say he is absent to the banana.

**L:** When you say he is absent to the banana, does that mean he has no desire for the banana?

**AP:** Desire is to the desirous one. The sage is not the desiring entity. There is a need that you have to keep the body afloat, and there is a need you have to keep the self afloat. The sage is now free of the need of the second kind. Most of our needs are not to keep the body afloat; we have needs to keep the self afloat. There is a great difference there.

It is not of much use discussing the state of the sage. Because as far as we are concerned, we need to actually have a relationship with things in the world. The sage has crossed over; he needs no relationships. We need relationships.

So, a pertinent question for us is: How to have the right relationships? How to choose the right thing to eat? Should it be a banana, an apple, a bread, or a burger? That is the question we should answer. And then, gradually, if you are resolute enough, you come to a point where the banana is to the body, not to you. Right now, it is just too far-fetched to be going into that.

We should be asking this. How to relate to food? How to relate to others? How to relate to work? How to relate to clothes? How to relate to family, to house, to money, to everything? What is discretion? What to say no to? What to say yes to? And out of these two, what to say no to comes first because you cannot be in a position to say yes unless you have firstly said no.

The inner vacancy is limited. If it is already occupied, you will not be in a position to afford a yes. To afford a yes, first of all, you have to say no to something that is squatting within. You may actually have to tear it away from your system because a polite no may not suffice. The thing has grown roots within. You will have to forcefully uproot it, and only then is there a vacancy or space for something to say yes to. That is more relevant to us.

What to relate to? What to keep in life? What not to keep in life? What to want? What not to want? How much to want?

**L:** When I ask those questions, it feels like there is some kind of a concept there. I end up asking, "Did I do this to further the self, or did I do this just because it is functional?" And I am confused with the intent behind the question. I don't know if the intent is to find out whether it is purely functional or whether it is about giving myself undue self-importance.

**AP:** Let there be no intent, let there be no question. Let there be just a subtle attention.

Because I am using words, what I am communicating is not getting diluted but over-said. When I say look into your relationships, see what to say yes to, what to say no to, and all those things, it does not exactly proceed this way. You just *attend* to it. You don't attend to it with an objective; you don't attend to it with a specific question.

If you have a specific question, all you can get is a specific answer, and specific answers won't suffice. You need something a bit from the beyond; you need to know that which has so far been unknown to you.

So, your enquiry has to be open-ended. You don't look at a face with the question, "Is he black or white?" If that is the question, the answer will be binary: black or white. But if you just look at him, just attend, you may come to know a lot.

We are talking of attention here. Don't make it a very regulated and predetermined kind of enquiry. There is no objective there. In fact, an enquiry with an objective or intent is no enquiry at all. You will only come to know something that you have already asked for.

Similarly, observation. You don't observe with a purpose. It has to be purposeless observation. You just open yourself to know; what to know is not your business. You are just opening yourself up, and that requires courage because now you can come to know anything.

There is a difference between answering the doorbell after peeping through the peeping lens, being already sure what you are opening yourself to, and wandering in a jungle. Now you are completely open to everything.

**L:** Even if I take away the intent of the question, I notice that there are conclusions in the mind, things coming up this way, that way.

**AP:** That has to be avoided as much as possible, and that is coming to you because of your purposeful life and purposeful education. The kind of life and occupation you have had has taught you to be businesslike with everything. At the end of the day you want to ask, "So, what did I get out of this? How much did I make? What is the benefit?" and you bring over that attitude into this as well.

"I observed. What did I come to know?" You don't have to determine what you came to know. In fact, it is quite likely that this passive attention that you have—J. Krishnamurti used to call it 'choiceless awareness'—may not yield any visible fruits at all, and that is the beauty of it. You are just attentive, and you do not even come to know what attention has yielded to you. And then suddenly, one day you find that you know something very precious. And you wonder with a smile, "How exactly did I come to know this? From where did this knowledge come to me? I have never read such a thing, I have never heard such a thing, I have never thought of such a thing, and yet I know this."

And that is the joy in living: to know without knowing, to know without training, to know without education or purpose, to just know. To know without conditioning—that must be added. A lot of that which we know, we may have been just subconsciously conditioned for it. And that is not what I am calling as meditative knowledge.

Meditative understanding is a different thing altogether, and it offers you such immense freedom; you don't have to be prepared. You just have faith that you will be up to life and up to the occasion and up to challenges when they come.

So, you ask me a question. I just do not know where I would come from; I leave myself free and loose to come from anywhere, and I know, I rest in peace, that whatsoever would come forth would just be the right thing. And there is such security and comfort and effortlessness in it, you do not get tired. The body does, you do not get tired.

And if you can respond to everything in life by not having it upon you to respond, you are not responsible for anything now; you are just letting it happen. As if a greater power beyond you is in charge.

**L:** I guess I feel scared at times, that I might be losing control. I guess I am cautious of whether I am really being meditative or just being taken in by Maya. Because that is what I am trying to avoid.

**AP:** Yes, and that is a good thing to ask because in the name of attentiveness you may even become absent-minded. And that is a danger you have to accept. Maybe after every ten or fifteen minutes, you will check yourself and ask, "What was I doing? Was I attending or was I dreaming, hallucinating?"

Slowly, it becomes a way of life. Things start opening themselves to you—very subtle things, very little, very delicate things. And when things open up, all that they have to say is: "Use us to go past us. There is nothing in us of such great value that you must stay with us."

In fact, nothing in the universe ever wants to deceive you. It is our own infatuation and ignorance that deems things as extraordinarily lucrative. Things by themselves are not, and nothing ever carries a conscious intention to deceive you.

And by 'thing' I mean every object in the world—money, things, people, matter, relationships. When you pay attention to them, they just open their doors, fold their hands, and say, "Great. Now that you have come to us, please carry on. Walk past us. Leave us behind."

---

Anything and everything that you have trusted has either already betrayed your trust or is vulnerable to betrayal. And that is the reason we remain so suspicious and insecure: because we know that vulnerability. Your very insecurity is the proof that you do not see anything. Otherwise, why would you be insecure?

---

*Course in Realization, BodhSthal, 2021*

# 11

# She Is the Little and the Big

*All things are little. Some are little, some are littler, and some are littlest. But there is nothing big. There is nothing big around here.*

यथोर्णनाभिः सृजते गृह्णते च यथा पृथिव्यामोषधयः संभवन्ति ।
यथा सतः पुरुषात्केशलोमानि तथाऽक्षरात्संभवतीह विश्वम् ॥

As the spider puts out and gathers in, as herbs spring up on the earth, as hair of head and body grow from a living man, so here all is born from the immutable.

~ Mundaka Upanishad, Verse 1.1.7

**Acharya Prashant (AP):** "As the spider puts out and gathers in, as herbs spring up on the earth, as hair of head and body grow from a living man, so here all is born from the immutable."

"All is born from the immutable." The Upanishads have no two things to tell. There are no two Truths. There is not even one.

As the spider puts out the web and then takes it in—mythically at least—so does everything arise from that one source and goes back to that one source. "As herbs spring up on the earth, as hair of head and body grow from a living man, so all comes from the immutable."

All mutations arise from the immutable. At the center of everything that is going around is the immovable. What does this mean? This means that if you are to consider something as the source, then please do not consider the movable ones, the mutable ones, as the source.

Negation is always important. So, what is being negated here is to be understood.

The movable and the mutable ones are not to be taken as the source, the first, or the highest. Please don't be so respectful towards these intermediaries, these dwarfs, these perishables. Don't offer them such high regards, they don't deserve it.

It is not about disrespecting the stuff around us; it is not about disrespecting the world. It is about acknowledging that if you respect these little things too much, then you will be left with no respect to offer to the real. If you allow stuff to fill up and dominate your life, how will you allow the central seat, the place of respect, the seat of honor to the real thing?

And the real is a bit pricey, a bit finicky, and immense. The real won't accept an inferior seat. The real is too large to be accommodated in a corner and too pricey to accept a corner. You will have to keep the center vacant, and wait with immense patience and tireless efforts and folded hands and teary eyes. You will have to wait. And not merely wait: I said tireless effort. We are not talking of a passive kind of wait here. Waiting, here, implies the time taken in clearing up. You have to make space, you don't just sit and wait. You take time because there is stuff to be done, mess to be cleared.

Why must you accept anything worldly as the source of wellness or goodness? Be a little contemptuous. Healthy contempt is what you must have. Not the kind of contempt that mocks and derides but contempt that keeps the little thing in its little place, the contempt that you have for the little thing when it starts acting too big for itself.

That is the kind of contempt you must have towards the world. Yes, it is a thing, but a little thing. Let it not throw its weight around; let it not try to dominate you. You cannot allow it to sit on your head. It is a little thing.

That healthy contempt translates into a carefree nature, which in turn translates into joy. You cannot have joy without having that kind of rebellious attitude. You cannot be joyful if you care too much for every little thing.

And all things are little. Some are little, some are littler, and some are littlest. But there is nothing big. There is nothing big around here.

**Listener (L):** If there is nothing big, then why does it appear to be that way?

**AP:** Because it is hiding something big behind it. A little speck of dust in your eyes can screen the sun away. That little thing is able to screen something as big as the sun. Why? Because you have allowed it to come too close to yourself. If you allow a little thing to come too close to you, it will screen away the immense.

So, be very careful about who is entering your intimate space. One sand particle from the beach, and the sun would be lost to you. Let it enter your eyes and then see—the sun is gone.

And suns are suns; they have to be at a distance to keep you safe. And sand is sand; that thing is so small that you carelessly feel like allowing it to come too close to you, it appears harmless. The sun—you won't even try to dream of going too close to it. Sand—you want to allow it: "Okay, sand. Nothing! Come over, come over kiddo!" and the thing comes over. Sun is gone.

What do you think, the face of Maya is the face of some demon or a witch? The face of the Maya is the face of a cute baby. You just can't resist hugging it, caressing it.

And remember, the baby doesn't walk or crawl up to you; *you* go and actively pick it up. Just as the sand won't enter your eyes on its own; *you* must have done something. There is sand in your hands and you rubbed your eyes or something.

And once these little things occupy your life, you can forget the real or the immense. Your entire day, your entire life is now held hostage to such trivia. Entire life becomes a tale of moving from one trifling thing to the other.

Figure out what it is that you have allowed intimacy but doesn't deserve to be intimate with you. No, no, no. Resist, resist, resist. Block, block, block.

**L:** Is trying for the sun, for the immense, a painful practice? If it is, why should we even go for it?

**AP:** *(Sarcastically)* Probably because a sunless life is blissful. If trying for the sun is painful, then living without the sun must be blissful!

Be kind to yourself.

We are conditioned to live sunless lives. To most people even those sporadic moments of joy come almost as a rude shock. We have become such strangers to joy that if it ever does come accidentally to us, we are taken aback by it. We respond even with aggression: "Why the hell has this unwanted stranger come to us?" We call it names. It is not as if you will welcome joy with open arms. When it comes to you, you will abuse it and kick it out. Yes, some flimsy, cheap happiness, that we are open to.

Now do you see how joy and strength go together? Do you see that? Joy is only for the ones who love their strength, who awaken it, summon it, and want to exercise it. If weakness is your trademark... *(Shakes head)*

**L:** I want to discuss these three words: perception, the divine, and karma. When we are talking about the spiritual path, I think it is a life we have chosen. So, in this path, I have realized that our perception has to be improved so that we can see that the divine is all around us and...

**AP:** No. There is nothing called 'improvement of perception'.

*Perception by itself is the projection you inflict upon yourself.*

This word 'perception'—and 'better perception' and 'higher perception'—is just too much in circulation, and one has to watch out. There is a great difference between perception and attention or realization. Perception everybody has, and each one perceives as one is. You see how you are, you get what you are.

So, there is nothing in perception. In fact, the Buddhists, therefore, use the exact opposite: they say 'apperception'. When they want to talk of seeing rightly, they say, "I apperceived," not perceived, because perceiving is always false.

*Perceiving is always false, perception is always false, because the perceiver is false. Full stop.*

Similarly, the divine. Forget the divine. Look at the worldly, the humanly, the mundane. That is important. That divine, as we know it or talk of it or read about it, is just another human fancy. At times, the word can be usefully used to point at something outside of yourself. But in general, looking at something outside of yourself doesn't help. There is so much work to be done inside.

So, talk of your humanness; talk of what you really are living with and living as. And if you do not see what you are living as, there is no question of change in perception or anything.

Perception follows the state of the self, the ego. And the ego is too resistant to change itself. Therefore, it happily agrees to changing things *about* itself or *around* itself, but not itself.

So, it will happily say, "I want to change my perception!"

Sir, change yourself. Your perception will follow you.

"I want to change my behavior!"

Change yourself. The behavior will follow the change.

But that is one thing we rarely want to change: the self itself. Because that is where our stubborn ego sits.

As far as the Upanishads are concerned, very rarely—if ever—do they bring this word up, 'perception'. In my memory, never; probably once or twice somewhere. But these days it is in very, very thick circulation. "Perception, perception, perception!" Won't help. You may train yourself to look at a banana as an apple. Won't help. The one being trained is still the same. The one being trained is still a trained one.

It is one thing when the patient does not want to take medicines; he is at least being honest that he has fallen in love with his disease. It is an even more dangerous thing when the patient admits the disease and starts taking false medicines. Now he is not only diseased but also cunning.

Be very, very alert against false spiritual notions. There is the mind, and there is just the mind, and there are games that the mind plays against its own welfare, against its own interest. See how the mind becomes restless and squirms when its deep-seated beliefs are questioned and attacked. See how you resist. See how your listening just drops to zero.

Not being spiritual is alright. Being a victim to pop-spirituality is lethal, fatal.

Unfortunately, that is the situation. When we talk of Upanishads, people come over on social media and they say, "Where do we get the Upanishads? We want to buy a copy. How do we get them?" That is a very tragic state of things, you know. Because there are bookstores and they have spirituality sections, but they won't have the Upanishads. They would have all kinds of random and nonsensical stuff in the name of spirituality—this doctor, that author, that bestseller—but the genuine thing is just absent. Probably, that is the way things should be, no? The real has to be rare.

Spirituality is not about projecting your hallucinations upon others. You already have enough beliefs, you don't need to gather more from a guru or an author. Don't you have enough of your own? Why do you want to accumulate his garbage as well? Thing is to clean up.

If you want to see something, you will see it. If you want to find something, you will find it. Your world follows your desires, but facts don't. If you really want to see something, project something, just try hard enough and the thing will appear.

Autohypnosis. Spiritual masturbation. Learn to say no to these tendencies.

'Belief' is one word you have to be very, very cautious against. Whenever you find yourself uttering a sentence that begins with "I believe that..." Two hoots to beliefs, yours or mine! How does it matter? Each is entitled to his beliefs. It doesn't serve anybody. Ever found any fellow not having beliefs? But Truth is another thing.

Be guarded against beliefs and see how your beliefs exist just to protect the existing state of the self. Whenever you want to utter something very confidently, whenever you want to say, "But this is the way things are! But this is the way things move!" pay attention. Why are you so assertive that the world is this way? What are you getting from it?

After the session, some of you may feel, "Ah, sounds good... par aisa kar thodi sakte hai (but we can't do this)!"

Why not exactly?

"Nahi, aise thodi hota hai (No, it doesn't happen that way)!"

What is this 'aise thodi hota hai'? How many lives do you have? Inside how many people do you live? Where do these rules come from? What do you get by following these rules, "Kya hota hai, kya nahi hota hai; kya chalta hai, kya nahi chalta hai (What happens, what doesn't happen; what works, what doesn't work)"?

So, I am leaving you with not a conclusion but a challenge. May the challenge be daunting but not insurmountable. May you not pick a small challenge for yourself. Pick a worthy battle and fight it heartfully. And don't worry about anything.

---

"If you allow stuff to fill up and dominate your life, how will you allow the central seat, the place of respect, the seat of honor to the real thing? And the real is a bit pricey, a bit finicky, and immense. The real won't accept an inferior seat."

---

*Course in Realization, BodhSthal, 2021*

# She Conceals, She Reveals

# 12

# How to Know Someone's Real Face?

*Real beauty is not only an absence of ugliness but also a total absence of that which we usually call beauty.*

**Listener:** Why does everything seem so attractive when covered or coated, but the moment the thing is revealed, all the attraction and excitement disappears?

**Acharya Prashant:** It is because you have not yet taken the coat off fully. It is because you have not yet taken off all the coats. Man wears a pretty mask because he thinks that his face is ugly. Otherwise, why would he ever wear a mask?

When the mask is taken off, indeed, what you see initially is an ugly face. But if you can go closer to its factual and apparent ugliness, you discover that what you are calling the face of the man is yet another mask. Remove this mask as well.

We have no real faces. There is nothing such as the real face of a man. What you think of as the correct face of a man is always the next mask. Keep removing the masks. Do not bother about their relative beauty or lack of it. Just because a particular face appears relatively beautiful, do not stop at it. Keep unmasking.

As you keep unmasking with no regard for likes and dislikes, with no regard for beauty and ugliness, with no intention of ever stopping at any favorable face, you come to a point where there is neither beauty nor ugliness in the other one. It is something that your eyes may have never seen before. When your eyes look at this third possibility—the possibility of neither a beautiful nor an ugly face—your eyes themselves get renewed because they are looking at something totally new. When you look at the non-face of the other person, you find that you are looking with non-eyes. Similarly, you too are a non-person when you look at them as a non-person.

Why do you stop at ugliness? Because ugliness is favorable to you in some way. You are quick to unmask the beautiful façade, but why are you not equally quick to unmask the ugly face? Why do you stop there? Why are you comfortable with stopping at ugliness? Don't you see that you stop there because it helps you maintain your worldview and, therefore, yourself? Your worldview is that the world is an ugly place. Any worldview that you hold only upholds the viewer's concept. Your inner concept is that you are an unfortunate soul, a timid and hapless victim in a bad and ugly world. You must somehow keep inventing facts to uphold your concept. You must somehow keep on building, manufacturing, conceptualizing and perceiving ugliness to convince yourself that what you have been thinking for so long is indeed truthful.

You think that the world is a deceptive place. If the world turns out to be a reliable place, then you will be considered stupid. You don't want to be considered foolish, and you don't want to be called out. Everything that you do, the entire foundation of your life's building has been on the premise that the world is ugly. If the world is not ugly, then it will be proved that your personal building is standing on a sorry foundation, and you will have to demolish your building. You will have to move to the open skies. Who likes that? Many people continue to live in their houses even when they know that their houses have shaky foundations. They will not take the risk of moving out into the unknown. They will move out only if, first of all, they are given an alternative house of their choice.

It is good that you like uncovering and unmasking. But you must fully unmask. Do not stop when you see ugliness. If beauty was not real, then ugliness is not real either. Man is layer upon layer of masks, and you should stop at none of those layers. Is it not obvious to ask? If you had to stop somewhere, why did you not stop at the beautiful mask? If you did not want to unearth any further, why did you not stop digging in the first place? If you want to live deluded, then why not simply be deluded by the outermost façade? The outermost is glitzy and glamorous anyway. If you want to be fooled, then be fooled by the outermost sheen; why do you take it off? And then, with self-fulfilling and self-vindicating sorrow, you say, "See, I knew there is only ugliness all around." There is ugliness all around only because you knew in advance about it.

Don't you see that your unmasking is purposeful? You unmask beauty only to reach ugliness. When you reach ugliness, you conveniently stop there. You say, "I need not disclose and unmask anymore." You say so because your purpose has been served, your worldview has been upheld, and you have seen what you have wanted to see. You wanted to convince yourself that the world is horrible, and you have convinced yourself of that. Don't you see that you just want to maintain your own horrible ways by calling the world horrible? Don't you see the self-interest involved there?

If you are to justify your ugliness, it becomes important for you to prove that the world is an ugly place.

I am not rallying for the sensually beautiful. I am not a sentimentalist or a romantic who would say that every man is beautiful, nor will I tell you to look into the eyes of a man or a woman before you, be captivated and say that you see God. I am not talking about all that hormonal nonsense. I am saying that there is a vast silence, a great purity that is beyond our concepts of beautiful and ugly. That is what has been called real beauty. But you need not call that beautiful. To be exact, you can call that an absence of both beauty and ugliness. It is an absence of all conceptualization, purposefulness, and preferences.

Beauty is that which relaxes you and in whose lap you can conveniently go to sleep. Obviously, that beauty cannot be one that excites you. Real beauty, in that sense, is not only an absence of ugliness but also a total absence of that which we usually call as beauty. It does not scintillate or arouse. It makes you uninterested and, therefore, relaxed. Come to that; it is one's real nature and divinity.

If you are unmasking, unmask fully. This unmasking is parallel to uncovering your own eyes. To see the other's real face, you will have to have real eyes. The real eyes are non-eyes and the real face is non-face. That is extremely beautiful. That has been the essence of all sacredness. That is religiosity and spirituality: to have no eyes and to look at no face.

---

"To see the other's real face, you will have to have real eyes. The real eyes are non-eyes and the real face is non-face. That is extremely beautiful. That has been the essence of all sacredness. That is religiosity and spirituality: to have no eyes and to look at no face."

---

*Advait Shivir, BodhSthal, 2017*

# 13

# Mind Invents Dummy Problems to Escape Looking at Itself

*The game of Maya is to give you something important in life. And of course, whatever Maya gives you as important is false, but it will not declare itself to be false; it will declare itself to be very real. It will demand all your concentration.*

**Listener (L):** Sir, being a teacher, I often fear a student who would fully surrender and dislike a student who is not attentive. If both the states and anything in between are only reaffirming my ego, how can my class be of any use to the student?

**Acharya Prashant (AP):** Who is facing this problem? Is the student asking this question? Right now, whatever you are saying is a concept of your own mind. When you say, "Can the session be of any use to the student?" the definition of use is coming from...?

**L:** The teacher.

**AP:** From the mind of the teacher, right? You would regard one particular thing as useful to the student, and she *(addressing another listener)* would regard another thing as useful to the student. You might say, "If I could get the student to laugh, it indicates that the session was useful." She might say, "If I could get the students to silence, then the session was useful."

So, when I say that my session is useful to the students, what do I mean? Whatever I will mean will be an indicator of my own life. What I think of as useful for myself, that I will think of as useful to the student.

If I live in one room which would be hardly 7 feet by 15 feet and you come to me and say, "Sir, I wanted to buy a 3,500 square feet house but instead I could get only a 2,500 square feet house," will I say that you have met a great calamity? When I am living in something which is 100 square feet, will I feel great sympathy for you if you had to live in just 2,500 square feet?

Let us assume that I find money very useful to me. All the time I am thinking of it, it features in all my mental activity, and the mind is calculating all the time. Now, if a student comes to me and says, "Sir, you know what, I could not get that higher paying job; instead I had to settle down for this average one," I will surely feel that the student has lost out on a great deal.

A student comes to you and says, "Sir, I cannot attend your session today because I have to prepare for that particular interview and that company pays me so much. So, the preparation is very useful to me." You will surely allow the student to be absent from your session if you yourself are money-minded. If you are money-minded, then you will immediately feel the need to allow the student to be absent. Do you see this?

You are standing here and the student says, "You know, sir, they are paying so much. I need to go and prepare." And impulsively you say, "Yes, yes, go and prepare! It's a great opportunity." Do you see why you allowed him away from your class? Because to you money is important. Forget about the student—money is important to you. So, the moment the student says that a high paying company is coming, you immediately let the student go.

All of these are purely your own concepts. Even the problem that you have mentioned, "I fear a student who would totally surrender..." I am not asking whether one must fear; I am asking, do we know what fear is? Have we really known what fear is? Had we really known what fear is, how could we have said that we fear surrender? We don't know fear, and we also don't know surrender. And if I am afraid, will I be able to know whether there is a surrendered mind in front of me or not? What am I to do?

Forget about the student, firstly, because only in forgetting about the student can you give the student the best you can.

You see, the best method that the mind finds to escape looking at its own fact is that it...?

**L:** It looks at someone else.

**AP:** It finds somebody else to be occupied with. I have a student, I have a very important task, somebody's ill in my house, something to achieve—you don't even realize that all of these are only shrewd escapes of the mind. Can the false declare itself to be false? Will the false ever come and say, "I am false"?

**L:** No.

**AP:** What is the only method for the false to survive?

**L:** Not to say that it is false.

**AP:** So, it will say, "I am real, I am important, I am the truth." Will it say, "I am false, yet be attached to me"? Will it say, "I am false, yet keep thinking of me"? What will it say? "I am important."

So, all of you have something important in your lives, and you think that it is genuinely important. You have to think that way; otherwise, how can it remain important in your life? How can the false remain important to you without telling you, of course falsely, that "I am important"? Can you come up to me and say, "Sir, I am not coming to the session because I have something unimportant at home"? Will you come and say that? What will you say?

**L:** I have something important.

**AP:** So, that is the game of Maya: to give you something important in life. And of course, whatever is important is false but it will not declare itself to be false; it will declare itself to be very real. It will demand all your concentration. It will say, "I am the object at which the mind should be centered, I am important. I have something important in life. There is something important, I must take care of it." And you will say, "I am genuine, I am sincere about this. There is something important!" Is it important? Don't be too sure that this is important. Is it really important?

Nobody is wicked. Nobody is evil. It's just that we don't summon up our power for attention. Attention has to be called. You have to decide to be attentive. You don't decide to be attentive because you are already sure that you know what is important in life.

You are asking a question. Please check your assumptions. You know what an assumption is? That which is already taken as proven. When something is already taken as proven, that becomes the foundation of all further perception. If I ask Mr. Dhavan *(referring to a listener)* what is this *(pointing at the wall)*, what will he say?

**L:** A wall.

**AP:** He will say, "This is a wall." But will he say, "This is a wall in my frame of reference. This is a wall because I am Mr. Dhavan"? Will he say that? No, he will not say that. He will say that this is a wall. And there is a great underlying assumption which he will not even talk of. What is that assumption? If this is a wall, for this wall to be there something has to be there. What?

**L:** 'I'.

**AP:** The perceiving personality. But that personality is already been taken as a conclusion—as a foregone conclusion. So, he will not talk of this.

*And that is the game of Maya: you make assumptions and then you believe they are real.*

So, what are your assumptions in this question? What is it that you are assuming as the truth? What is it that you are not talking of? What is it that you are not writing, just assuming and conveniently believing in? What is the belief? Ask that. What is the belief, hidden belief?

**L:** When I am taking a class, it should be of some use to the students. They should get something from it, and...

**AP:** ...and I know what usefulness is.

**L:** Yes, and I should be able to know that.

**AP:** The central point you are making is, "If both the states and anything in between are only reaffirming my ego"—you are assuming that you know this. You are assuming that you are in control of this. You are assuming that you know that these are reaffirming your ego.

You know, there are these dictators in countries and everybody wants to kill them, just as in this room everybody becomes a sharpshooter and wants to kill the ego. The dictators in various countries—there was Saddam Hussein, there was Gaddafi—all these people are on the hit list of organizations, countries as well, and the individuals they might have harmed. So, they want to kill them. They are always under threat. So, what do they do? The dictator, so that he may not be killed, would create look-alikes. So, one Saddam Hussein would have twenty Saddam Husseins walking across Iraq, and that dummy is often targeted and killed.

That is a beautiful way, a very successful way of defending yourself: create a dummy, and let the dummy be targeted.

Now you know what I am going to ask. How would the ego want to defend itself? Name some small thing as ego and kill it, and believe that ego has been killed. Now, the dummy has been killed, the real thing is hiding somewhere, but you are happy. "What have I done? I have killed the ego!"

"You know, sir, I am greatly egoistic."

How?

"Sir, you know, I do not talk properly to my driver."

Ah! Here you are. You have identified ego and you have also confessed. So, now you are a saint. Now, today you go and share a meal with your driver, and then you are free from ego.

Now, the bugger is greedy, obnoxious, vicious, hateful, insecure, accumulative—he cannot look at all these monsters in his mind. What did he find as his ego? "You know, I don't talk properly to my driver." A dummy ego has been identified. Now, this can be easily shot down. "I am such a big sinner. And what is my sin? I do not talk properly to my driver!" Ah! Talk properly to your driver and then you will be eligible for the kingdom of heaven! Dummy has been shot and the real one is laughing. Dummy has been conveniently shot.

"Sir, I am such a sinner..."

Why? What have you done?

"Sir, I eat meat."

Ah. Great sin. Thou must repent. So, what will you do from today? You will not eat any flesh.

Now, this bugger drinks the blood of so many people around him; he is an exploitative employer. But he has become ego-free by giving up on animal flesh. The dummy has been shot.

"Sir, there is nothing in my life. It is so dry, I am living a wretched existence."

Why?

"Sir, I do not talk properly to my wife!"

Yes! Son, you figured it out! Today evening, you will gift a black rose to your wife and take her out for dinner, and that way you have dissolved your ego.

Now, this bugger is corrupt in all ways. He is violent towards the entire world; he hoards, he kills, he terrifies. But he has identified his biggest problem as not having dinner with the wife. Now, if the problem is this, then it can be easily rectified;

the dummy can be easily shot. Is this the real problem? Where are the real ones hiding? Why don't you bring them out?

It's like going to a brain surgeon and saying, "Sir, you know, there is some problem with my nail." And he says, "Here is a nail cutter and we will trim your nails. Yes! Now the tumor in your brain has been cured. Go!" And he comes back with very nice nails. Where is the real problem? Don't you see that by presenting dummy problems you are only hiding the real ones?

And that is the reason why we need to have small, miniscule problems in our lives. "Today the milkman didn't come. You know, the electricity fluctuates too much. My son has got only 74% marks!" These small problems are important—very, very important. They are important so that you never look at the real issue, so that your mind is always filled with this little stuff, with these petty problems. This pettiness is needed.

"The car needs to be serviced"—existential problem.

"One of my teeth is aching. It's raining. My son's diapers are still wet! How can I go to the clarity session?" These problems are so important.

"Today she didn't wish me. Oh my God! I am heartbroken! Call the ambulance!"

"I haven't shaved today!" Great problem.

"What will be the result of the upcoming Lok Sabha elections? Existential crisis for me!"

But all these things are important, very important. Why? So that that which is deeply sick in our lives, the central rottenness, can be defended. To secure that we create all these dummies. That is hidden like an assumption: just as the assumption is never seen, only the words are seen, similarly that is never seen.

So, this is nothing. Identify the real question, the real problem.

Isn't it a good tactic to fill your mind with so much trivia that there is no space for anything else? You are busy, and you can also get the feeling of being a conqueror. Because if it is trivia, you can probably do something about it easily. Even without any change you can do something about the trivia. The milkman didn't come? You can call him up and rough him up. So, what do you feel like? "I am strong and I can solve the great problems of life. The milkman has been admonished. Yes! I am Caesar, the admonisher of all milkmen! I have solved a great problem." The mobile is not working? Solve this problem and feel like a winner. "I am not getting a cab." Feel deeply terrified. "Oh! There are no cabs!" Feel terrified. And there is great use in feeling terrified. "I am not getting a cab," and you feel a great sense of fear. Work yourself up, psyche yourself up! "The heavens are about to crash down. I am not getting a cab!" And then you get a cab. How do you feel? "Yes! The great existential mystery has been solved. I have hired a cab!"

You need all these problems. Such trivia is needed so that you may overcome it and feel like a winner, so that there is some meaning in life, so that you don't feel absolutely wretched. The more you are afraid, the more will be the occasions when you are able to do something about that fear; the more will be the chance that you will feel like a full man.

"You know what, yesterday there was a disaster..."

What was the disaster?

"A monkey came and he was eating my tomato! Now I bought ammunition and targeted that monkey, and the monkey is gone! Now give me a Padma-Shri for that. How great do I feel!"

Let me give you an example. Before entering this session hall, we ask you to switch off your mobile phones. Just for two hours, your phone is unreachable. I was informed that when you are asked to switch off your phones, many of you first message your loved ones—so-called loved ones—"I am switching off my mobile. Darling, please don't feel insecure!" After all, it's night time, and you know...

Now, for two hours your darling is unreachable, and what does it become? A great problem! And then how does it feel when you are again able to contact him after two hours? How does it feel? Great relief! "Darling is still within reach. I can still lay my hands on him. He hasn't escaped!"

Now, to feel this sense of relief, what is important? What is needed? That you first must be terribly worried, that there must be a problem. What is the problem? Darling is unreachable.

So, first create a problem out of nothing, and then solve it and feel good, "Life is worthy!" That is the mantra of living. Spend the first half of the day creating the problem, spend the second half of the day solving it, and do not see that this mind that wants to live in this escape is itself the biggest problem. Hide that like an assumption. Keep that buried. The real dictator is hiding and all the time creating dummies so that you can keep shooting the dummies and feel like a winner.

Look at that which really bothers you. Look at the core of your fear. Go to your innermost pain point. See what it is that makes you cry out without any apparent reason. Touch your innermost suffering. Only that can be true relief, not that "I am greatly happy because I got 2% discount on my new sweater."

Touch your innermost suffering, not surface trivia like "These days I am suffering greatly because the temperature is in the range of 15 to 19 degrees. Whenever the temperature is in this range, I suffer!" This is not suffering; this is an escape.

What is the problem of problems? What is the mother problem? Can we find that out? What is the soil in which all these problems germinate? Can we find that out? Or will we keep ourselves occupied with rubbish?

What is the problem of problems? Look at that. Who is the real dictator? Not the dummy ones.

**L:** Our fear.

**AP:** Of what? What is that one mystery which, when dissolved, will dissolve everything? What is that one question of consequence?

**L:** Ego.

**AP:** Then why not look at that directly? Instead of this and that, here and there, and several diverse questions, why not go into that?

What is that? The problem of problems, what is that?

**L:** Maya. Like, "I am what I am."

**AP:** The person that I consider myself to be—*that* is the problem of problems. The person that I consider myself to be.

**L:** And I want to remain like that.

**AP:** That person will want to remain like that, not you. That person wants to remain like that; that's his basic property.

What is the problem of problems? Something is hiding. What is the problem?

**L:** The identities which we want to have with us all the time.

**AP:** And who wants to have that identity? The Atma? Who wants to have that identity?

**L:** The outer self.

**AP:** Which is itself an identity. So, an identity wants to have identity. Then what is the problem?

**L:** It is creating the problem, the attachment.

**AP:** Whose attachment?

**L:** Of the identity.

**AP:** Of the identity. Identity is attached to identity. But what is your problem?

**L:** We want to come out of it, but we...

**AP:** Who wants to come out of it? The identity?

**L:** I myself, the capital self.

**AP:** Another dummy—the capital self. This one is called the Atma Saddam! And whenever the actual Saddam is under threat, the Atma Saddam says, "That is the Saddam with small 'S'. I am the Saddam with capital 'S'. Kill me!"

What is the mother problem?

**L:** I think I am the mother problem, the 'I'.

**AP:** Isn't it a good, funny game? Everybody is happy. You have shot down ten dummies so that you are happy. You are happy thinking what?

**L:** I have done it!

**AP:** And Maya is also happy. Why?

**L:** She has also done it!

**AP:** Everybody is happy! It's a good game. Win-win situation. You think you know, so you are happy. Maya knows that you don't know, so she is happy. Good game. Keep feeling nice about yourself and your life.

"I was unemployed, I got a job. Yes! I solved the problem."

"I felt lonely, I got a wife. Yes! Solved the problem."

Keep feeling good. You are happy, she is happy, everybody is happy. That's why the world is like this. That's why there is no or little possibility of change. When everybody is happy, why should there be a change? Every day you are solving problems. Every moment you are solving problems. So, everybody is happy.

And the bigger a problem-solver you are, the more pride you take in yourself. "You know, there were so many challenges, I conquered them. I married off my eleven daughters!" The bugger first gave birth to eleven daughters, and then he is taking great pride in… "I am somebody who has done something in life, ask me. *Eleven* daughters!"

---

"Spend the first half of the day creating a problem out of nothing, spend the second half of the day solving it, and do not see that this mind that wants to live in this cycle is itself the biggest problem. That is the mantra of modern living."

---

*Advait Shivir, BodhSthal, 2018*

# 14

# Stop Searching for Truth, Look for the False

*The job of man is to just shadow. It is not given to man to do, decide or understand. Real doing happens in your absence; real understanding too happens in your absence.*

छायया स्पृष्टमुष्णं वा शीतं वा सुष्ठु दुःष्ठु वा ।
न स्पृशत्येव यत्किंचित्पुरुषं तद्विलक्षणम् ॥

If the shadow of a man is touched by heat or cold, good or evil, it does not in the least affect the man who is other than his shadow.

~ Vivekachudamani, Verse 504

**Listener:** Sir, I understand that I'm not the shadow when I read the scriptures and listen to you, but I forget this understanding in my daily life. What should I do? Please help me understand.

**Acharya Prashant:** Why do you act contrary to your own understanding? You're saying that Adi Shankaracharya has told you that you are just a shadow, and now you're saying that you forget the understanding.

Does a shadow ever forget anything? What is the job of the shadow? The job of the shadow is to shadow. It is not supposed to do anything but shadow.

And what does the word 'shadow' mean? Shadow means 'to follow'. When you say you are shadowing somebody, that means you are following him. You are only supposed to follow. And here you are asking, "What should I do?" Has a shadow ever asked this question? How would you feel if one day your shadow springs up from the ground and asks you, "What should I do?"

I feel the same way when you ask me this question. I'm surprised, how is the shadow attributing doership to itself? Why is it determined to take on the role of an active agency? Shadows don't talk, shadows don't do, and remember, shadows don't even understand. It is not your job to understand. Then how can it be your job to remember the understanding?

You are saying, "I miss and forget this understanding in my daily living." If you feel that you are the one who misses, that you are the one who understands, then you are not considering yourself a shadow; you are taking yourself as the active doer—and the active doer is just One.

You are trying to act like that One. That is not good at all.

The job of man is to just shadow. It is not given to man to do, decide or understand. Real doing happens in your absence; real understanding, too, happens in your absence. You are not supposed to remember anything.

I repeat, you are not even supposed to understand anything. Relieve yourself of all burdens. You are not obliged to act or even know. Such is your freedom. Such is the freedom of the shadow. The shadow is free of all burdens and responsibilities. It has to follow just one dharma (right action), and the dharma of the shadow is to shadow. That is also what is called discipleship. Just follow the discipline of being a student, stay behind and just follow.

Do you see that following and shadowing are the same?

What does the shadow do? It always follows you. The shadow has no will of its own, no direction of its own, and no decision of its own. If you turn left, will the shadow say, "No, I want to turn right"? You turn left, the shadow turns left too. That is also called surrender. You turn right, the shadow turns right. You are now letting things happen. You are not causing them to happen, you are letting them happen.

So, when the active internal agency called the ego is prepared to consider itself the shadow, then the one that you are is not the shadow. Please understand this.

Atma and you are distinct. Atma has no name. Ego has a name, and we will call the ego as 'you'. So, there is Atma, and there is 'you'. You try hard to act like Atma. The thing called 'you' tries hard to take Atma's place and she doesn't want to do this by merging with the Atma. She wants to remain herself and yet be one with the Atma, even supplant the Atma.

Adi Shankaracharya is telling you, "Let yourself be the shadow." When the 'you' is the shadow and she realizes that she must remain as the shadow, then she does not try to act as the doer. Then the real one, who is so purely you that she can't even be called you, acts and nobody else acts.

Ordinarily, you act, decide, understand, and remember. All that is no good. Adi Shankaracharya is requesting and reminding you to give that up which you are not entitled to have or handle. You will not understand by trying to understand, and you will never be able to remember any understanding.

I have been repeating that for a very long time and you still say that you do not want to forget the understanding. You still feel that you are the one who understands. The one who understands is the real One. The shadow neither understands nor is supposed to understand.

So, if you do not understand, that is fine. Not only do you not understand, you also cannot understand. There is great pleasure in lying flat on the ground like the shadow. That pleasure is called joy.

A man's head is higher than his feet when he stands ordinarily. But look at a shadow—the head and the feet are both at the same level. That's joy, and that can only come in total surrender. There is no burden—the head and the feet are one. The shadow doesn't mind where the master goes either—it is just a shadow. And where are the shadow and the master connected? At the feet, not at the head.

That's the task of 'you': to be connected to Atma, the master, at the master's feet. No other relationship is possible.

Have you ever found a shadow hugging his master?

Have you ever found a shadow disobeying its master?

Have you ever found a shadow having a will of its own?

Have you ever found a shadow threatening to leave the master?

No, that can't happen. The shadow never goes away as long as there is light. But in total darkness, the shadow can disappear.

As long as there is the light of Truth, the shadow refuses to leave the master.

The truthful ego refuses to leave the Atma. Neither would it leave nor would it try to climb up the master. It stays connected at the feet. It says, "I will not go away nor will I forget my real position and try to act too high." That's the dharma of the shadow. Man must remember that his job is to just shadow, and then he would be joyfully guided by the real one.

You must be wondering why Adi Shankaracharya seems to be telling you that you are not the shadow. He is telling you that all those things that are happening to you are actually happening only to your shadow, so don't mind them—you are untouched by all happenings. And here I am telling you that you are purely the shadow. Don't consider these two approaches as contradictory.

Adi Shankara is telling you that you are pure Atma. I'm telling you that you are just the ego. And if you can say that you are just the ego, then in the intensity, depth and truth of this declaration lies the Atma.

You can never directly say or claim that you are the Atma. Atma is light. You can perceive it only when it is reflected. So, when you truthfully declare that you are just the ego, the Truth lies in that declaration. On the contrary, if you try to declare that you are the Atma, then in that declaration lies the ego. It's strange—when you say that you are the ego, then in your saying lies the Truth, but when you swell up and say that you are the Atma, then it is nothing but the ego talking.

Spirituality has long been the unfortunate victim of the ego masquerading as Atma. Therefore, I greatly desist from telling you that you are Brahm, Atma or Truth. I rather want you to acknowledge that you are continuously functioning as the ego. I see nothing wrong with the ego as long as it is a servant ego—a shadow. After all, anything and everything that is done in this world is done only by the ego. It is the material doer, the servant, while the Atma is the master. The master orders the servant to do stuff.

The greatest works have been done by the ego, and the most debauched crimes have also been committed by the ego. High or low, good or bad, left or right, it is the ego in action everywhere. Without ego, there is no action. It's just that the ego should not feel like an actor. The ego, as I said, must be a servant ego. The ego must say, "Though I seem to be doing, the real doer is my master." That should be the ego's humility. It should remind itself: "Though I seem to be doing, the real doer is my master." And that would not be wrong. For example, if a shadow seems to be running, who is actually running? Is it the master or the shadow? Similarly, if a shadow appears to be climbing steps or stairs, who is actually climbing? The master is climbing.

So, you are the ego. Please remain as the ego, but remain as a servant ego, as a surrendered ego. The ego will remain as long as there is the body, because you will differentiate between your hand and the table till there is the body. The moment there is a differentiation between oneself and the world, there is ego. Ego means 'I', and 'I' exists only in the context of the world. The moment you say, "This is me and this is the cup," it is the ego talking.

So, you can never say, "I am the pure Atma." You will have to be honest and accept that you are the ego. Man does not have a choice in choosing between ego and Atma; man is the ego. If he says, "I am the Atma," then he is lying.

But man does have a choice in choosing between a stubborn ego and a servant ego. That's where your real choice lies. The true man is not the one who keeps saying, "I am Atma." The true man is the one who keeps saying, "I am the servant ego." If someone calls himself the Atma, he is grossly mistaken. Please be very cautious of people who keep uttering that they are Brahm, Atma, Truth, or whatever.

You are born as an ego. You may even say that you are condemned to live as the ego. The best that you can then be is a servant ego. Don't try to act like the Truth, which is beyond you. Just be contented to act as the servant ego, the shadow ego.

When you are acting as the shadow ego, then you are in the loving, benevolent, and compassionate custody of the master, the Atma. The moment you have accepted that you are a servant, you have allowed the master to lord over you. Thus you have gained the company of the master. That's how one reaches the Atma.

If you are searching for the Truth, then search for the false instead. If you can successfully see what's false, then in that seeing lies the Truth.

In the name of spirituality, man has been searching for the Truth for ages. But it is beyond man's capacity to find the Truth. What should man rather hunt for? He should hunt out the false.

Strangely enough, people's lives are full of falsehoods, yet they cannot see even these immediate falsehoods. What do they claim? "We are searching for the Truth, and we are going to India, to the hills, to the Himalayas, to Rishikesh looking for the Truth." You can't even see the falsehoods—how will you see the Truth?

First of all, please see the falsehoods for what they are. The day you say, "I am false"—I'm repeating this—the day you say, "I am false," that declaration is powered by the Truth. And now the Truth is yours. You now belong to the Truth, having surrendered yourself to it.

So, please just remain the shadow, and remember that the shadow has total freedom because it is always prostrated at the feet of the master. That's what we need: an ego that is always prostrating at the feet of Atma, the Truth.

---

"If you are searching for the Truth, then rather search for the false instead. If you can successfully see what's false, then in that seeing lies the Truth."

---

*Course in Realization, BodhSthal, 2018*

# 15

# The Elimination of False Knowledge

*You know how to live, you know what your core value is, yet you do not live by it or do justice to it. You betray your own realization and choose to live by second-hand knowledge.*

**Listener (L):** Ramana Maharishi says, "The individual is miserable because he confounds the mind and the body with the Self. This confusion is due to false knowledge. Elimination of false knowledge is alone needed. Such elimination results in realization."

What does he mean by false knowledge? What is the knowledge that should be eliminated?

**Acharya Prashant (AP):** All your knowledge comes from the world. It gives you this knowledge in various forms, structures and fields. But there is one underlying theme in whatever knowledge provided to you by the world through your senses.

And what is that underlying theme? It is that knowledge can be had only from the world and knowledge is possible only about the world. All objects of knowledge are present in the world.

So, the world keeps asserting that the world and knowledge are one. It keeps the possibility open that one may not have complete knowledge about the world, yet it maintains the strong identity that all knowledge is worldly. When I say 'world', I also include the body and the mind.

Look into your mind. Isn't whatever you know, from whichever field, always about something in the world?

If you know geography, you know about the mountains and rivers of the world. If you know polity, then you know about the countries, systems, and constitutions of the countries; all of these are in the world. If you know physics, then you know a lot about the properties of the matter in the world.

You may know this and that. Your range of knowledge may be broad, the fields may be diverse, and there may be a lot of depth to your knowledge. But it is certain that whatever you know is always *about* the world.

So, the world has taught you many things, but along with everything that it has taught you, the world has been parallelly teaching one common thing: that the world is the only possible object of knowledge—if the world is not there, knowledge cannot be there—that the world and knowledge go together.

This is proven wrong when you start knowing instantaneously, without the aid of the world, without any source of knowledge outside of yourself and without any experience or cause whatsoever. That instantaneous knowing proves that the world's assertion that knowledge can only be had from the world was false.

There comes a moment when you suddenly know that grace has blessed you. Where did this knowledge come from? Nobody from outside came to teach you, it was not written in any scripture and you've had no previous experience to draw from. Yet you know with total certainty that you are blessed—that this is grace.

This proves that the world was lying to you. The world was saying, "Only I will give you knowledge. Only I will tell you whatever is there to be known." No, not true. Even without the help of the world, certain things are just known.

For instance, you look at a goat's kid and just know that you cannot be violent towards it. You just know that this little vulnerable thing is worthy of love and protection, and by protecting it you are not doing it a favor; you just know that it is your dharma to be with it, not to harm it and treat it gently. You act like this even though you were not taught to do so. Now you know that there is a certain knowing that arises from within.

This shows that you don't have to depend on the world for knowledge—that the most precious thing does not come from the world. Knowing has a certain quality which is different from knowledge. It is an instantaneous realization without cause or proof and with total certainty. You cannot prove that what you have just learnt is the right thing, yet you are totally certain about it. You are certain without proof.

All your worldly knowledge is doubtful and uncertain. You keep asking for proofs, and even after getting them, your knowledge is tentative. One contrary piece of information can prove all your accumulated knowledge wrong. One little piece of evidence can prove all physics theorems wrong. One bit of news can destroy all your trust or shatter a fifty-year-old relationship.

But knowing which arises from Heart is not so fragile; it does not crumble so easily. It has a great certainty about it.

Let's say you come across a scripture that you have never read before. It may not even belong to your organized religion. Nobody has ever recommended it to you, yet you read it and know that something worth worshipping is in front of you.

Similarly, when you meet someone and fall in love, nobody has tutored you to do so. The person may not even be attractive. You do not know what pulls you there, and you are neither drunk nor an ignorant being. You are awake, in your senses, yet you know that what is happening is not sensual.

If someone asks you to explain this phenomenon, you will not be able to explain it. But you still know that you're doing the right thing. It is causeless, unsubstantiated, yet certain. This is the quality of knowing.

Faced with this knowing, all the knowledge that the world gave you appears weak, trivial, and also deceptive because it had been lying to you all the while.

What was worldly knowledge suggesting to you? That all knowledge will come only from the outside, will always have a cause and be something that can settle in the memory. All worldly knowledge was always transferred from memory to memory.

On the other hand, knowing is so subtle that even your consciousness fails to detect it sometimes. How will it then move into memory? As a result, knowing neither arises from nor enters memory.

When you live with grace, love, and a reasonless devotion, you are free from the bondage of worldly knowledge. This is what Ramana Maharishi calls the elimination of false knowledge.

Such a person says, "Now I live in the knowledge that arises from my Heart, so I do not listen to the knowledge that the world has given me." This is being referred to as the elimination of false knowledge.

All that goes around in the head, the total stuff of consciousness, is false knowledge. If you live by that, you will live in fear and insecurity because that knowledge is neither certain nor total, and obviously not final. Things get added to and deleted from it. What appears so perfectly right in this moment is discarded the next moment.

Worldly knowledge frequently springs up and settles down. That which you just know never deceives you. It never fails you. It is another matter that you may fail it by not being faithful enough to it.

That is the story of our lives, is it not? We know, yet we do not live by our knowing. We have no faith in that which we directly know; we rather have faith in that which others have told us.

You know how to live, you know what your core value is, yet you do not live by it or do justice to it.

You betray your own realization and choose to live by second-hand knowledge. You see security in others; you see security in numbers and crowds. You say, "So many people of the world have verified the external knowledge, so it must be true! Everybody is following it. All the great teachers, researchers and respectable people have given their stamp of approval on the books and on the worldly ways of living. Surely, it must be something right. If I feel uncomfortable, then surely it must be my fault. I would rather accept that which others are pushing onto me and I am uncomfortable with. I would dare not live by that which is totally mine, that which is arising from my own core, from my own self, which is clean and untouched by anybody. It is gentle, vulnerable, smaller than a newborn baby—and as easy to kill."

This knowing, this realization is something that arises from earth, from us. It is our own child. We don't nourish it or raise it. Instead, we silently, secretly just kill it.

If you raise it and nourish it, you will find that it is raising and nourishing you in turn. If you live by it, you will find that there is no better way to live. But all of that is revealed only to those who have faith, first of all. Those who live by fear will live by what the world tells them to do.

Nothing stops you except your beliefs. And all your beliefs are coming from outside.

There is nothing that I say that you do not already know. It is just that I know far less than you do. I only have that which I know purely and by myself. You have that which you know by yourself and you also have that which the world has stuffed into you. So, you are far more knowledgeable than me.

*That is my little secret. I do not know a lot of things like you do.*

And that is why Maharishi is saying, "Kindly be free of your knowledge. Don't be so knowledgeable. Don't be such a scholar. Don't be so world-wise. Remain a little empty, remain a little foolish!"

**L**: Is this notion put into us by the world?

**AP**: Obviously. Don't you see what the world is telling you? The world is telling you that everything is limited. Is not all worldly knowledge about objects? And every object is limited.

So, the world is telling you that everything comes to an end. That's what limits mean, don't they? Everything comes to an end. And if everything comes to an end, then you'll have to live in fear. So, you are suffering.

All the knowledge that ever comes to you comes along with the message of suffering because all knowledge is about limited stuff. That is why one must live by the Heart: because limitlessness only exists in the Heart. And only if there is limitlessness will you refuse to suffer.

It is not for nothing that you are called identical with the infinite Brahm. Don't you see that your appetite is infinite? Don't you see that you do not settle for anything less than the limitless?

And the world can never satisfy you because whatever the world offers is always exhaustible. And that is why knowledge from the world is so dangerous if you make that knowledge the center of your living.

The world will tell you, "This will disappear, that will disappoint, this will end, and that will die."

And your appetite is infinite. So how will the world satisfy your appetite? You are then forever hungry and suffering, and that in turn validates what the ego had already been saying. What did the ego start out with? "I am suffering." And the world has proved the ego right, so now the ego has reason to claim that it is indeed suffering.

Do have worldly knowledge, but don't live by that. Live by something else. In small matters, follow reason; in matters of life and death, be completely reasonless. You want to decide which bus to take to reach home? Apply reason, see which bus takes the least time, compare the fare, etc. But if you want to choose whether or not to love and live with somebody, don't apply reason there. Such decisions are not to be taken based on reason.

The mind is petty and little, so it is perfectly alright for matters that are petty and little. When you want to decide which shirt to wear, apply your mind. That is alright. Look at the season, look at the occasion, and accordingly you may pick a shirt.

But if you are deliberating on what to do with your life, what work to choose, and what mission to choose, then please don't apply your mind. Don't start being calculative in matters that define your life. There, you must be nonsensical and act without reason. Doing so will make you appear foolish, but it is alright. This foolishness is great wisdom.

You must know the right place of the mind and apply the mind there, and you must also know the right place of the Heart and there you must not apply the mind.

The Upanishads put it very beautifully. They say that you must know both vidyā (knowledge of the subject) and avidyā (knowledge of the object). If you miss out on either of them, you will suffer badly.

Where calculation is needed, be calculative until the last penny. But there are also matters where you must not pick up the calculator at all. Usually, we are overly calculative. We use the calculator even in matters of our basic freedom. We live by numbers and digits. This is not good. Not good at all.

Let the Heart take the first position. Let the Heart decide on all matters that are important, and then let the mind, like a servant, figure out the details. Let the Heart decide who you are. Let the Heart decide where to go, and then let the mind work out the itinerary. The mind is good for that.

The mind is a useful machine designed to analyze, compare, dissect, calculate and conclude. It's a good and useful machine. But no machine can ever be a master. Let the master be the master and let the machine be used by the master. Both will be good if the master is in his own place and the machine in its own place.

When that happens, you remain with the master and don't become identified with the machine. When you remain with the master, you are the master. Then the machine becomes your servant. That alone is mind control. That alone is Yoga. That alone is 'citta-vṛtti-nirodha', or control of mind.

How are you so certain that you do not know? Sometimes, just changing the name helps. Instead of saying, "No, no!" say, "Yes, yes!" Your entire body is already saying yes. The body is more intelligent than the conscious mind. Just change the word!

I will repeat this a thousand times: you already know all of this. This is not knowledge that is hidden in some esoteric scripture. This knowledge is not the privilege of a few gurus, enlightened, or awakened people. All of this is commonplace. All of this is your own essence. All of this is just the teacup, the chair, table, and the bed that is found in your own home.

What I am saying is as common as the cutlery found in our homes. Is there anybody here whose home has no cutlery at all? If you have cutlery at your place, then you also have that which I am talking about. It is so very simple, common, and all-pervasive. You cannot not have it!

Do you have blood in your veins? If you do, then you also have that which I am talking of. You cannot not have it.

And that is why your question, "Sir, how do you know all this?" often perplexes me. You are asking me, "Sir, how do you have a teacup at your place?" Is it difficult to have a teacup at home? It is not difficult in India. Is it difficult in France? I don't think that it is difficult to have a teacup at your place anywhere. So why do you ask me with such amazement, "Sir, how do you know all this?" I have all this just as you have teacups.

It is absolutely simple. It is just that you are far too clever for your own good. You are like someone who has eaten a lot and is now squirming, "I have only eaten as much as I need!"

You have consumed too much knowledge and now your tummy is bloated. Spirituality is about having a clean stomach. But you keep eating because of greed, fear, and taste; the world keeps feeding you, and you keep eating. Yoga, then, is not about having a lean body; it is more about having a lean mind that has no excess fat. What is the mind's fat? It is knowledge.

Kabir Sahib puts it very beautifully. He says that the man of Rama is reduced to bones. You understand this? He says he is left with no fat at all. Please understand what he is pointing at. No fat! Why do you hear so much? Why do you watch so much TV? It is the biggest cause of an obese mind. Do you see that all of that is making you fat? Now do you see how deeply meaningful Kabir's statement is?

Even physical obesity is caused by television. And mental obesity is far more dangerous than physical obesity. All the knowledge that the television is feeding you is making you terribly sick.

When you're listening to the television, how will you listen to the Heart? Why do you listen to gossip? Why do you listen to others instead of being with yourself? Why do you spend so much time with people who are sick? Don't you know that your friends are sick? And if you sit with a sick man, what will you get? Sickness.

And you too are sick. Your immune system is so weak. Should a sick man sit with other sick people? Only a healthy man has the right to sit with sick people. The sick one should avoid more sickness like one avoids death.

Why do you keep gathering knowledge?

---

"All that goes around in the head, the total stuff of consciousness, is false knowledge. If you live by that, you will live in fear and insecurity because that knowledge is neither certain nor total, and obviously not final."

---

*Course in Realization, Uttarakhand, 2017*

# 16

# What Is Bondage?

*Maya remains as long as there is darkness about the nature of Maya. That darkness is itself exhibited in the form of the question. Where there is light, there are no questions, or are there?*

**को बन्धः ।**

**बन्ध इति च अनाद्यविद्यावासनया जातोऽहमि-त्यादिसङ्कल्पो बन्धः ।**

What is bondage?

Bondage consists in imagining due to the beginningless latent impressions of nescience, 'I am born', etc.

~ Niralamba Upanishad, Verse 18

**Acharya Prashant:** Bondage, the Upanishad says, is the thought, the imagination, 'I am a body and I am born, I will die.' This, the Upanishad says, comes from anādi-avidyā (beginningless ignorance). So, we will go into what the imagination 'I am born' is all about. But before that, it is important to understand why avidyā (ignorance) or Maya are being called as beginningless.

Brahm is called beginningless, so is Maya. Why is Maya beginningless? Why is Brahm beginningless? To know this, we will have to go into the questioner.

What is being said is that the questioner can never reach the beginning of Maya nor the beginning of Brahm. So, to the questioner, it is said that Maya and Brahm are beginningless for *you*—for you because the question is coming from you. So, to you these two are beginningless.

Why are these two beginningless? Why can't their origin be known? Because Maya does not comprise of an entity called Maya. Maya is verily the questioner himself. Maya resides in the questioner. All questions are Maya. A question implies lack of knowledge.

So, the questioner is Maya. If you can reach the beginning of Maya, then you say, "I have reached the beginning of Maya, and here Maya is no more." When you reach the beginning of something, is that thing there anymore? No, you have reached the end of that thing. If you have reached the end of that thing, who is still remaining there now to say, "Oh! I have reached the end of that thing"?

See, you are the one who is trying to trace the origin of Maya. So, you trace the origin of Maya and you, let's say, let's assume, reach the origin somehow. And upon managing to reach the origin, what do you exclaim? You say, "Oh, I have found the beginning of Maya!" So, you found the beginning of Maya, and you still remain to say that you have found the beginning of Maya. If you indeed do still remain to say that the beginning of Maya has been found, then what remains alive and intact in your form? Maya itself. If Maya still remains alive and intact in your form, have you reached the beginning of Maya?

So, the beginning of Maya is, therefore, reached only when the quest to reach the beginning of Maya is dropped.

Maya remains as long as there is darkness about the nature of Maya. That darkness is itself exhibited in the form of the question. Where there is light, there are no questions, or are there? Remaining yourself—which means remaining Maya-bound—you cannot receive an answer to the question, "From where did Maya or avidyā begin?" The beginning is the end. How is the beginning the end? Because if you have reached the beginning, you have reached the point beyond which there is no more the same substance of which the beginning is being sought.

Let's take a rope. There are two ends to a rope, right? If you reach the beginning of the rope, what have you de-facto reached? The end of the rope, right? If you have reached the end of the rope, how will you know? Who will survive to know? Because you are the rope, you are the questioner, you are the darkness. If that darkness still remains, then there is a contradiction in the claim that the end of darkness has been reached. You cannot say that you survive, you remain, and yet Maya has ended.

Even the question to know about Maya is Maya.

Even the one eager to know the origins of Maya is Maya.

The one who perceives Maya is Maya.

The one eager to know the end of Maya is Maya.

So, if there remains someone to receive the answers to all these questions, or to receive success in his efforts to reach the end of Maya or know the origin of Maya, then Maya has not ended. Therefore, Maya is called beginningless.

If at all you have to ask, "From where did Maya come?" then the only answer is, from your question. That's the answer. When did the world begin? When you ask this question. From where does Maya come? From the same point your question comes.

So, Maya is beginningless because if you can reach the end of Maya, you have reached your own end. If you can reach the end of Maya—which is the beginning of Maya—you have reached your own end. As long as you remain, Maya remains.

Equally, how is Brahm called anādi? Why is Brahm beginningless? You are Maya and Maya cannot know anything. Least of all Maya can know Brahm. When Maya cannot even know itself, how can Maya ever know Brahm? So, how can Maya know the beginning or the middle or the end of Brahm? It does not know its own whereabouts—what will it know about Brahm?

Therefore, to the seeker, it is rightly said that Brahm is the origin, the middle, and the end. And in the same breath it is said that Brahm has no origin, no middle, and no end.

Now, the Upanishad says that when you are in the thrall of anādi-avidyā, then you have the belief that you are the born body, and that is bondage.

Yes, that is bondage because there is no bondage that you experience, that can survive without the assumption or the belief that you are the body. Show me one bondage that can survive without the body. You will say, "But without the body, even I cannot survive! How will my bondages survive?" That's what.

The 'I'-sense identified with the body is the principal bondage.

You see, it is quite interesting here. There are two questions that the Upanishad is addressing: 'What is bondage?' and 'What is liberation?'. It is instructive, insightful to see that the question 'What is bondage?' has been answered in eleven verses. The question 'What is liberation?' has been wrapped up in one single verse, and even that single verse, all that it says is, "Liberation is the cessation of bondage." It says nothing about liberation per se at all.

So, all that has been dealt with in great detail is bondage. If you know bondage, you are liberated. And talking a lot about liberation is bondage. And eleven verses are dedicated to bondage, and of these eleven verses, the first one says the principal bondage is, 'I am the body'; from there all the other ones ensue.

The feeling, the foolhardy certainty that 'I am the body' is the progenitor of all other bondages. I am calling it foolhardy because if you apply a little mind, it is not difficult at all to see that you and the body really cannot be one, that the body as a machine and you as consciousness just cannot be identical. The very nature of the body, if studied, makes it clear that it is something a little alien to you. What remains a mystery, however, is the fact that you are apparently tied to the body. That is the mystery of mysteries. Given two such disparate alien entities, how did this unlikely union become possible? How did you end up in a knot with the body? Who caused this wedding? How have oil and water managed to mix together? That is the wonder of wonders.

The body is a conditioned phenomenon. It comes from two bodies much like itself, undergoes a predictable cycle of growth, development of all kinds, and then decay and death.

And that's all that the body knows—passing through its lifecycle with very predictable characteristics associated with each phase of the lifecycle.

And that is how medicines can be, and are, developed. All medicines are either fully generic or generic to an extent. There is hardly any medicine that applies only to just one individual. Have you seen how one medicine that will be effective on your body will be equally effective on someone belonging to another gender, race, continent, nation, age? So, all bodies are similar to each other to a great extent. There is nothing unique about bodies.

And then you come to consciousness. Is there any medicine that is applicable to the body equally applicable to consciousness as well? Think of it. There is so much that can chemically affect the body—does that same thing really affect your consciousness as well? Many of you will be prompted to say yes. But wait! Consciousness is affected by material or chemical substances only to the extent the consciousness is identified with the body. There are so many things that you can give to the body that will render it almost fully healthy. But can any of those things render health to the consciousness?

The needs of the body are predictable, known, and similar, and universal.

The needs of consciousness are non-material, mystical, almost unknowable.

Two entities, each having needs, existence in two very different dimensions—would you call them as one, identical? The body feels hunger, the consciousness too feels hunger. Can the same thing satisfy both of them? Is there even a remote similarity in what satisfies the body and what satisfies the consciousness?

In fact, we know what satisfies the body. As for consciousness, we do not even know what satisfies it.

The body never says, by itself, "I exist." All existence, all being pertains to consciousness. Consciousness says, "I am." When you are not conscious, is there anybody to say, "I am"? The body is still there lying unconscious. Does the body say, by itself, "I am"? The consciousness says, "I am."

Now, this consciousness that says "I am" exists in one particular dimension. The body exists in a totally different dimension. And yet it is quite wonderful that the consciousness somehow ends up saying, "I am the body."

It is this absurd combination that is at the root of all human misery. Two entities that just cannot have any convergence, any meeting ground, somehow come to meet in the form of a human being. A human being is, in some sense, an impossibility. We shouldn't exist. Even animals—when I say 'human being', I mean all sentient, all conscious beings.

The body could have existed on its own. Or consciousness—free of the body, pure and free—could have existed on its own. How come these two managed to meet and mate? One never knows how it happened. But irrespective of how it happened, it has resulted in great suffering as well as a great possibility.

There is great suffering because this unlikely union has happened.

The great possibility is that this unlikely union can be very beautifully brought to an end, a completion.

Consciousness is tied to the body. But when consciousness is tied to the body, then it cannot behave freely. How will consciousness then feel? What would be the quality of its experience? The quality of the experience of consciousness when it cannot be natural is called bondage or suffering. That's what the Upanishad says.

All suffering is the experience of consciousness when it cannot be its natural Self.

In fact, pure consciousness, non-dual consciousness becomes an experiencing consciousness only after it has combined with the body. Otherwise, the consciousness will not experience anything; it is full, complete, and non-dual in itself. Upon identifying with the body, pure and complete consciousness becomes incomplete and dualistic. It becomes an *experiencer*. It becomes an experiencer of other bodies, other things, the stuff in the universe. And therefore, all experience is of bondage or suffering.

We sometimes love to say, "Oh, I had a great experience! I am experiencing happiness or freedom or bliss!"

But the fact is, as long as there is the experiencer, all experience, directly or indirectly, will be that of suffering.

*Therefore, there can be no experience of that which is real. Only the unreal can be experienced. Truth or freedom, therefore, cannot be experienced.*

To have an experience, first of all, an experiencer has to be there. And the experiencer by definition is the partial, impure, ignorant, dualistic consciousness. If consciousness is still ignorant and impure and incomplete, how will it experience anything complete? Given the state of the consciousness, all its experiences will be of suffering of some kind.

Now, unless we want to say that the experience of Truth too is an experience of some kind of suffering, we should readily agree that Truth cannot be experienced. Similarly, freedom cannot be experienced.

Then how do Truth and freedom come to the human being, the human mind, the human consciousness? They come to us, if at all, in the form of the cessation of the experiencer. Not as another experience to the experiencer, but as the cessation of the experiencer. These are two very different things.

You are in the waking state of consciousness, let's say, and you are having certain experiences; that is one thing. Your consciousness is having experiences; that is one thing. And you pass into deep sleep; that is a totally different thing.

Now, there is a pleasure associated with having experiences in the waking state, and there is a deep bliss associated with retreating into deep sleep. They are different, very different. In one, the first one, the experiencer is alive, kicking, eager, hungry to soak in more experiences and gratify itself. In the other one, the experiencer has simply withdrawn, gone away.

So, that's how Truth comes to you—not as an experience to you but as an end to you. If you do not get the difference between these two things, then you will remain another one of those enlightenment chasers who believe that enlightenment too is some kind of an event, albeit a special event or a special experience.

There are so many people who claim or report extraordinary experiences during meditation or such things, and they deeply believe that these experiences have some metaphysical significance. They believe that it is a call from the beyond or some mystical dimension is calling to them. None of that.

Truth has come to you when you are left aghast. Truth has come to you or is coming to you when you are shocked out of your wits, when there is beauty so great that you are stunned, or when there is a realization so immense that you are left thoughtless. And if you are stunned or thoughtless or witless, then you do not call it an experience. It is some kind of a passing away. It is some kind of a coma. It is almost like your consciousness has been struck with an electric stunner; it has been rendered numb, it has been de-capacitated; it has been inactivated, at least for a while. To use a more shocking analogy, it is some kind of a paralysis of your normal self. That's when you know that something special has happened.

In fact, you cannot really know. That's the thing with Truth. When it comes to you, it does not leave you capable of knowing in the usual sense. It is all over you. It has taken possession of you. You are not left even to report that you are not left.

It is almost like an army post being run over by the adversary and each single one of the soldiers being put to death. Now, who is left to report back to the headquarters that the adversary has won? Such is the complete domination of Truth. When it comes, it totally runs you over. Not even one soldier remains to run back and deliver the news that you have been outnumbered, outgunned, outsmarted.

It would indeed be a strange situation if an entire battalion shows up to report that the battle has been lost. If the enemy has indeed so conclusively won, then each of you should have been put to death by now! If you are surviving, then it appears that it is not the enemy that has won; instead, some kind of charade is being played out. If the enemy is really an enemy, will he really spare you buffoons?

All of you are happily here and declaring, "You know, we are enlightened! Truth came, we experienced the Truth! It was coming, it was coming, and it was coming with heavy guns and armor, artillery, airpower. It came and it was infinite in its capacity, as Truth is. It came and it totally vanquished us!" So far so good. But if you all were totally vanquished, how are you still here grinning and happily narrating your fairytales?

That's the trouble with all experiences of Truth. How is the experiencer surviving? The Truth is the great destroyer. Remember Shri Krishna? "And now I am death, destroyer of the worlds." When the immense form is displayed to Arjuna, it is with these words: "And now I am death, destroyer of the worlds."

Truth is a great ending, a finality, a peak, a closure. If you indeed have had an encounter with absolute Truth, you will not remain. And if you still remain, then what you experienced is some kind of an ordinary dream—an ordinary dream appearing extraordinary, just as people with a weakness for cosmetics do. Any ordinary person can manage to appear extraordinary by virtue of cosmetic treatment. That cosmetic treatment, that dressed up experience is what most of our Truth and enlightenment experiences are—a simple ordinary thing showing up as something extraordinary.

So, why do we say that the Truth is the ending of consciousness? Consciousness as *we* know it. Consciousness, in the sense we are conscious, is consciousness adulterated with physicality. It is this consciousness that comes to an end, not consciousness per se. Consciousness by itself is eternal. But consciousness in the sense of us being conscious is born, and therefore it can come to an end.

Mind you, this unholy union does not really come to an end through physical death. Which union are we referring to? Consciousness and body. So, if we believe that this union ends when the body ends—no, that does not quite happen. The body might end but the universal tendency of consciousness to associate with bodily stuff remains; the personal consciousness does not remain. I am not talking of rebirth here. The tendency of consciousness itself—not personal consciousness—the tendency of consciousness itself to attach to a body remains. So, not much has been gained with the demise of the body.

What is liberation, then? Liberation is when, irrespective of the status of the body, the tendency to affiliate with the body is overcome. The body might be young, old, man's body, woman's body, healthy body, diseased body—doesn't matter. The body is there, and consciousness has seen that it is not the body; there is no point uniting with the body.

Now, it is the supreme way to be alive. The body is alive, and you are not bodily. The body is alive, but the body is now not dictating terms to consciousness. What is the body for then? Consciousness says, "Well, you see, my purpose is freedom from the body. I have seen that I am not the body and it is an absurd union that I am tied to the body. I am seeing that I need to bring this union to an end. How do I bring this union to an end? By using the body properly."

So, the body is a resource. The body is a resource to get rid of body-identification. Human life, then, is a resource to gain liberation from bondages in life.

Once you are no longer dominated by the body, once you become the master of the body, once you start using the body as a good resource, you find that the body can be a very useful servant. Now life is not something random; now life is not a sequence of chance events. Now life is really purposeful. That should have helped you see something important.

Randomness or being subjected to randomness is bondage, and life is all about random things happening to you. Who can predict what will happen the next moment? If you are controlled by random events, if you are taken in by chance happenings, then you are living in bondage. To test your degree of freedom, just see what unpredictability of life does to you. If the vagaries of life upset your consciousness, then you are not free. However much we may like to plan, things seldom go as per the plan. Your freedom is tested by your response when things do not go as per the plan—which means always.

Isn't it a pathetic state to be in? Buffeted by unknown forces from all directions, not knowing what is going to come next, and yet having to bear the consequences of whatever comes next. Most of us live that way—very, very vulnerable, very much at the mercy of situations and, therefore, always afraid.

To be free is to be free of the tyranny of randomness. "Come what may, I am. You will come. And because you will come, you will go. But I am."

Will you remember this?

*"You will come. And because you will come, you will go. But I am."*

---

"If you are controlled by random events, if you are taken in by chance happenings, then you are living in bondage. To test your degree of freedom, just see what unpredictability of life does to you. If the vagaries of life upset your consciousness, then you are not free."

---

*Course in Realization, BodhSthal, 2020*

# 17

# How to Drop All Fakeness and Masks?

*You never lose your masks accidentally. It requires a certain frustration and disappointment. You need to turn heedless and become unconcerned of the value of the mask.*

You ask me how I became a madman. It happened thus: one day, long before the gods were born, I woke from a deep sleep and found all my masks were stolen—the seven masks I have fashioned and worn in seven lives—I ran maskless through the crowded streets shouting, "Thieves, thieves, the cursed thieves."

Men and women laughed at me and some ran to their houses in fear of me.

And when I reached a marketplace, a youth standing on a house-top cried, "He is a madman."

I looked up to behold him; the sun kissed my own naked face for the first time and my soul was inflamed with love for the sun, and I wanted my masks no more. And as if in a trance I cried, "Blessed, blessed are the thieves who stole my masks." Thus, I became a madman.

And I have found both freedom and safety in my madness; the freedom of loneliness and the safety from being understood, for those who understand us, enslave something in us. But let me not be too proud of my safety. Even a thief in a jail is safe from another thief.

~ Khalil Gibran

**Listener:** How can I drop all fakeness and masks?

**Acharya Prashant**: Your masks can be stolen only if you become a bit careless about them. How can somebody steal your masks if you keep them safe in your locker? Become a little careless and give a thief a chance. If they still do not respond to your invitation, tempt them. Hang your masks out on your gate.

You never lose your masks accidentally. It requires a certain frustration and disappointment. You need to turn heedless and become unconcerned of the value of the mask. When your thoughts come to you and say, "Your mask will be taken way," and you say, "Two hoots"—it's then that your mask is taken away.

Have you ever heard of a mask that is right and tight on a person's face being stolen? Who will dare steal such a mask? It will be secure as you have plastered it on your face with all kinds of adhesives. It will become your very face since you are wearing it to perfection. After all, who will steal your face away?

Become a little forgetful. Go, visit a jungle to watch the birds. As it's not possible to see through the tiny slits in the mask, take the mask off. Then, you keep the mask under the tree and become engrossed watching the birds. As the birds fly, they will take you further and further away from the tree, and you will follow them captivated. Soon, it will be sunset. The birds will decide to go home, and then you remember that you have come very far away from your mask. Now there is some possibility that you will lose the mask. You will have to encourage the thief this way.

Or, if you fall in love madly, and the one you are in love with has no taste for things fake, and she says, "Masks won't do; I need real lips." And you say, "No, this is all I have. The world tells me that it's quite a handsome face. These lips are not plastic either; they are real. Let's proceed to kiss." And she says, "No, fakeness doesn't sit well with me; I will have to go."

Now, it's either the mask or her. Since she won't tolerate fakeness, you will have to remove the mask and then a little peck might turn into an embrace. Then you sink into the depths of being memoryless. After long hours of trance, when you recover, you will realize that you have had bliss and lost the mask—some fellow came over, found you lost in union, and did away with the mask.

Oh, wait! Was it you who invited the theft? Was it you who did not want to ever be out of the union again? You feel strange in the beginning. Your skin has become accustomed to the protection; it has become pink and tender. When you lose the mask, the wind and sunlight touch your face for the very first time, and it feels very odd—you want to return to the safety of the masks. It is then that you require someone like the youth in the story to pep you up with a cute quaint name, somebody who, without repugnance, without rejection, calls you the Madman. And you love your maskless face. You love your new name.

And now, who are you? You are nobody. The masks were somebody. They are gone. Now you are nobody. There is freedom in that state. Do you know why? It is because the world knew only the mask. Therefore, the world was able to manipulate the mask. Your unmasked face is entirely new and unexpected. Nobody knows it, so nobody can own, possess or comprehend it.

Freedom from masks is freedom from yourself. It's not a matter of luck; it's a matter of love.

First, you must love somebody or something so much that you are forced to take off your masks. Then, you must love your maskless state so much that you decide to stay maskless. The first step is typically the love for the guru or a mortal beloved, second step is love for the Truth. The first step has been called as Ishq-e-majazi or apara-prema. And the second step is called Ishq–e-haqiqi or para-prema.

Find someone on this earth who will make you drop your mask by any means. He will have to sometimes tempt you or threaten you, since you only understand the language of temptation and fear.

But whatever his instruments, he will succeed, and you will do away with the masks. But that is not sufficient because masks can be again put on. You may still decide to return to the old masked self. Therefore, you must develop a great love for maskless nothingness. Unless you have great love for the nothingness that your unmasked face is, you will find your old masks or even a new mask to put on.

Love, difficult love, demanding love—that's what is needed. Easy love is puppy love—of no avail.

May you choose a very, very difficult one to fall in love with.

---

"First, you must love somebody or something so much that you are forced to take off your masks. Then, you must love your maskless state so much that you decide to stay maskless."

---

*Course in Realization, BodhSthal, 2018*

# 18

# Learn to Cheat the Ego

*Habit is not the problem. The problem is that we are habituated to wrong things. Habits should exist where only one right decision is possible. In all those matters, be fully habituated.*

**Listener:** I think I am very possessive about things, and I am very rooted in this habit. I procrastinate real work by thinking that the real happens on its own. Right now, I feel I'm trapped in habits much more than I actually realize.

Please talk about breaking habits and living a more aware life.

**Acharya Prashant:** Habits will remain. As long as you are alive, habits will remain. Do you know what your most primitive habit is? The breath and the heartbeat. These are the most primitive habits. They will remain.

Why did Prakriti give us habits? It gave us habits so that certain things can happen without thought. It is for the sake of efficiency. Habits are a timesaving measure in Prakriti.

There are so many things that you do out of habit. If you do not do them, you will have to think over them and that will waste your time. That is the logic of Prakriti.

Prakriti says, "Because these things have to be done anyway, why mull over them? Why keep pondering? Why involve decision-making where there can be only one decision?"

So, Prakriti has given you habits. She has given you habits so that you continue physically. But do look at the rationale of habits again: where there can be only one good decision, why spend time in taking the decision? Let the decision be automatic. This automaticity is called habit.

Do you see how the argument is shaping up?

Be habituated. Habits are good if you know what that one right decision is. Then habits are what you call thoughtlessness, transcending thought or nirvikalpata (choicelessness).

Be fully habituated. If you do not have a habit, what do you have? You have choice. Then you operate using your consciousness, by using the faculty of decision-making, weighing the pros and cons, looking at this alternative and that one, and then you come to a decision. That is called normal decision-making. With habit, there is no decision-making involved. You just do it.

So, habit is not the problem. The problem is that we are habituated to the wrong things. Habits should exist where only one right decision is possible. In all those matters, be fully habituated.

In fact, if you are not habituated in those matters, then it's a problem because you will create alternatives for yourself where there must be no alternatives. You will start thinking of things that should not be thought of; those routes, those ways will open up to you that lead only to misery and hell.

Be habituated to the Truth.

Be habituated to freedom.

Be habituated to keeping it simple and straight.

Let these be your habits.

You have talked of procrastination. It's a wonderful thing! Procrastinate everything that is nonsensical.

Why am I asking you to procrastinate? Why am I not asking you to kill it? Because you cannot kill it. As long as the last cell in your body is alive, you cannot kill the tendency to procrastinate. Every cell in your body knows procrastination. If it did not know procrastination, then you would not stay alive.

The entire physical organism works on the principle of right timing. Everything has a right time. So, you have to wait for the right time. Even if there is an urge to do something right now, you suspend it for the future. In some sense, that is procrastination, and that is ingrained in the body.

So, use your tendency to procrastinate. Don't take it as an evil burden. It is useful, provided you know how to use it. Procrastinate the nonsense.

The body too does that. It procrastinates all the nonsense. But in the body's lexicon, what is nonsense? That which is a physical threat. Only that is considered nonsense because the body is physical.

You are a bit beyond the body. You are consciousness—consciousness with an unfinished agenda. So, in your parlance, what is nonsensical? That which deviates you from your real agenda. What is your real agenda? To come to a standstill, to reach a conclusion, to reach an end, to reach a completion.

Procrastinate nonsense. Procrastinate it because it will keep coming to you again and again. It's there in the system, the world, the body, and the tendencies. It's there in our conditioning. All nonsense keeps coming back to you, even if you push it away repeatedly.

What is the solution, then? To procrastinate it. Tell it, "Come tomorrow." You cannot tell it, "Don't come." You can only tell it, "Come tomorrow." Procrastination is useful.

You have to learn to deal with yourself. Spirituality is the art of cheating the ego. Unless you know how to cheat yourself, how can you be spiritual?

If you try to be honest with the ego, you will never be able to deal with the ego. The ego has to be deceived.

When you tell the ego, "Don't come," you are being honest but stupid.

When you tell it, "Come tomorrow," you are being dishonest, but it will be effective.

Learn to cheat yourself. If you are to be loyal to the Truth, you must learn how to be disloyal to yourself. If you are loyal to yourself, you cannot be loyal to the Truth. Pick your side.

How to break habits? By consciously developing useful habits. Learn to say an unconditional and instantaneous 'yes' to the Truth. That is a useful habit.

It has happened before. Here's the story: There was once a student who was given to sleeping a lot. He would sleep with such abandonment that nothing could wake him up.

So, the Guru said, "Your only sadhana (spiritual discipline) is, whenever I take your name, you will have to respond immediately. It does not matter whether you are awake, asleep, conscious, or in a coma; if I take your name, you will have to respond immediately."

It is said the student took many, many years to master this one. But there did come a point when in the middle of the night the fellow would be in deep sleep, and yet deeply aware. When called out, he would immediately get up and say, "Yes, master." That was the only practice given to him, and he mastered it and succeeded.

And then the Guru probably started having fun! He would whisper, "Son," and this fellow would be so alert, he would get up and say, "Yes, master."

Done! You are free. You are free of yourself now.

---

"If you are to be loyal to the Truth, you must learn how to be disloyal to yourself. If you are loyal to yourself, you cannot be loyal to the Truth. Pick your side."

---

*Advait Shivir, BodhSthal, 2019*

# 19

# The Ninety-Nine Floors of Consciousness

*When you understand Prakriti as Prakriti, then Prakriti is merely Prakriti. When you take Prakriti as yourself, then Prakriti is Maya.*

**Listener (L):** I do not want to ask philosophical questions, as you have rightly stopped me from doing so many times in the past. But here are some thoughts knocking about in the head, and I want to know how to make them practical and behaviorally relevant. So, I am asking these three questions only with the purpose of understanding how to live the answers. The first question is, what is the difference between Maya and Prakriti?

**Acharya Prashant (AP):** When you understand Prakriti as Prakriti, then Prakriti is merely Prakriti. When you take Prakriti as yourself, then Prakriti is Maya.

Just a while back I read a joke sent by you. That joke was Maya because you were confusing Prakriti with yourself. You know what that joke said? "Human body is eighty percent water, so we are just cucumbers with anxiety," which is good, the wit is appreciable. Human body is eighty percent water, so we are just cucumbers with anxiety. But do you see the underlying assumption there? Yes, the human body is eighty percent water, but what did you term the human body as? Yourself. Don't you see that? You are not merely comparing the human body to a cucumber; you are also saying, *we* are cucumbers with anxiety. So, there you have taken Prakriti—the body is Prakriti—as yourself, and that is Maya.

You said that the human body is eighty percent water and cucumbers, too, have eighty percent water. Instead, you could have said, "The human body is just a cucumber with anxiety." But you didn't say the human body is a cucumber; you said *we* are cucumbers, and you failed to notice the subtle trap. I looked at that and I said that you are confusing, conflating Prakriti with 'I', and that is Maya.

*When Prakriti is taken as 'I', that is called Maya.*

Ashtavakra tells you, "Bodho'haṃ Prakṛtiḥ paraḥ—I am merely realization, I am separate from Prakriti." Very clearly he says that you are not Prakriti, but see how quickly you label the body as 'I', and that is Maya.

Is the question answered?

**L:** Yes. My second question is, why does God's Prakriti seem opposed to realization of God or peace? Surely, Prakriti and its laws exist by his will and Prakriti is not running a parallel empire of its own. Then why must we be subjected to fluctuations of time, age, mood, hormones, physical needs, etc.?

It has become even more necessary to understand this as I observe how the things I want, the people I love, and my definitions of all these are due to my physical condition at any given time in the day and the brain chemistry of my particular age. They can make us so helpless, so enamored, so willing to surrender to false gods. And then one day all the definitions change because something in the body changes, all these drivers that control us because we took birth or because the species must continue. I can tell myself not to be its puppet at a particular moment, but when I have to do it moment after moment, consistently, then I feel as if I don't fully know what I am saying no to, and that I lack an understanding of the nature of the thing that I am to resist.

All the study of psychology, social psychology, evolutionary biology, and anthropology, etc. seems to be lacking something from which I can distil wisdom about my own true nature. What am I missing? It is not even about faith because there is no fear and I am resolute that this inquiry must be completed, that I will go down this road. I am not even asking for the next step or assurances of what happens or is achieved at the end of the road or if it is worth it, but there is confusion that if I had to be punished by being encaged in a body, why is the body designed to find the false gods beautiful in any way at all? The body's processes have the power to influence the mind itself.

I am not scared; whatever it is inside that used to shy away is standing its ground now. It is not a lack of faith. Sanskriti (social conditioning) can be easily resisted somehow, but Prakriti is feigning innocence and wants to be indulged. "It is only natural," it says. "Not acting on it impulsively would be repression," it says. And apparently that would amount to insulting one of the many forms in which divinity exists. But even I know it's a trap and I am just being used by nature like a machine. It has its own reason and agenda for every chemical secretion and consequent mood that I experience. Please tell me, during Neti-Neti (not this, not this; the Vedantic method of negation), what am I supposed to hold on to?

**AP:** You are questioning about the hormones, the body, its effect upon the mind and such things. First of all, let me rephrase your question to the specifics.

You are saying we are conditioned in two ways: social and biological. The social way you call Sanskriti, and you say that it is easier to resist because you can see what the society is doing, and that is perceivable: its ways change across cultures, across time periods. And the ways of the society have also been studied and captured in literature, in the various social sciences. So, you know all that, and you can cut through the stranglehold of Sanskriti. Your question pertains to Prakriti; you are saying that it is very difficult to get rid of. You are deeply identified with it. How do you know which chemical, which hormonal secretion is affecting your mood in what way? That's the question.

Even this question is not you.

You are trying to say that the society is not you, the body is not you; hence, how to figure the real you out? You have said you can fight the society, but what to do with the body? The body says, "My impulses are natural," and you have said that if you do not cater to those impulses, then they shout, "Repression! Repression!"

Even this question is not you. Without the play of the three prakritik elements, the three guṇas, even this question won't arise. You can go as far and as back in search of yourself—

you will never find yourself; you will never see yourself lying somewhere at the end of the tunnel. You are just the seer.

Look at this question. Even though it sounds inquisitive and carries the halo of spiritual enquiry, it is not much different than any other social enquiry. You might find this shocking or difficult to take, but in one sense all spiritual inquiry is no different from any other activity of a human being. A drunkard is mouthing obscenities, and a genuine seeker is asking the most profound of questions. It is true that they exist at different levels of consciousness, but it is equally true—and more importantly so—that they both are just operating *within* consciousness.

You have to watch them both with an aloofness. You have to look at them both as a child looks at a new and alien object—just with passive wonderment. Passive wonderment, no active indulgence, no trace of knowledge; mere wonderment.

The drunkard is uttering the foulest of words; the spiritual seeker has asked the most profound of questions. Look at them both with equal detachment.

*You are not the fallen one, you are also not the sublime one. You are nobody. You are just nobody.*

At the end of your question, you have asked, "What do I hold on to?" The answer is, nothing. Nothing.

*You don't have a true nature.*

You are asking me, "I am rejecting everything, Neti-Neti. What do I hold on to?" The answer is, nothing. Nothing.

When it comes to rejection, look at all rejectables as equal—all. Be a watcher of everything. Watch the most beautiful of flowers and an ugly carcass in the same way. Here you have an enamoring aroma, there you have a foul stench. It's okay. None of them is fundamentally true. In a relative sense, one might appease the mind, calm you down, and the other might agitate you, work you up. Attraction or repulsion—doesn't matter. You are in a very, very comfortable seat; you are just supposed to laze around. Doing is all happening in Prakriti on its own. You are the super cause who just watches. His is the office on the 100th floor, and the 99 floors are the various departments and sub-departments, sections and such things.

On his 100th floor, he is alone. From there he just watches.

The 99 floors are one dimension. The 99 floors together can be clubbed into one single dimension. Look at them all as one.

The 99 floors are the 99 layers of consciousness. They are the 99 levels of Prakriti. Relatively some of them are inferior and some of them are superior—yes, relatively. Compared to each other, some are inferior and some are superior, but in an absolute sense they all are one and they are all false. In an absolute sense they are all one, all 99 are one, and all false. Only the 100th one is true. And the wise ones have said that these 99 are just the projection, the game of the one sitting on the 100th floor, or let's say, the only floor really possible.

We live on the 99 floors. We sometimes ascend, we sometimes descend. And we are advised to try to ascend; we are advised to be on the highest floor possible to the mortal form. But even if you are on the 99th floor, truly speaking, you are as distant from the 100th floor as you were when you were on the first floor. Having come to the 99th floor, you haven't come any closer to the 100th floor.

Even the best word is just a word, incomparable to silence. But yes, it is still better than a misleading word. You come to the

99th floor, but absolutely, it is still very, very, very distant from the 100th floor. But when you are on the 99th floor, then you, the being, the little creature caught in this maze of floors, is demonstrating, certifying that she is eager to go beyond the murky business of floors. Then, for want of better words, I say that magic happens.

The 99th floor is really the same as the first floor, but when you are on the 99th, you are demonstrating that you are eager to rise. You haven't done much, but you have demonstrated that you want something. It is your want that you have demonstrated, not that you have earned the eligibility to now break away from the system of floors. You have just demonstrated your desperation, your utter desire.

**L:** Is the one who is desiring still the ego?

**AP:** It is still the ego. Even on the 99th floor, the one who is desiring is still the ego. And if it is ego, it is unreal. That's why I said that 1 to 99 can all be bundled into one as false.

So, falseness there is, but falseness can at least demonstrate its love for the Truth; it cannot do any more than that. You are false on the first floor, and remember, you are *equally* false on the 99th floor. But on the 99th floor you are saying, "I am false. Yes, I know I am false. But please, please, please, can I have a taste of Truth?" Then magic happens; you are picked up. It's like a magical ladder dropping from the heavens. You are picked up, a mighty hand descends and just takes you away. Takes what away? That which deserves to be taken away. The body still remains there. All that which is false will remain false. That of you which belongs to the 1 to 99 will remain in 1 to 99, but something else is touched and sanctified; something else gains ascension.

That does not mean that you disappear from the system of floors; you still stay there. You still stay there, but now something about you is up there and from there it can say, "Ha! Riya (the questioner) is there on the 88$^{th}$ floor right now!" Now Riya is there *(points down)* and Riya is there *(points up)*. Riya is at both places. Now Riya is false and Riya is true as well, and the true Riya is watching the false Riya.

Does any floor exist there *(pointing upwards)*? No. If you ask me the address of that place—"Is there any address of that place up there?" No. Is there a place like that at all? No, not at all. No place like that exists. You cannot even say that it is a thousandth floor; it is not.

So, Riya is saying she needs an understanding of the nature of the thing that she is to resist. Who will resist, Riya? You are still taking yourself as *somebody*, somebody who will resist. Can empty space resist? Who are you offering resistance? This is exactly what you must watch. Not resist, watch.

What is to be watched? That there is a force of Prakriti within me that wants to fight something else in Prakriti. A fellow one the 83$^{rd}$ floor wants to fight a fellow on the 45$^{th}$ floor. Ha! You want to take sides? You want to favor one of them? Seriously? The two rascals are both jail inmates. It is just that one is a little senior compared to the other; one of them has been in the jail for eight years, the other one is a little fresh, and the two of them are quarrelling. And here is Riya saying, "I want an understanding of the nature of the thing that I am to resist." Surely she is siding with one of them. Why do you want to favor one of them? Let them fight. Those are things within consciousness. Let consciousness do the resolution. If you are really compassionate about helping your consciousness, which means helping yourself, just be a spectator to the fight.

The one who deserves to win, will win; you don't interfere. As they say, let the best man win.

And within those layers, of course, there are gradations; there are levels and hierarchies, and there are inferiors and superiors. And the game continues. Something is sometimes better than something else, of course. Don't I advise in my sessions, do this and do not do that? All of that is within the 99 floors. One thing is preferable to another thing, and all of that is within the 99 floors. Let all of that happen, don't try to suppress that. You stay where you must.

Yes, you have a body, somebody has a man's body or a woman's body, and you experience that which a human being does, a woman does. You mentioned hormonal surges, chemical secretion, and mood swings. Yes, of course, all of that would happen. On some days you will find the world beautiful. Somebody is finding something beautiful; it might just be due to hormonal effects, fine. Why do you want to tell her, "Listen, it is just that time of the month"? Why? And on other days, for no ostensible reason, the world appears wicked and the lady is upset. She is upset, fine. The Riya of the building is upset and the Riya of the skies must watch. Fine. All of that is happening within the case of the 99 floors.

It is not as if realization will take away your social and biological prejudices or conditioning; it is not going to happen. It is just that you do not identify with them, you do not provide your life energy to the nonsense that is happening there. To what extent can you fight your fate, Riya? It is not going to be possible.

What if you were genetically coded to be more susceptible to cardiac disease—and there are people who are genetically more vulnerable to diabetes, to cardiac disorders, and to many other things in the body. They haven't really done anything in this lifetime to deserve a heart attack. There are so many people who are very physically fit but they would suffer a heart attack at the age of thirty-five; they haven't really done anything to deserve that heart attack, but it comes because it is there in the body. You didn't just watch that; that is going to happen.

So, kindly do not live in the illusion that by being a witness you will be able to eliminate all the pain. The pain will be there, because the pain is contained in the body. The day you were born as a human being, you were born in the world of pain. We all are born in the city of delusion, as we said the other night.

*We are born in the world of pain.*

Now, it is a choice available to you—it is not a very proper word but let me use it—whether to identify with the pain or not. If you identify with the pain, the identification results in resistance. If you identify with the pain, then you suffer. You can either identify, or you can watch. And it's a surreal thing to watch pain. Riya on the floors is in agony—and agony she will face, it is her fate, nobody can fight fate—and Riya from the skies is watching. Riya from the floor is in pain, she is cringing, her entire demeanor has been distorted by angst—and that is inevitable, that is going to happen—and sometimes she will be in utter delight as well. "Ah! A butterfly on my shoulder!" Great delight, a sunny day in the mountains. And those things will come and go.

If you think that spirituality will give you an everlasting tranquil state—as you might have read in some of the books and biographies and descriptions and also autobiographies—then you are just being fooled. It is not going to happen.

*You are born human and to be born human is to be born in pain, disorder and chaos.*

Riya from the skies can watch even as I talk right now. This is your test. If you are there, answer me from wherever you are, who is being addressed right now?

**L:** Riya in the sky.

**AP:** No, it is the Riya on the floors. Riya in the skies is beyond any address; she cannot be talked to. She is just beyondness. Whom am I talking to? Riya on the floors. And when I am talking to her, what is the best that can happen? When I started talking to her, she was on the 70$^{th}$ floor.

**L:** She can come up to the 99$^{th}$ floor.

**AP:** She can come up to the 99$^{th}$ floor, and then from the 99$^{th}$ floor she can be picked up. But that is not in her discretion. That may happen, that may not happen; that only the Riya in the skies knows. Even the guru does not know that. He can at best pull you up to the 99$^{th}$ floor and then you have to wait for the magic to happen.

Then she is saying, "Why does Prakriti seem opposed to God-realization?"

Prakriti is neither opposed nor in favor. How can something on the floors oppose something in the skies? Where is peace?

**L:** In the skies.

**AP:** And where do you find opposition and support? On the floors. How can 'I', a phenomena within the floors, have a bearing on the one element in the skies?

The floors, as you know, are a self-contained phenomena; they are a self-contained delusion. Do the floors have it in their powers to touch the sky? Then how can Prakriti oppose peace? Prakriti doesn't support peace; Prakriti doesn't even oppose peace. Prakriti simply does not know peace. Prakriti and peace are different dimensions altogether.

Prakriti only knows its own ways; there is no question of peace or lack of peace there. Prakriti and peace are like sweetness and red color. Is there a relationship between these two? What is the relationship between sweetness and red? They are different dimensions. You keep doing something in one dimension, it doesn't affect the other dimension.

You are asking, "Prakriti exists by God's will and Prakriti is not running a parallel empire of its own. If it too is subject to God's mighty will, then why are we subjected to the fluctuations of time, age, mood, hormones, physical needs, etc.?"

Who said that *you* are subjected to these things? You are the Riya of the skies. The Riya of the floors is subjected to all these things. And the Riya of the floors is not Riya at all, she is just Prakriti.

So, Prakriti is subjected to itself. You are not subjected to anything, you are there up in the skies. Now, Prakriti is subjecting itself to what it is. Elements of Prakriti are being subjected to the laws of Prakriti. This is an element of Prakriti *(points to the body)*, is it not? So, it is subject to the laws of Prakriti. For example, it is subject to gravitation, it is subject to decay, it is subject to heat, cold, so many things. It is subject to the laws of Prakriti only because it is an element of Prakriti.

Why am I calling this *(points at the body)* as me? Prakriti is operating upon Prakriti. Prakriti is not operating upon me.

The lion is killing the deer. The lion and deer are elements, entities and forms in Prakriti, and killing is a phenomenon in

Prakriti, correct? Now, Riya thinks that she is the deer and she starts crying, "God, why are you meting out this injustice?" The fact is that Riya is not being killed at all; it is the deer that is being killed. But Riya thinks that she is the deer, and because Riya thinks that she is the deer, so now she suffers.

Similarly, there is a woman's body and that body is subject to time, age, disorder, pain, etc.—the laws of Prakriti. The thing in Prakriti is subject to the laws of Prakriti. But Riya thinks that that body belongs to Riya, and now when something happens to that body, like when something happened to that deer, Riya started crying aloud. See how stupid it is.

And it is going to happen because lions would always keep killing deers. You cannot stop that. Just as lions keep killing deers, similarly there is going to be pain to the body. The deers can make merry in between, and they do. Have you not seen them galloping and mating and enjoying the grasslands? Just as they would have pleasure, they would also have pain. The deer that is frolicking today gets killed tomorrow.

If today you say Riya is happy, tomorrow you will also say Riya is sad. All of this is happening within the 99 floors.

So, your fundamental assumption that you have been subjected to—all the things in time and space and all the phenomena—that assumption itself holds no ground. And when you feel pain, then just visualize the lion killing the deer. The lion is killing the deer; why are you jumping about? And even as you sit here, some deer somewhere is surely getting killed. Even as you sit here, aren't lions doing their work? Even as you sit here, aren't deaths happening somewhere? Somebody is always dying somewhere, and if you start identifying with that death, then your life is hell.

Similarly, something wrong is always happening either in your physical universe or in your mental universe. And if you keep identifying with that, then life will be hell. Even as you sit here, you may not know but something is going wrong. See how alert you already feel. Just as some death is happening somewhere in the universe right now, something is going wrong with your personal universe, in your personal universe, right now. And if you start identifying with that or thinking of that, then can you stay attentive? Can you stay in the skies?

**L:** In one of your earlier talks, you even proved that we are not alive, that we are just elements being attracted and giving reactions. So, what is really going on? Am I alive or not?

*(Everyone laughs)*

**AP:** That which you call as life is happening only in the floors, and that is why when you call that as life, life is full of suffering. Life is up there. And the life up there is not subject to the vagaries of time and death.

In the 99 floors, there would necessarily be birth and death. You have a funeral floor here and you have a maternity floor there. And due to your prevalent value system, you place the cremation floor in the basement—not even on the first floor, not even on the ground floor. Where do you put it? In the basement. According to you, it is the lowest thing that can happen. And where do you put the maternity floor? $99^{th}$. Wow! A wonderful thing has happened! And the result of that is that all your life you live in the fear of death because, according to you, birth is the best thing and death is the worst thing, and all that happens in between them you call as life. Death is in the basement, birth is at the top—according to you—and in between is life. This is false. What is false? Not that merely death is false; birth too is false.

And it is a random assignment by you to place birth on the 99th floor. Life is not here; life is there, up there. Riya is asking me is she alive. Depends on who is asking. If the one in the floors is asking, then she is not alive. She may call herself alive; that is just a social convention. If you are breathing, you are alive. You go to a hospital; how do they confirm whether you are alive? They check your pulse, they check your heart rate, they check your brain, and finally they declare you are brain dead or whatever.

So, you may keep telling yourself you are alive according to the medical conventions. But if you listen to the masters, they say that as long as you are in the cycle of birth and death, you cannot call yourself alive. Saint Kabir says, "Sadho ye murdon ka gaaon (Saints, this is the village of the dead)." You are already dead. You are not going to be dead; because you live in the floors, so you are *already* dead. Life is only up there. Up there.

*The more entangled you are in the various states of consciousness, the more dead you are. Only the witness is alive.*

The witness is the one whose state does not change according to what he witnesses. That's the difference compared to the subject-object duality. There is the subject-object combo, and then there is the witness and the witnessed combo. There is a difference there. What is the difference? The subject looks at the object and the object changes the subject. You look at money or a woman and your state changes. That's about the subject and the object. The subject-object combo is found in the floors. And what is it about the witness? He keeps looking at everything and his state does not change—because he does not have a state. Had he had a state, the state would have changed.

The witness is nothing; therefore he cannot change. The subject is something or somebody; therefore he changes. The moment he looks at something, that something changes him. The witness is a nobody. The witness does not change.

If the witness does not change, it means time does not exist for the witness. Time can exist only where there is change, and if the witness is the one who by definition does not change, then time does not exist for the witness. If time does not exist for the witness, the witness cannot die. Therefore, the witness alone is alive, the witness alone is eternal.

If you change, then you are living in time, and if you are living in time... Ha! Death.

The only eternity possible is unchangeability. Don't change. The Riya of the skies must remain forever untouched, unchangeable. The scriptures say virgin, virgin in the spiritual sense.

**L:** When we started this conversation, you said that from the 99$^{th}$ floor Riya gets pulled up, that it happens by itself, the ladder gets dropped down so to speak. But now that we are talking, it is almost like Riya is already there even when she says she is here. So, even when we are here, we are already there. Or are we there only after that pull happens?

**AP:** You are already there. But unless the one there chooses to touch the one here, she will keep feeling that she is merely here.

**L:** If I have never witnessed anything without my judgements, that means that I have never even touched ways with the one there.

**AP:** Yes, yes, yes!

Riya is both here and there, Taru (another listener) is both here and there. But unless the Taru here decides to ascend to the 99th floor, she will keep feeling that she lives only on the floors; she will never become a witness of herself. She will just remain a subject and an object indulging in the floors, in the various phenomena and such things.

**L:** And whose decision is it to indulge? Is it of the Taru of the floors?

**AP:** This decision, you must suppose, is of the Taru of the floors. In reality, it is not of the Taru of the floors. But in your best interests—and I am talking to the Taru of the floors—you *must* keep assuming that she does have the power to ascend to the 99th floor. You must exercise choice because you live in choices.

Choice is an illusion. Absolutely speaking, no choice exists. But then, why does Acharya Prashant keep talking of choices? The fact is, absolutely no choice whatsoever exists. I keep talking of choices because choice is a phenomenon of the floors, and it is your only hope or your only savior. You keep choosing, and because you keep choosing, you can also choose to rise to the 99th floor. So, that's the choice you must make.

**L:** And when you say that evil and virtue are the same...

**AP:** Same in the sense that they both are within the floors.

**L:** But still, virtue is better than evil.

**AP:** Relatively better. Absolutely, not at all better. If you ask the witness if one is thing better than the other, he says, "Ha! Come on. They all are merely objects to be witnessed, and hence all of them are at par, at the same level."

**L:** Are we picked up to the skies only from the 99$^{th}$ floor or from the lower floors also?

**AP:** No, that's the condition. That's why tapasya (austerities) and sadhana (spiritual practice) are needed. What is the definition of sadhana? That which takes you from the fifth floor to the 99$^{th}$ floor. He will not pick you up from the fifth floor; the pick-up point is on the 99$^{th}$ floor.

**L:** I have a question on choosing virtue over evil. When we were speaking the other day, you mentioned something about clearing of the Karmic account. Is it related to this discussion?

**AP:** This is that clearing of the Karmic account. *(Moves his hand up implying ascension within the floors)*

**L:** So, you rise only once those are cleared?

**AP:** In the process of rising you clear the Karmic account.

**L:** So, in the process of rising, you have to choose virtue?

**AP:** Yes, yes. But when the Riya from the sky looks at all this, she says all of this is just nonsense.

**L:** But she doesn't mean anything to me right now.

**AP:** She doesn't mean anything. For you, I said, it is in your best interest to assume, to believe that you do have a choice and exercise that choice.

**L:** At one place you were saying, don't be fake. So, even if we are feeling hurt, we shouldn't be fake. Is this being said to the Riya of the 100$^{th}$ floor?

**AP:** Nothing can ever be said to her. Who can address her? Nobody. Only she can address herself.

**L:** Is watching the Riya of the floors the meaning of 'don't be fake'?

**AP:** 'Don't be fake' and 'be real'—both these statements are within the 99 floors only. When you are being honest to yourself, even then you are in the 99 floors, and when you are faking stuff, even then you are here. All that which you can perceive, experience, and name is in the floor domain; it is not outside of that. It's just that relatively speaking—only relatively speaking—honesty is better than feigning. In that world *(points up)* there is nothing called honesty. Honesty is a virtue only in the phenomenal world. But because you take yourself as belonging to the phenomena, so you better be honest.

**L:** What is awareness? Is awareness playing cards, cricket, watching movies, doing nothing? And why is there the fear of being alone?

**AP:** Awareness is when none of this matters to you. You may play cards, you may play cricket, you may watch a movie, or you may be alone or whatever. When none of that matters to you, that is awareness.

Matter must matter only to matter, not to you. There is you, the matter, and there is you, the You. And matter must matter only to you, the matter. That is awareness. To you, the You, matter must not matter. And cards, cricket, movies are just matter.

When to you, the You, no matter matters, then you are aware.

Being aware is just about being you, the You; not you, the matter.

Should matter matter? Of course, to you, the matter. If an insect comes and bites here, it should matter, and the hand must jerk the insect away. But You must have remained unmoved when this phenomenon was happening. The hand should have quickly moved and protected itself, but You should have remained unmoved. You, the matter, should have reacted to insect, the matter; but you, the You, should have remained unmoved and untouched by insect, the matter. But you can remain untouched by insect, the matter, only when you are also untouched by hand, the matter.

When you are someone your own hand cannot touch, then you are aware.

**L:** Thoughts, feelings, emotions, everything is matter?

**AP:** Of course, all is matter. That which can be named is matter. Mind is matter. That which can rise or appear or show up as something in mind is matter.

**L:** How can I increase my intellect so that I will take the right decisions in life?

**AP:** Keep listening. All this is an arrangement just for that, for the right decisions. Just that your question is a little misdirected.

Right decisions appear to be coming from intellect, but for the intellect to make right decisions, the intellect must be guided by something beyond itself. If the intellect is its own master, then it cannot make right decisions. For your logic to be well-directed, for your intellect to move in the right direction, the intellect must be subservient to something immense.

But for now it suffices to say, stay put, keep listening.

**L:** When we go to the various gurus belonging to the various cults and communities, they do not motivate us to go to the 99th floor; they are assuring us that even from the second floor we would be picked up, and this is the most hurtful of deceptions.

**AP:** That's true. If you realize this, you will never ever be found in front of a false guru. The very mark of a false guru is that he will not encourage you to make the disciplined effort to rise to the 99th floor. He will never say sadhana and tapasya are needed. He will say, "Wherever you are, God's grace will shine on you." It is not going to happen.

Let me explain. When you are on the second floor, then God's grace shines on you to encourage you to move to the 99th floor. That's how God's grace shines on you when you are on the second floor. It shines on you and it tells you, go to the 99th for more help. If God's grace is shining on you, you cannot make the second floor your home.

And if a teacher is telling you, "Wherever you are, you are alright. If you're sitting in the shop, stay there and you can be liberated. If you are subject to various obsessions, intoxications, infatuations, you need not give them up. It's okay. In the eyes of God all are equal. He doesn't differentiate between black and white, saint and sinner. So, stay where you are, feel comfortable. You don't need to make any effort. Enjoy your luxurious home, and from there you will be picked up," that guru is just cheating you, he does not want to disturb your comfort zone. The fellow just is a creature of the floors.

And when you want to stay in the floors, then you are hardly ever targeting That *(points up)*. When you are in the floors, then you are only targeting something that is relatively beneficial to you according to your own value system. Don't forget, the value systems too are just a delusional phenomena within the floors. Outside the floors no value system exists.

*All values exist only within the floors, and since they exist within the floors, they are all false.*

I repeat this: If God's grace shines on you when you are on the second floor, then it will only encourage you to move to the 99th floor. If you say, "God's grace is shining on me and I will be straightaway picked up from the second floor," it is not going to happen. God has only one pick-up point. I repeat, the helipad is on the 99th floor; it cannot be on the second floor, you know that. Can there be helipads on the second floor? Not going to happen.

Make a disciplined effort. Ascend.

Yes, the plane is waiting for you, but you have to go to the airport at the right time before your death, and get the boarding pass. The flight is indeed waiting for you, but you have to move to the airport, and the airport is on the 99th floor. Reach there in time—and you don't know how much time you have. Better hurry up.

**L:** The boarding pass is...?

**AP:** Once you reach the 99th floor you get everything—the security check, the boarding pass—but first of all you must reach the 99th floor. You will not get a boarding pass where you are, and once you are on the 99th floor, you need not worry about the boarding pass. Just reach in time.

**L:** What is the 99th floor?

**AP:** Sitting on the second floor, you cannot know that. When you are on the second floor, talk only of the third floor.

**L:** What can I do to make that grace fall on me?

**AP:** Remain open to that. On the second floor, on any floor, you make choices. Choose to receive grace. Choose to invest your time, resources, attention, energy towards receiving grace rather than in miscellaneous pursuits.

**L:** Receiving grace means...?

**AP:** You know that. On every floor that choice is there, which means that knowledge is there. You cannot have choice without knowledge. Of course, all that knowledge is bogus and all those choices don't mean anything in the absolute sense. But if you are on the second floor, then you surely know at least what is worthy of being done on that floor itself. You cannot know too much, but I said you can know a bit about at least the second and third floor.

I am sitting here. I may not know what it means to be absolutely liberated. But if a thorn is pricking me in my back, I at least know what to do with the thorn; I at least know what to do with this prick right now.

I may not know absolute liberation, but I know what to do on this floor. What to do on this floor? Get rid of that which is pricking your right now—and there is a lot that is pricking you, right? Get rid of that. You have that knowledge.

**L:** It's almost like you become lighter when you go up...

**AP:** Good. It is like a gas balloon!

*(Everyone laughs)*

Rockets, as they move up, what do they do? They keep shedding their load. To go up you have to keep shedding your load; otherwise, you will just be bound to gravity.

"The more entangled you are in the various states of consciousness, the more dead you are. Only the witness is alive. The witness is the one whose state does not change according to what he witnesses."

*Advait Shivir, BodhSthal, 2018*

# 20

# Helplessly Riding a Powerful Horse That Obeys Its Own Whims

*We do not exist. We are products of a factory we know nothing of, let alone have any control over. We are utterly predictable like pre-designed factory products. There is nothing called Atma within us. There is nothing called the Self within us.*

A horse suddenly came galloping down the road. It seemed as though the man had somewhere important to go. Another man, who was standing alongside the road, shouted, "Where are you going?" and the man on the horse replied, "I don't know! Ask the horse!"

~ Zen Koan

**Acharya Prashant (AP)**: "Anatta," said the Buddha once.

We do not exist, we are not.

The horse is, we are not.

The horse knows, we do not.

For if we are not, how will we know?

We are galloping, obviously, and if we are not galloping, then we are just gallivanting and loitering. Some movement is always there. But is the movement yours? If you are not galloping, then you might be flying, diving, stuttering, or just hobbling. Sometimes, you are stationary and at rest. But even if you are at rest, is the rest yours?

Neither the movement nor the rest is yours. The horses are doing everything. And when things are not happening, it is because the horses are not doing anything.

The man on the horse is the one who calls himself 'I'. The horse is the entire system—mind, body, and universe. The horse is the within and the without. The horse is the tendency within and the universe outside, and the 'I' is merely the horse's slave.

We do not exist. We are products of a factory we know nothing of let alone have any control over. We are utterly predictable like pre-designed factory products.

There is nothing called Atma within us. There is nothing called the Self within us.

We are not. There is no real 'I'.

We are being carried hither-thither by situations alone. And when I say 'situations', I do not merely mean external situations. I also mean that which is situated within us in the form of hormones, emotions, thoughts, tendencies, and conditioning.

We are not. We are purely situational and accidental.

So, the man is not in the rider's seat; the man is just being carried along.

And the horse! Why is it galloping? Because the horse knows nothing better than to gallop. It is the horse's prakriti to gallop, it is the horse's physical nature to gallop, and the horse is doing just that. The man is just being taken along. While it may appear that the man is on the top of the horse, it is really the horse that is on the top of the man.

Hold your horses—even one horse is so difficult to rein! You have half a dozen, right? That which carries you away is your horse. Name your horses! Name your horses before the next session. I want the entire gang to put their fingers on their horses. That is your Koan.

The man on the horse is already a Zen practitioner. This is because he at least knows that he does not know where he is going. Thus, he very honestly says, "Ask the horse."

We are very dishonest people. We claim that we set the direction and the speed, don't we? The horse turns towards the tavern and you claim that you want to get drunk. Do you really want to get drunk? No, it is your horse that is deciding that you will get drunk, and you are neither careful nor honest enough to know that. Anything can happen in this state.

On the way towards the tavern, the horse crosses the temple and stops there for a reason known only to horses. And then you say, "I want to get married." Do you want to get married or is it your horse talking?

You neither want to get drunk, nor do you want to get married because you do not exist, and that is what the Buddha called anatta (non-self).

Do you know what you are? We are not even bad; we are just not. It would have been comforting had we at least been consistently bad. We are not even bad! Situations change and we become good. Forget about being good; we are not even bad. We are just not!

Yesterday, I was telling someone that neither are we of one color, nor are we even a rainbow.

Kabir Sahib said, "Ek rang me jo rahe aisa birla koi (The man of one color is rare)."

Forget about being of one color, we are not even of multiple colors. We are a hologram! Look at it once, it is one thing; look at it differently, it is another thing. We are a kaleidoscope. We are not even loyal to our vices; forget about being consistent with virtues.

We do not exist.

What you call a man is just a bundle of his conditioning, his production and his experiences. Of those experiences, there is no set experiencer either. The experiences form the experiencer, and therefore the experiencer himself is a flux, constantly changing along with the experience. Or, you could say the experience and the experiencer are one.

What is constant, then? Nothing. The game is constant. Everything else is so very fluid.

When somebody asks you, "Who am I?" reply, "Are you?"

To ask, "Who am I?" first of all there must exist an 'I'. There is no 'I'. There are just buttons. Press this button and the man is happy; press that button and the lady will start sulking; press the button of respect and the old man is delighted. Consciousness is very predictable and, therefore, controllable.

How can you get angry at someone? They do not exist! Obviously if you can listen, if there is someone to listen to, you would have already heard that there is nobody to love. To love someone, first of all, someone must exist.

We are not even split personalities; our personality is a predictable flow, like wisps of smoke rising and making shapes and faces in the process.

"Do you love me, darling?"

"Love whom? Who are you? *Are* you? You were somebody else twenty minutes back, now you are somebody else. And if I utter one predictable statement, you will change into somebody else. Who is there to be loved?"

That is also the beginning of compassion because you realize that there is nobody to love, and equally there is nobody to be angry on, there is nobody to hate.

The man on the horse is helpless. How can you be angry with him? How can you hate him? He is not deciding the wrong direction. He cannot even decide the right direction because he does not exist! Only the horse exists, and the horse makes no decisions; the decisions of the horse have been decided since the beginning of time.

Prakriti decides the gallop of the horse. Sat-Raj-Tam (the three qualities of Prakriti) decide the way the horse will go and the distance it will travel. When ammonia meets chlorine, you get ammonium chloride. Who did anything? Was there somebody to do anything? Are we anything other than our chemicals? It is a sorry question to ask, but I need not feel sorry because there is nobody to answer. Why is there nobody to answer? Because nobody exists.

There is laughing gas and there is tear gas—you can be made to laugh and you can be made to cry. Now, do your tears have any value? Just chemicals. Chemicals! Does your laughter or smile have any value? Horses, horses!

And obviously, in the ultimate sense, the man on the horse cannot do anything right; he cannot be held responsible for anything either. That brings us back to compassion.

Potentially, the man on the horse could have been so much, but actually, he is a nobody. He does not exist. And that is compassion: to see that you could have been so much, but right now you do not even exist. There is the flesh, there are the bones, there are the chemicals, but there is nothing called 'you'.

That 'you' could have been the one who really understood. But is there understanding in your life? There is the horse, and that is all. And when the horse gallops, who can hold it? When the emotions surge and the prejudices operate, they are unstoppable. Where are you?

Compassion is to see two things. Firstly, that you cannot be blamed, and secondly, that you could have been so much, but you have wasted the opportunity. Both these things must be seen parallelly.

The first thing is that you have made a total mess of yourself. Only the mess exists, you do not. And the second thing to be seen parallelly is that the mess was not necessary. Was it necessary?

I ask you, couldn't you have lived another way? Couldn't you have decided another way? Was it all so essential? Isn't there a better version of you? Isn't there anything called 'you'?

The man on the horse meets someone along the way and says, "I have come to you." Has he? He has come to no one because he is no one. The horse has carried him to the other person.

Just as the horse has brought him to the other person, the horse will also take him away from that person. The only way to really be with someone is to jump out, drop out, fall down, climb down, whatever is possible for you.

Is it any fun riding a horse you do not own or control? Just suddenly, things happen to you. Just suddenly, your mood changes. There is nothing called a self that decides. Things just happen.

Where is the self? Where are you?

---

"What you call a man is just a bundle of his conditioning, his production and his experiences. Of those experiences, there is no set experiencer either. The experiences form the experiencer, and therefore the experiencer himself is a flux, constantly changing along with the experience."

---

*Course in Realization, BodhSthal, 2018*

# 21

# All That Shines Is But the Shadow of His Shining

*The brain is the vessel, pure consciousness is infinite. But if the vessel is dirty, then anything that you put into it will also get dirty, and that dirty consciousness is called personal consciousness, and that's what we live in.*

**न तत्र सूर्यो भाति न चन्द्रतारकं नेमा विद्युतो भान्ति कुतोऽयमग्निः ।**
**तमेव भान्तमनुभाति सर्वं तस्य भासा सर्वमिदं विभाति ॥**

There the sun shines not and the moon has no splendor and the stars are blind; there these lightnings flash not, how then shall burn this earthly fire? All that shines is but the shadow of His shining; all this universe is effulgent with His light.

~ Mundaka Upanishad, Verse 2.2.11

**Acharya Prashant (AP):** Beautiful. One does not even feel like speaking on the verse; it is almost an act of irreverence and also an act that cannot ever fully succeed. It is probably enough to read it and re-read it and keep reading it. Anyway, I will attempt to say something.

"There the sun shines not and the moon has no splendor and the stars are blind; there these lightnings flash not, how then shall burn this earthly fire?"

All objects that you have in this universe are no more there—where? In the purest state of the mind, because the purest state of mind is a point of pure subjectivity. What is pure subjectivity? The subject and the object merge into one. The fundamental separation that is at the root of our misery is dissolved. So, neither are there objects, nor is there the light that acts as the bridge between subjects and objects. When objects are not there, when light is not there, how can any separation be there. How can the universe be there?

In some way this is the most honest description of pure subjectivity, and in another way this is a great method to shock the mind out of its regular patterns of perception. Mind has a pattern, it imagines. Even in its imagination it cannot conceive seeing something sans light; it cannot conceive existing sans objects or space. And here the sage is shocking the mind out of its regular mode of experience. He says there is that possibility in which there is nothing that you know of, not even time. This befuddles the mind, and when the mind is befuddled, then it becomes a little receptive to something that is not in its usual patterns, in its normal habit.

"All that shines is but the shadow of His shining; all this universe is effulgent with His light."

All that you experience in your dualistic perception arises from that something special that we just referred to. Otherwise, you can have the fire, you can have the stone, you can have a great wall just behind the fire, and you can have a body exactly similar to yours but without any consciousness, and there would be no fire experienced by the body.

You can have a body, a sensory mechanism that is a total replica of your body in the material sense and yet it would know nothing, see nothing, hear nothing, experience nothing. Brahm is that special something at the foundation of all your experiences, and you experience the world; therefore, Brahm is said to be the foundation of the world.

There is no objective world sans the subject who experiences it. And in spite of the presence of the objective world, the subject would experience nothing were it just a material entity arising out of the material world. Had the subject been just a material entity born out of the material world, the subject wouldn't have been able to experience the material world. Some reactions might have happened. This mic is gathering my voice right now; the sound waves are hitting some electronic and mechanical systems within, but you cannot equate it to the ears. The camera is gathering my image, but there is a fundamental difference between the quality of the eyes and the camera.

There is a fundamental difference between the quality of the brain and the mind. The brain is absolutely material, and we agree that it can be replicated one day. We are already cloning cells, right? But what about the mind? There is something related to the mind that is just not material, and that is everything because everything is in that. Is the universe there without consciousness? So, everything is in consciousness, and consciousness is from that which we are calling as Brahm, that special something, that miracle. Therefore, we are saying that the entire universe arises from Brahm; in other words, consciousness arises from Brahm.

When you say consciousness arises from Brahm, what you are actually saying is that consciousness does not arise from material alone. Like everything else in the Upanishads, read this statement also in negatival. Consciousness arises from Brahm is to be read as, consciousness does not arise from material alone.

**Listener (L):** You said consciousness is not dependent on material...

**AP:** Material *alone*.

**L:** Still, consciousness can be considered as a function of the material, because if someone's brain is damaged or someone dies, consciousness ceases. How is consciousness independent of the material then? What is the role of the material in consciousness? Or is this the case just for me?

**AP:** It is just for you. See, your material, which is your brain, determines your particular consciousness. What we talk of or what we experience is not pure consciousness but personal consciousness, and personal consciousness obviously depends on the person, which is the body. So, no more body, no more personal consciousness. What we are saying is that the mere presence of the brain is not the presence of consciousness itself. Neurons, the entire nervous system is necessary, but not sufficient. Remove the brain, and the entire sense of personal 'I' is gone, no doubt about it. But the brain by itself doesn't suffice to produce the 'I'. You could take it like this: Consciousness is impersonal but personalized through the brain.

**L:** So, this verse is referring to the impersonal consciousness?

**AP:** Impersonal consciousness, and that is called pure consciousness or Atma. Which means, the more your consciousness is dependent on your brain, which is your body, the more you are in a state of bondage. Therefore, liberation is about liberating your consciousness from the bundle of conditioning that your body is.

**L:** The personal consciousness could be the forces which are driving me—for instance, fear, anxiety, lust etc.

**AP:** Everything, all of that.

**L:** Is it because the material is heavily driving that consciousness?

**AP:** But do not ask what then is impersonal consciousness. Do not ask what is pure consciousness, because pure consciousness is actually simply a dissolution of all that which you know as normal consciousness. Limited vision, limited perception, the fear, the greed, the lust that you just talked of—all that is personal consciousness, and all these things are introduced as stains or distortions in the consciousness by the brain.

So, the brain is the storehouse of the various impressions and the various latent tendencies, and when the brain exports all these things that it has into consciousness, what you get is your impure or personal consciousness.

**L:** So, the pure consciousness is trying to manifest itself through the brain.

**AP:** See, the brain is the vessel, pure consciousness is infinite. But if the vessel is dirty, then anything that you put into it will also get dirty, and that dirty consciousness is called personal consciousness, and that's what we live in. The dirt in the personal consciousness comes from the brain, which is the body. Therefore, the scriptures talk so much about disidentifying from the body, because the bodily tendencies are what is distorting or corrupting the consciousness.

**L:** You said consciousness cannot arise in the case of cloning. But the natural way of birth is also an application of genes; it is almost like cloning. There, by default, the personal consciousness is evolved. So, a personal consciousness could also be cloned.

**AP:** Obviously.

**L:** So, is there any chance that pure consciousness is still there?

**AP:** No. When you say pure consciousness is still there, you are locating it in space somewhere; you are trying to talk of pure consciousness from within the impurity of your brain. So, that kind of speculation is bound to fail. The maximum we can do is talk of the impurities.

See, that is the reason why Buddha's teachings were successful in a space where classical Vedanta was corrupted: because Buddha would only talk of that which needs to be disallowed or falsified. He would not talk of what Atma is. He would rather talk of how the ego masquerades as the Atma. He would, therefore, not talk of pure consciousness; he would only talk of how impure our consciousness is.

The moment you start talking about pure consciousness, you get into this particular trap. You start speculating, imagining, and you start conducting thought experiments like: "If a thing is cloned, will it have pure consciousness, impure consciousness?" The problem is that when you are conducting all these thought experiments, you do not realize that you are sprinting, galloping within the boundaries of conditioned space-time. And from within these boundaries, you are trying to speculate about something that is beyond the brain by definition.

So, it suffices to say that our consciousness is impure, our consciousness is stained by all the stuff that the brain is carrying as memory, as conditioning, as impressions. What will happen if consciousness is liberated from the unworthy company of the brain? Let's not talk about it.

I was once asked: When one is no more body-identified, where does his consciousness live? The fellow was happily imagining that consciousness is something that floats in space, pure consciousness, and impure consciousness is something that you absorb from space; because you have absorbed it, now it comes in contact with the brain and, therefore, gets stained. Whereas, pure consciousness is like waves and those waves are floating in space.

This kind of speculation just doesn't help. Therefore, I say we should talk of falseness. We should not venture too much into the Truth. It won't help.

Somebody was giving this example that, you know, pure consciousness is like radio waves and your brain is the receiver. So, just as voice is heard from a radio set only when the radio set is there—when the radio set is not there then, irrespective of the presence of waves, you will hear no sound—similarly a fellow is conscious only when the body is there. When the body is not there, consciousness will still be there, just as the radio waves are there even if the radio is not there. Consciousness would still be there even when the body is not there.

This is a very flawed example. You are assuming that consciousness is something that floats in space, whereas the fact is that space is a construct of your brain. What you are saying is, here is the brain and pure consciousness is floating in the space. So, you are imagining that space is distinct from the brain. You are saying that impure consciousness is in the brain, in contact with the brain, and pure consciousness is floating in the space, and you think that this is a great model. This is a stupid model because the space you are talking of is itself a construct of the brain. So, what do you mean by space *outside* the brain?

There is no space outside the brain. Space is all inside the brain. No brain, no space.

But we like to construct smart models like these. They don't help. Therefore, let's restrict ourselves to the negativa.

---

"There is no objective world sans the subject who experiences it. You can have a body, a sensory mechanism that is a total replica of your body in the material sense, and yet it would know nothing, see nothing, hear nothing, experience nothing. Brahm is that special something at the foundation of all your experiences."

---

*Course in Realization, BodhSthal, 2021*

# Only She Can Lead You into Reality

# 22

# Don't Deceive Yourself by Calling the Ego False

*Spirituality is not merely about stating absolutist concepts. Spirituality is firstly about helping the petty and suffering ego. Help is even greater than the Truth. There is no truth bigger than compassion.*

**Listener (L)**: A non-dualist author says, "Any attempt to reduce or transcend or discipline what is only a concept can only affirm its illusory appearance of reality. When all concepts are seen for what they are, that is, are recognized as such and nothing more, the ego finds itself in the waste-paper basket with the rest."

Sir, you say that we know concepts to be concepts. But intellectual understanding does not bring about any lasting fulfilment. Even if the fact of no-self is momentarily perceived, it quickly reverts to being just a concept. The ego-self always quickly regains its rule. At the same time, there is a whole neo-spiritual movement around the assertion that there is no ego-self or 'I' at all.

**Acharya Prashant (AP):** We need to remember the fundamentals. What is all spirituality for? To whom are the sayings of the sages addressed? The ego might be an illusion or a concept, but is it a concept to itself? Does the ego ever accept itself to be an illusion?

Please understand. The ego is just a concept, vacuous fiction or an absurd story only from the point of view of the Absolute. Are we the Absolute? Conceptually, yes. Factually? Not at all.

And why do we not have the right to speak as the Absolute, or on behalf of the Absolute? Because our lives do not permit that. Our lives do not stand testimony to our Absolute nature. We do not choose to live as the Absolute. Since we do not live in absoluteness, it would not be honest to take an absolute point of view. It does not behove us.

It's like a frog talking the language of the elephant. What does the frog live as? A frog. It would befit and benefit the frog to honestly acknowledge its frogness. In the heart of the frog, there might exist a latent elephant, agreed, but the elephantness is latent, dormant, asleep; it does not manifest, neither in action nor life. Then what right does the frog have to speak as the elephant would?

Absolutely speaking, the frog does not exist, and the elephant is the Truth of the frog. But from the vantage point of the frog, the little frog itself is the Absolute.

You know what we are referring to. The frog is the ego. The elephant is the True Self, no-self, Brahm, Atma, Śūnyatā, the Absolute, the absolute fullness or the absolute emptiness, as you please. However, for the frog, is the elephant or the frog real? The frog is. Some of you might contest this. You may say, "No, no, no! Whatsoever the frog may say, ultimately only the elephant is real." If only the elephant is real, why are we writing and reading books? If only the elephant is real, who is the guru and who is the disciple? If only the elephant is real, what is the point of the Buddha's teachings?

The elephant is non-dual, right? Then the elephant cannot have anybody to talk to. If only the elephant is real, there is no point in having this discussion here. Honesty demands that we acknowledge that the elephant might be real, but as frogs, we are far too removed from that infinite reality. As frogs, all we do is croak in our little wells.

Croaking—this is how the little thing lives. And then, when it comes to spirituality, this petty fellow wants to declare: "I am the great void. I am nothing. I am no-self. I am Brahm." What nonsense! Look at your life. You are just croaking all the time. And then you talk big. Then you say, "No method is needed, no practice is needed, no discipline is needed because I am not a frog at all. Since I am not a frog at all, I do not need to reduce my frogness, I do not need to transcend my frogness, I do not need to discipline my frogness."

You are saying that if the frog tries to transcend its frogness, it is further confirmed, proven and cemented that the frog is indeed a frog. But in the frog's eyes, the frog is indeed and already a frog. What is the purpose of self-deception? Who are we trying to fool? Does the frog seek a lady frog, or a lady elephant? How many of you have seen frogs chasing she-elephants? And here you are saying, "No, no, no, if we try to discipline the frog, that effort testifies its frogness even more."

But the frog is indeed a frog, sir. Let's talk facts.

You will say, "There is no earth at all; only the great void exists." Nonsense. If there is no earth at all, you don't exist. Then why do you talk so much? Why do you write such big books?

Remember, spirituality is not merely about stating absolutist concepts. Spirituality is firstly about helping the petty and suffering ego. Help is even greater than the Truth. There is no truth bigger than compassion. Regurgitating the absolute Truth again and again, if it does not help, will serve no purpose. I repeat, there is no point in repeating and recycling the absolute Truth endlessly to the listener if it does not help.

The objective of spirituality is not the declaration of Truth. The objective of spirituality is to help the ego. We forget this fundamental thing. Therefore, we start chasing the Absolute. I ask these puritanical knights: Does that help? If that does help, continue what you are doing. Otherwise, just check yourself.

You quote, "When all concepts are seen for what they are, that is, they are recognized as such and nothing more, the ego finds itself in the waste-paper basket with the rest."

Who will see all concepts for what they are? Will the Absolute see anything, ever? Does the Absolute have anything other than itself to look at? Does the Absolute exist in a dualistic dimension? Does the Absolute ever know or recognize anything? Does the Absolute ever gain clarity? When you say, "When all concepts are seen for what they are," who is the seer here? Obviously, it is the ego.

You say that there is no need to reduce, transcend, or discipline the ego. Then in the very next line you say, there is a need to see concepts as mere concepts. That is exactly what you call reducing, transcending, or disciplining the ego. Transcending the ego is nothing but seeing that concepts are mere concepts;

that we do not live with facts but ideas about facts; that we do not even live, we ideate about life. That is the ego looking at its own reality. For the ego to look at its own reality, it must first acknowledge that in its own eyes, it is real.

Finally, you quote, "And when all concepts are seen for what they are, the ego finds itself in the waste-paper basket with the rest."

But just a while back you said that there is nothing called the ego. If there is nothing called the ego at all, what is it that will find itself in the waste-paper basket? So, the ego does exist, right? And methods are needed to transcend it. It's just that you too are talking about a method called 'seeing'. And seeing may require practices of many kinds, a lot of discipline and transcendence.

Transcendence is nothing but the process of teaching and training and advising the ego to look and go beyond itself. Good old selflessness is nothing but transcendence.

Let me take this occasion to talk about the no-self, because to quote your question, "There is a whole neo-spiritual movement around the assertion that there is no egocentric self or 'I' at all..." So, you say there is no 'I' to begin with. Now, who is saying there is no 'I' to begin with? Isn't the ego itself declaring that there is no ego? Will that help the ego?

Similarly, when we say that the Truth is actually just a no-self, are we still not talking to the ego in the language of the ego? When we say the Truth is no-self, this self is the fictitious self, the egoistic self. When you say yes and no, to which world do these words belong? These are dualistic words that belong in the ego's world. So, when you say no-self, the self is ego, and the word 'no' also belongs to the world of ego.

You stay in the dimension of the ego even when you talk about no-self. But we go on preaching that the Truth is no-self. When you say that the Truth is no-self, you have brought down the Truth to the level of the self, because 'no' belongs to the world of the self. And self obviously belongs to the world of the self. Therefore, no-self also belongs to the world of ego.

Does the ego know absolute no-ness? Does the ego know absence? When the ego says yes, it is an affirmation. When the ego says no, even that is an affirmation. The ego does not know negation of any kind. Even when you say no, you are pointing at an object because the one who is pointing, the subject, has no option but to point only at objects. Even the absence that we talk of when we say no is a positive affirmation of something. What is that something? It is an absence.

You will have to understand this. Even an absence is an objective thing. What is an object? That which can be perceived by the subject is called an object. For example, I say, "You are sitting here." I perceived that with my usual sensory mechanism. This mechanism and the 'I'-feeling sitting at the center of it is the subject of which you are the object.

Now, I change my statement: "You are not sitting here." But when I say that you are absent, even the absence of you is an object. Yes and no are both objective. How did I perceive his presence? Using my sensory mechanism. How did I perceive his absence? I have no option but to use my sensory mechanism. Even when I am saying that he is not here, I am using the same faculty that I used to confirm his presence. That's the problem when you start talking in negation or no-ness. The ego cannot talk in no-ness. For the ego, 'yes' is yes, and 'no' is another kind of yes. 'Yes' is a presence, and 'no' is another kind of presence.

When you are present, you are present as an object. When you are absent, you are present as another object. That does not mean that the objectivity has disappeared. That does not mean that I am dealing with another dimension. Whether you say self or no-self, you are still dealing in the world of self—the little self that is the ego.

To illustrate further, whether I say you are present or you are absent, I am talking about something happening within this room. When I said you were present, didn't I point at something within this room? When I said you were absent, didn't I again point at something within this room? Or did I talk of something beyond or transcendental? When I say you are absent, has it taken me to another realm? So how would no-self point towards the Truth?

Yes and no are very earthly, very worldly dualities. Whether you prefix something with 'yes' or 'no', you are keeping the thing very much on the earth. Therefore, there is no point in referring to the Truth as absence, void or no-self. This is simply because the ego does not know the word 'absence' or 'absent'. Remember that the ego can only know presence. It is designed and cognized to perceive only presences, not absences. You cannot cognize an absence. All you can ever know of is a presence. Even when you talk about an absence, you are referring to something being absent. It's still a dealing in objectivity, memory, and worldly stuff.

When you tell someone that the Truth is no-self, what do you think will happen? Will his mind respond to your statement? Will his mind be cleared of all concepts just because you said that the Truth is no-self? He will instead create another concept called no-self. The ego can only have concepts. We forget that the ego is a thirsty being; you cannot leave it with absences.

Don't call the ego fictitious. Look at our lives. Don't we think of ourselves as a presence? Do we say that we are absent and hence don't exist? We are living beings talking to each other. And this is not a conversation between a pair of Absolutes, it a conversation between living beings, and living beings are thirsty entities. Anything that is thirsty is neither absent nor looking for an absence; it is rather looking for a presence.

Just as thirst needs water, which is an objective presence, the ego is designed to know and detect only something that is present. Therefore, it will turn even an absence into a presence. Otherwise, it cannot cognize. Mere negation will not give you any relief. You have to give the ego something affirmative.

Constant negation will just keep the ego thirsty. You are being defeated in two ways. Firstly, you are actually giving the ego something to cling to even when you are negating it. In affirmation, you give the ego something to hold on to. You teach the ego something, give it something to do. In the method of negation, you say, "No, I will not give the ego anything to do because it would mean that the ego is real. I will turn a blind eye to the reality of the ego. I will act as if the ego is not there at all." Even when you are doing this, you are giving the ego something to hold on to. What is it that you are giving to the ego in this case? An absence.

So, you have been defeated in attaining your objective of not giving anything to the ego. You have unwittingly, inadvertently, unknowingly and unconsciously given something to the ego. While the others were giving something affirmative to the ego, you are giving something negative to it. Maybe the ego is now dabbling in nihilism. Maybe that's what you have given to the ego. You are telling it that nothing exists, nothing matters, and nothing is meaningful.

Nevertheless, the ego's little hands are full and occupied. You have not been successful in emptying the ego of all that it has and holds. The ego still has something. That is the first defeat. And the second defeat is that you have given the ego something useless. You said, "No point giving anything to the ego because if I give anything to it, she feeds upon it. If I give anything to her, that makes her appear more real, more certain and more powerful." So you say you will give nothing to the ego. What you don't realize is that you have given it a big thing called 'nothing'. You stand defeated. You have given something to the ego through the backdoor.

It's a compulsion. You have to give something to the ego. Like entropy, it increases, irrespective of what you do. If you say, "I will come up with a method that decreases entropy," you do not know science. Similarly, the ego can only be given something; it cannot be emptied of all that it has. Why? Because the ego is a thirsty being.

Do not say that the ego does not exist. I am talking to all the great writers who keep harping on zeroness—you too are thirsty. Look at your face. Look at your life. How many dreams have you chased? How many women have you chased? Are you still not eager and desirous after writing all your books? Do you write as the Absolute or the great void? Does the great void bother to write books? Does the great zeroness bother to affirm or deny principles?

*You are the thirsty one. Because you think you have little, you cannot be emptied of the little you think you have. You are desperately clutching. You will clutch either this or that.*

I once saw a little boy who was holding trash in his hands. His father came to him and snatched away the trash. And as soon as his hands were freed of the trash, the boy clutched his father's thighs. He needed something to hold on to. He would grope until he had something, and then he would latch on to it. That's the ego. It always requires something. Kindly do not think that you can deny its existence or deny it what it needs. The only way to fulfil the ego is to fulfil it, not empty it. If you empty it, it will attach itself to emptiness. It needs something.

And an ego attached to emptiness is more dangerous than an ego attached to run-of-the-mill worldly objects. Emptiness too is an object. It's the kind of an object that does not appear like one. Normal objects are easy to point towards. Emptiness, because it describes itself as a non-object, is very difficult to point towards. Therefore, it easily remains a very stubborn object of attachment. If you are attached to fame, money, a man, woman, or any other worldly thing, you can see or perceive them. But what if you become attached to nothing? It's a huge problem then.

You will be attached to something because you are a thirsty being.

Look at your life, and you will realize that you are a thirsty being. We aren't talking about principles here; we are talking about reality. Let none of us, even the highest ones, even the Buddhas of this world, dare say that we are not thirsty. Every embodied being is thirsty. To have a body is to be thirsty. And if you are thirsty, you need something. Spirituality is the art of giving the ego something that would really fulfil it. You cannot dispossess the ego. It already lives in the feeling of deprivation. It says, "Oh, I am so sick, unwell, poor, needy, incomplete, and thirsty." And how are you responding to it? You are telling it, "Give me whatever you have." How will that assuage it? Instead, give it something that would fulfil it.

Things that can fulfil the ego do exist. The art of devising objects that can take you beyond your infatuation with objectivity also exists. Furthermore, a world exists that can take you to silence. Is that not what the Buddha has said clearly in the *Dhammapada*? Only those words are useful that can take you to silence. That's the knack—give the ego an object that will make it drop all objects. Give the ego a world that will make it forget all other worlds. Touch the ego in a way that will make it lose all its obsessions with senses and touches. Deal with the ego in such a way that will raise it beyond all worldly dealings. Be involved in such a way that you go beyond all involvements.

The path to beyondness does not bypass involvement. You have to enter the thick of involvement to go beyond it. And you don't have to enter separately. You are already in it, but in a superficial way. You are swimming in shallow waters. You must dive deep and only then will you find that you have surfaced.

It's a strange thing. Those who remain in shallowness because they don't want to be too far from the surface find that all they ever get is shallowness. They never cross the river or fully experience it. That is the fate of most human beings. That's how we live life, right? We neither transcend life nor do we even experience it. This gives us a hint: probably to transcend life one has to fully experience it. And what does it mean to fully experience it? It means to experience objects that can bring fullness to you.

If you live for eighty years, you are experiencing for eighty years. The Buddha too lived for eighty years. He too was experiencing for eighty years. The duration of experience for both the persons is the same, is it not? Eighty years is the same time duration for you and Buddha. Then what is meant by experiencing fully? Your experiences are mundane and run-of-the-mill. You do not want to dive to the core of life. The Buddha wanted more and more. The Buddha wanted to know the essence of it all. He said, "I want a special kind of experience. Life would anyway keep ticking, moment after moment, whether I experience it fully or whether I deal in shallow waters. So, why not make the best use of life and make every second count?" He left the palace and went to scores of teachers. You, on the other hand, keep dreaming of the palace.

Were those teachers available where he already was? No. Remaining where he was, would he be able to have the experiences that he had when he went out? No. That is what experiencing life fully means. We all experience life. We eat, walk, deal, and chit-chat with the same old fellows in the same old ways—these are all experiences. But there is a special quality of an experience that can rid you of your obsession with experience. That is spirituality.

Spend your time where time comes to a standstill. Be in a place which makes you forget where you are. Live in a way that you stop caring for whether you are alive or dead. That is what the ego wants—something big that will make it forget its thirst. Once the ego forgets its thirst, it also forgets its petty concept about itself. The moment the ego forgets its petty concept about itself, the ego is no more.

Can there be a limitless ego? No. The ego exists only as long as its limits exist. If you can make the ego forget its limits, forget time and forget space, then the ego is not dead, but it is fulfilled. Never talk the language of killing the ego. You will not be able to do that. It cannot be killed. The ego can only be fulfilled. There is no point in decrying the ego and unnecessarily ridiculing it as fictitious. It is dishonest to do so. In saying that the ego does not exist, you act like kids playing hide and seek, who declare to each other, "I'm not here."

Remember these basic things. We are not here to discuss Truth; we are here to be helped. Help is bigger than any principle pertaining to Truth. Truth that does not help is merely fiction, some conceptual principle. We are not here to dabble in principles. Spirituality starts when you experience suffering. We are here to get rid of suffering. We are here to be helped. So, we will first respect and acknowledge the one who is suffering. And who is suffering? The ego. So, the ego is real. Otherwise, there is no need for spirituality. Spirituality can't even begin in the absence of the ego and suffering. There is suffering.

For instance, take the story of the Guru and the student. The student comes to the Guru and the Guru says, "You do not exist."

The student says, "I'm burning in hell."

The Guru says, "You do not exist."

Student: "But I experience myself. I think I am."

Guru: "Everything that you experience is fiction. It does not exist."

Student: "That means there is no reality?"

Guru: "None at all."

Student: "Anything that you say, experience, see, hear, touch, verify, or ratify is all nonsense?"

Guru: "It does not exist."

Student: "Then what do I do with my suffering?"

Guru: "You do not exist. Suffering does not exist."

Student: "Anything that I experience or look at does not exist and does not suffer?"

Guru: "Obviously."

Student: "I am looking at you, and you have just said that everything that I am looking at is fictitious. You have also said that fiction cannot suffer."

The next moment, the Guru is on his toes, and the student is hot on his heels. Fiction is chasing fiction—and now fiction has become very serious.

Just a while ago, it was all in abstraction: you do not exist, that does not exist, this does not exist, I do not exist, and you too do not exist.

If you do not exist, what's the harm in beating you up? After all, fiction cannot suffer.

---

Real or unreal, suffering exists. And we want to treat it. Sometimes, suffering can be relieved by telling the sufferer that your suffering is just a myth or a story. This method will not work most of the time, and then we have to come up with something better, more compassionate and more humane.

---

*Advait Shivir, BodhSthal, 2019*

# 23

# Keep Moving, Even If It Is Dark

*There is the city of Maya; it is a beautiful city, enchanting, appealing, bewitching, but it survives on your lifeblood. It gives you a few good moments, but at the cost of the essence of your life. It gives you pleasure at the cost of the essential. And then there is the city of the Beyond. That city, when looked at from the city of Maya, is not very attractive. It is a calm, serene place, but it does not have too many flashy attractions. It is the city of bliss, and the city of Maya is the city of blitz.*

**Listener:** Sir, I have lived my life in images. In the past, I have kept myself away from experiences with the excuse of not being sufficiently prepared. I realize now that I was wrong. How could I ever be prepared without practice?

But I am still afraid of not having the proper logic to debate with my opponents, of losing respect, people, chances of a good life. I have the opportunity to save myself but instead I am asking you what to do. It seems like I want to surrender and live like a slave. Why am I letting somebody have an edge over me? Is my self-image so low that I just cannot stand up for myself?

**Acharya Prashant:** This is a classical case of "Duvidha mein dono gaye, maya mili na Ram (In doubt, both are lost: the material and the Truth)."

It is a phase of transition; it is an intermediate stage, and right now you belong neither here nor there. When somebody is in this kind of situation, I advise him to keep moving forward with greater speed and greater determination. Don't just stop there. And if someone repeatedly tells me that he can't move forward, then I advise him to turn back.

There is the city of Maya; it is a beautiful city, enchanting, appealing, bewitching, but it survives on your lifeblood. It gives you a few good moments, but at the cost of the essence of your life. It gives you pleasure at the cost of the essential. And then there is the city of the Beyond. That city, when looked at from the city of Maya, is not very attractive. It is a calm, serene place, but it does not have too many flashy attractions. It is the city of bliss, and the city of Maya is the city of bling, the city of blitz. Most of us care for the blitz rather than for bliss.

In between these two cities is a great jungle. The city of Maya does not teach you how to cross the jungle. It does not even give you the required strength to be prepared to cross this jungle. This city survives on your life-energy. And if you are living in that city, you won't have the energy required to cross that jungle; it is going to be terminally tough.

But somehow, sometimes, magically, the impossible happens: a few chosen ones are struck with the desire to cross over. When they will start, they will start with their feeble steps because they too, after all, have been the residents of the city of Maya for long. So, they don't have too much of a strength, but they have a certain heartfelt inspiration.

So, they set off. How would they feel upon entering the jungle? Weird and terrible! But even as they are entering the jungle, silently, unnoticeably, something healthy is happening. What is happening? Their lifeblood is no more being sucked out by the Maya city.

The dangers are obvious, the benefit is hidden.

The jungle is full of huge elephants, leopards, and tigers and whatnot. So, the dangers are all very loud and apparent. In the din of those dangers, it is easy to not see that your health is being slowly restored. Your blood that was being diverted, extracted is now healthily flowing in your veins. But you won't sense that because that is a very silent phenomenon, and the bears and the lions are all roaring loudly; that's easy to hear. The difficulties that you face will be very noticeable and hence very daunting, but the benefits that you are getting will be very imperceptible and, therefore, undervalued.

From there you call out to me and ask, "What do I do? I am afraid and I am losing out. There were so many pleasures to be had in the Maya city. I am no more having those pleasures. And not only that, I have news that my competitors in that city are all prospering. They have taken over my house, they have taken a lead over my business, and they have stolen a march over me in all possible ways. And here I am losing in every sense!"

And of course, you do appear to be losing in every sense because your legs have been enfeebled by the city you have lived in. You are no more capable of crossing over, or so it seems. But slowly, vigor is being restored to your legs. How? Because your blood is no more being sucked out, so your legs are slowly gaining their natural strength. But it will take time. You have been a prisoner of delusion for so long that total restoration of health will take time. And till then, it will be a bad situation to be in.

Therefore, I say, if you are in that jungle, then keep moving. If you are in darkness, then keep moving ahead in darkness. Move through darkness, move in darkness.

As you move ahead, as you get more and more away from the city of Maya, you find that your competitors and the happenings in the Maya city are mattering less and less to you. The news themselves stop reaching you. The news of the Maya city can reach only the fringes of the jungle. As you get deeper into the jungle, what is happening in the Maya city matters less and less to you. Now your consciousness does not receive the news from that city; they become immaterial.

So, many good things start happening. One, what is happening in the city of delusion does not matter to you. Secondly, you now know the jungle. Thirdly, your legs now are regaining their power because your blood is now flowing in the right place, so you can surge ahead with greater vigor, and greater determination, and more speed.

But the initial few steps, the initial few days, are going to be very, very difficult, and that is why the city of delusion is immortal. Even if people want to leave that city, they enter the jungle, find it too much to cross, and return.

It is, I repeat, the first few steps which are going to be the most daunting, the most deterring. Don't fail then, and the battle is mostly won. Just don't fail then.

And if people come to me and they say—they repeatedly say—it is too much for them to bear separation from their beloved city of delusion and the jungle appears so dark and desolate in comparison, and if they stubbornly refuse to press ahead, then I advise them, "You turn back, you go back to the Maya city. You stay there. You stay there till you get fed up. Maybe your time has still not come."

Nobody can just get up and beat Maya. It requires a lot of grace and a lot of determination from the person's side. If that determination is missing, then you better let more blood. The bloodletting should continue till you see the bloody affair for what it is. That may require centuries. Fine! Keep paying with your blood; that is the price that you pay. That is the price that you pay for not making your way through the jungle.

Choose carefully—and I know it is going to be a difficult choice.

On one side are the glamorous, enamoring lights; on the other side is the anonymity and bleakness of the jungle. But you must enter that jungle. The city of delusion is not your home.

You must cross over.

---

"On one side are the glamorous, enamoring lights; on the other side is the anonymity and bleakness of the jungle. But you must enter that jungle. The city of delusion is not your home. You must cross over."

---

*Advait Shivir, BodhSthal, 2018*

# 24

# Guru and Maya

*If you desire what everybody has been desiring, you will get what everybody has been getting. And what everybody has been getting hasn't been too good, or has it?*

यः सर्वज्ञः सर्वविद्यस्य ज्ञानमयं तापः ।
तस्मादेतद्ब्रह्म नाम रूपमन्नं च जायाते ॥

He who is the omniscient, the all-wise, He whose energy is all made of knowledge, from Him is born this that is Brahm here, this name and form and matter.

~ Mundaka Upanishad, Verse 1.1.9

**Acharya Prashant (AP):** Form, matter, name, all come from That who is omniscient, all-wise, whose energy is jñānamaya. He is the one who takes shape; He is the one who becomes all things; He is the one who becomes Maya and Prakriti and life.

You have to clearly see how agency is being attributed here.

You see, Maya becomes all things, correct? Maya becomes all things. So, you find it expressed in both ways: sometimes it is said Maya becomes all things, and here it is said Brahm becomes all things. Both of these are correct. Both of these are right statements expressed at different levels.

*Yes, all things are Maya. But Maya, we had just said, is nothing but a great power inherent in Brahm. Maya is the very freedom of Brahm to be and then not to be.*

So, when you say this is all the game of Maya, you are not at all wrong. And it is quite useful to say all of this is the game of Maya, especially when you feel quite charmed and enthralled by all this. Then it pays to say all this is Maya.

At the same time, it has to be remembered that Maya has no power or agency of its own. There aren't two competent Truths, Brahm and Maya. And this is where the Upanishads greatly differ from many other philosophical streams.

At the heart of religion is philosophy, right? And it has been commonplace to say that there is God and there is Satan, and God and Satan have been shown as adversaries. That is not the way in Vedanta. In Vedanta, Satan doesn't compete with Brahm; in Vedanta, Satan, who can be broadly equated with Maya, is rather the power of Brahm to do as Brahm pleases.

Therefore, just as Brahm is timeless and birthless, Maya too is called anādi, not having a particular beginning, because the beginning of Maya is the beginning of Brahm. However, Brahm cannot come to an end; Maya can come to an end. How does Maya come to its end? By involution. It retreats back into what it came from.

So, Brahm is the source of Maya, the father of Maya, Mayapati. Brahm isn't competing with Maya; Brahm is rather commanding Maya. Mischievous, no?

That is the reason I once said, after the session is over, guru and Maya take tea together: because both of these are just two names for the innate freedom of Brahm.

*There is the freedom of Brahm to forget itself. That is Maya. There is the freedom of Brahm to remind itself of what it has forgotten. That is Guru.*

Guru and Maya are one in a very fundamental way. Maya is trying to make you forget what you can never forget, and the guru is reminding you of something you have never forgotten. Both are just playing games with you. Therefore, they are hand in glove in the game which is called saṃsāra. One builds the saṃsāra, the other dissolves it. Both of them are needed to keep the show running.

You never know—it might be a double role.

What does that mean in terms of your day-to-day actions and decisions and everything? Be very careful when desire arises. Are you desiring to get rid of your shackles, or are you desiring a few more of them? Desire can work both ways, obviously; it does. Unfortunately, for most of us, desire works the wrong way.

Why do you desire? You need to desire because you are stuck and shackled. So, you cannot say, "I don't desire anything." That kind of spirituality is best avoided, where you just say, "I don't desire anything, I am above everything, I don't need anything, I am nothing." Sorry, you are much—at least in your own eyes.

So, you need to desire, you need to be resolute, you need to want. You need to want, and if you want wrongly or badly, then you have had it. So, you cannot not want, you are pushed into wanting, and if you want wrongly, the punishment will be that you will need to want more and more. That gives us a clue regarding the nature of the right want.

*The right want is that which will lead to progressively fewer wants.*

*The wrong want is that which will lead to more and more wants. Radioactive wanting.*

Do you know about radioactivity? Particles from one radioactive disintegration happening in one molecule hit five other molecules; therefore, one radioactive event leads to five more events, and those five more events lead to more and more. So, we are radioactive people.

Ask yourself: "If this particular desire that lords me right now is fulfilled, will that lead to freedom from subsequent desire, or will that breed a thousand more desires?" Ask yourself. And if you are honest in asking, then the answer will decide for itself. If the answer is: the fulfilment of this desire will lead to a thinning out of subsequent desires, then proceed, do as you wish. Or will wants lead to more and more wants?

Caution: don't think of yourself as some kind of divine exception—because you are not, because all of us are fundamentally manifestations of the same 'I'-tendency.

Therefore, others are a good example. See what happened to those others who took the same route that you are now contemplating. Because our lives are the same, because our fundamentals are also the same, therefore our desires are also the same, right? We are hardly unique in any aspect of our life or wants.

That which you are desiring today has been desired by a billion people ahead of you. See what happened to them. Don't just keep deceiving yourself by saying, "Well, you know, I know that if I fulfil this desire, I will not require anything else." There have been so many others who did what you are thinking of doing now. What happened to them? The same fate awaits you. You cannot escape the fact.

See, if right now you are desiring just the same thing that billions before you desired, are you really different from those billions? Aren't you desiring exactly what billions before you have desired? Tell me. Are you different from them? Look at the facts. Are you? No. So, then, how do you convince yourself that once you have fulfilled this particular desire, your fate will be any different from that of those billion others?

But that is the internal deceptive logic we offer ourselves. "My case is different." Your desire is the same but your case is different—exactly how? "No, no, no. All took the same road and vanished into the darkness, but my case is different. I will take exactly the same road and return, and not only return but return illuminated. They were fools who disappeared."

They were not fools, they were just like you. What is the proof of that? They took the same road. So far you have been exactly like them. How do you propose to be different a few hours hence?

That is the trick of future. Because the future is not upon us yet, therefore we get the dangerous freedom to hope. We hope that our fate will be drastically different from the others who went before us.

You are not unique in anything, not at all, which is bad. But then, we said let's make the best of a bad situation—which is very bad. You are not unique in anything, but what is the advantage it offers? Because you are not unique in anything, therefore you can use the example of others to see what is going to happen to you. Had you been unique, then new things could have happened to you.

Are you unique? Seriously? Look at the way you are looking at me. A billion people before you have looked exactly the same way at somebody. How do you think you are any different? Any particular thought that is original to you? Any particular act that you propose to patent? Yes? "I am the first one to come up with this." Any little small thing?

If everything about us is just a rehash of the primordial script, wouldn't it be better to read the script? It has been enacted again and again, over and over again, no? Why not make good use of the various number of times it has been enacted?

*So, be careful. If you desire what everybody has been desiring, you will get what everybody has been getting. And what everybody has been getting hasn't been too good, or has it been?*

And if it has been that good, why do you so often get disappointed and spit at the past? Why don't you like doing what all the people around you have been doing?

Strange is our situation. On one hand, we do not like what has been happening before us and around us; on the other hand, we do exactly what our ancestors and our neighbors have been doing.

Superficially, we want to be different. The brand of your jacket is probably not the same as that of your neighbor, but a jacket is a jacket nevertheless, irrespective of the brand, no?

We do not like what everybody does but we do what everybody else does, and then we hope for a different result. We do not like how people are but we emulate them, and to keep our dignity intact, we tweak our actions just a little bit.

"You know, my uncle chose someone who wore a sari, I am choosing someone who wears a skirt. See, I am different!"

It doesn't matter. You can hang yourself using a sari; you can also find ways to hang yourself using a skirt or something even shorter than that. There can be a million ways to die.

"But my death was unique, you see. My uncle died by hanging, I died by stuffing something down my throat! The thing was so little—I just gulped it and suffocated. I am unique! My fate will be different!"

**Listener (L):** If Brahm is the creator and the creation both, did matter always exist with Brahm?

**AP:** Matter exists only for the one who acknowledges matter. You cannot look at Brahm and matter objectively. When you say, "Did Brahm always exist or coexist with matter?" who are you that looks at these two? Who are you?

So, truly only Brahm exists. It is the power of Brahm to forget itself. Brahm doesn't quite create; it manifests. And when it manifests it gets divided into two: you and what you see.

*Non-dual Brahm manifests itself by dividing itself into two: you and what you see.*

And by 'you' I do not mean you, the name; I mean the 'I'-tendency. The 'I'-tendency is also the universe tendency, and the 'I'-tendency takes various shapes and forms. Those various shapes and forms are the individual persons.

Each person projects and experiences his or her own world—and I am not talking only of human beings. Every sentient being lives in the cocoon of its own experienced universe. Beyond that cocoon it knows nothing.

What do you think the universe of a firefly or gadfly is? Same as yours? Stretch your imagination and conceive the universe of a mosquito. What do you think? Same as yours? Or even that of your dog, pet dog. There it is relatively easier to appreciate the difference, to see that the universe of the dog can just not be the same as your universe.

It is not so easy to appreciate that your universe cannot be the same as her *(points to someone in the audience)* universe. And for you, your universe is, unfortunately, the Truth, and for her, her universe is, sadly, the final Truth. And that is the root of all suffering, including all human suffering.

Because we believe so much in ourselves, therefore we believe in the finality of our universe and, therefore, our experiences. That is the ego, no? "I am surely the Truth. Therefore, what I experience, how can it be false? Therefore, the world is as real as I am. I am real and the world is real."

But if you are real and the world is real, what is this reality so afraid of? Why do you live in perpetual fear? The real should be the last one to fear. That is the missing link in your entire narrative, the little gap through which we keep bleeding.

So, Brahm is not the creator. When you desperately want to invent a creator, then you come up with Īśvara. But Vedanta is not very enamored of Īśvara. So, Vedanta says Īśvara is just Maya. Just Maya. Because you experience the universe, therefore you feel the need to justify the origin of universe;

therefore, you must have an Īśvara. But how can the creator of a false universe be real? If the universe is false, what do you say about its creator?

So, Vedanta isn't very enthralled with Īśvara. The creator-creation theory goes more with God. God is comparable to Īśvara. Brahm is not God. Knowers of Brahm would say God and God's creation, both are just Maya.

Don't be deceived when you sometimes come across the word 'God' even in Vedantic literature. Be careful at such points. See carefully whether it relates to Brahm or Īśvara.

**L:** In the very beginning, you said that the complete Brahm evolves into an incomplete mind-matter-world, and later on you also told us that Maya can be triumphed by a process of involution. My question is based on this concept of evolution-involution.

Are you suggesting that evolution is something non-spiritual? Many modern philosophers, like Friedrich Nietzsche, Swami Vivekananda, and Shri Aurobindo have opined that the process of evolution itself can take us to Truth.

**AP:** From a pure perspective, evolution has never happened, nothing has ever happened; only Brahm is the Truth and nothing ever happens there. There is no evolution. But since you experience evolution, because you take yourself as the product of evolution, therefore, for you it is suggested further evolution or involution. *Only* for you.

If at this very moment you could see that you do not exist, then you do not need any involution or any spiritual progress. Nothing really happened; it is just that you feel that a lot has happened, and therefore a lot has come into existence.

But what do we do? Merely intellectually repeating that nothing really happened does not rid us of the impact of our sensory experiences. The world is announcing itself to be true by coming to us every moment through these senses. In fact, the world is beating us down into accepting itself. And how does the world do that? By making us firstly acknowledge that we exist.

Now, if you exist, then the ground beneath your feet surely does exist. Otherwise, how do you propose that you can stand? Because we believe in all these things, therefore some kind of progress is needed; therefore we need to decide on the way ahead. If with one blow of your resolute determination you could just in a flash see all this as false, then you don't need any progress.

Be very careful when you use the word 'happens', 'happened', or 'existence', or 'exists'. All these words are good only for day-to-day practical conversations. These words do not refer to the Truth. Nothing happened and nothing exists. The happenings and existence are your bondage. Illusion is another name for bondage. All happenings, all existence is illusory.

But it doesn't help us to merely verbally know that. Because as long as we are listening to this as persons, it is absurd to say, "I have just heard that I do not exist." Isn't it absurd? Therefore, let's keep this knowledge aside. Therefore, let's not entertain ourselves by saying, "Nothing ever happened, nothing exists, and neither do I."

We do exist in our own eyes, right? Then the topical question is, "Given that I exist, how must I exist? Given that I am alive, how must I live?" That is the beneficial question to ask. But never for a moment must you take your existence very seriously.

Now, it is a difficult thing to ask for. Because, on one hand, you have to take decisions as the existing one; on the other hand, you have to try your best to remember that you really do not exist. It is a very difficult balance to achieve, to act vigorously while remembering that no action is going to change anything at all—because no action is really happening. But that is the essence of all spirituality: to partake in these two opposites simultaneously, to concurrently act and know that all action is illusory. It is not even a balance, it is a concurrent happening.

*You have to exist simultaneously in two dimensions: the dimension of action and the dimension of non-action. In the dimension of action, you are a prisoner who must break free; therefore, he has to act vigorously to break free. In the dimension of non-action, you are the sky. Who can capture the sky?*

And you exist in both the dimensions. This is what I repeatedly emphasize. Remember that you exist in both the dimensions. Don't forget any or either of them.

If you forget that you are a prisoner, you will remain a prisoner because you will not even try to break free of the prison. And if you forget that you are the sky, then even if you break free from the prison you will have nowhere to go to; you will just land in a bigger prison because you have forgotten that you are the sky. How can there be freedom now? You will move from prison to prison. You will know that you are a prisoner, and yet you will remain a prisoner. You will be very, very eager for freedom, and yet you will just move from one prison to the other if you do not remember that you are already the sky.

So, you have to abide by both these things, which is very difficult to do. It requires a lot of practice and determination.

**L:** You said that our choices come from the unconscious. How can that unconscious be understood?

**AP:** You have no perception beyond what you consciously know. You can only operate within the zone of your consciousness.

How, then, do you know what is there beneath the shallow depth of the conscious mind? To know that, again, you have to just watch what is happening in your consciousness. You have no option, because what is happening in the conscious mind is arising from the subconscious, unconscious, whatever you want to call it.

So, let's say there is a well. Now, if you are throwing light into it, that light goes only up to a certain distance. Whatever you can see till that distance will give you a fair idea, a good indication of what is there beneath the illuminated area. You will have to make wise speculations. You have to keep watching what is available to be watched, and from that you have to infer what is not available to be directly watched. And if you can see what is arising from the subconscious, you will also know ways to penetrate deeper into the subconscious.

Watch your actions. See what they are pointing towards.

Watch your thoughts. See what they are pointing towards.

And the thing with the subconscious is: if you can decode it, you have illuminated it. It remains in the dark only because you are in the dark about it. It is the same thing, right? The more you know about it, the more it gets illuminated. So, know more about it. How do you know more about it? By doing what is available to be done.

All you can watch is your actions, thoughts, emotions, tendencies, reactions, biases, beliefs; watch these, watch the movement of life in general, and you will come to see what is there beneath the surface. But you will have to be inquisitive; you cannot just accept or dismiss things as usual.

*All the things that are apparently usual contain valuable information at their source or origin or in their depths.*

We breathe, don't we? Is breathing a conscious decision? There is nobody who wants to question why we breathe. Well, there are people who want to regulate the breath. But you don't decide to breathe, or do you? Why do you breathe?

There is somebody in the dark who is breathing and it is not the conscious you. The conscious you is hardly ever bothered about the breath. There is somebody in the dark depths of your mind who is breathing. Reminds you of some horror flick or something, some shady thing in the dark breathing heavily.

Now, hear your breath—that is not you!

Some shady thing in the recesses of our mind, that is breathing. Why does it continue to breathe? What is it breathing for? What does it want? Do you decide to impact your breath when you get angry or excited or depressed? Do you decide that? You don't consciously decide, right? But the breath does get impacted.

So, the one who is breathing is also the one who emotes. The breath and the emotions go together, don't they? The moment there is an emotional affliction, the breath is the first one to tell. So, where are the emotions coming from?

These are the questions we have to ask. We don't ask these questions because we are just too convinced that this is regular stuff, not worth enquiring into. That which we consider regular is exactly where the secret is and where it would be understood or revealed.

Why do you wake up every morning? Do you consciously decide to wake up? How many of you do? Keep aside cases like setting up an alarm or something. But everybody does wake up, right? Nobody keeps sleeping continuously for forty-eight hours or something. You sleep and you just wake up; you don't consciously decide to wake up, or do you?

You wake up. Who wakes up? The same fellow who is breathing, that silhouette in the dark—and that is not you. There is somebody sitting within, and he weeps and wakes up and breathes and asks for food. What does he want?

And mind you, irrespective of who you are, you wake up. We might have an illiterate fellow or we might have the greatest scholar here, but both of them do breathe and both of them do wake up in the morning. Which means, the one sitting within has no relation to knowledge. The one sitting within has no relation at all to knowledge. All knowledge is limited to your conscious self. Therefore, all knowledge is very shallow.

Who is the one sitting within, then? What does he want? He doesn't want knowledge. The rich one wakes up, so does the poor one. Ah, so he doesn't even want money. The old one wakes up, so does the young one. The healthy one wakes up, so does the unhealthy one. The one sitting within wants neither knowledge, nor money, nor health, nor wealth. Interesting character, right?

What does he open his eyes for? I am not saying what does he open *your* eyes for; your eyes are not your eyes. Who wakes up in the morning? You don't.

The one sitting in the dark is influencing, rather commanding everything that is happening in the lights. Therefore, it is not at all difficult to know him. Lights and shadows go together, and shadows are useful. In fact, light helps you see things through shadows.

Look at your face in the mirror and be astonished. And you *will* be astonished if you have not just bored yourself into a lazy acceptance of yourself. If you have some wonderment left towards yourself, the very look of your eyes would astonish you. What are these eyes searching for?

What do you think, the eyes are just some kind of biomechanical device to gather information from the external world? No, sir. There is a difference between these eyes and this camera. The camera just looks at stuff, the eyes are looking *for* something. There is a dimensional difference there.

Do you get this? The camera *just* looks, the eyes look *for*. What are the eyes looking for? The camera can't look for anything, and you can't just look at anything. It is impossible for the camera to look *for* anything; the camera cannot do that. And it is equally impossible for you to *just* look at anything; you cannot do that.

Whenever you have looked at something, you have looked *for* something. What are you looking for? What is he looking for?

You might train a camera to look for something, but still the camera would look for something that it already knows to look for; it is programmed to look for something in particular. And your eyes are looking for something they are not destined to ever find. The camera knows what it is looking for—if at all it is programmed to look for something—and you will never know what you are looking for, but still you keep looking.

It is said that some indeed do find what they are looking for. Though you can never know what you are looking for, still, miraculously, a few end up finding what that shady chap was all the time looking for. How does that happen? We don't know. Maybe the Rishis know! So, may we go back to them now.

**L:** If the eyes are always looking for something, is that a proof that everything is Brahm?

**AP:** What you are saying is quite right, but still the eyes would continue to look. One wishes that any of the things the eyes look at and any of the words we use to describe the looking one and the looked one would suffice. *(Shakes head)* Nothing is enough, nothing suffices. We might manage to explain the phenomena brilliantly but that brilliance fails to help. The eyes still desperately continue to look—look *for*.

Yes, we know the one looking at stuff is Brahm, the stuff he is looking at is Brahm, yet the separation remains. The eyes keep longing for some particular sight. That is what makes the eyes so evocative and so beautiful. They contain the essence of what it means to be human.

Human being is someone who is looking for something. The eyes decide, the eyes roll, the eyes blink, the eyes get dilated. All that doesn't happen with your nose or your ears, and that is why there is so little poetry around noses and ears.

The ears have no discretion, or do they? The eyes, they have discretion. You cannot close your ears to something, can you? But you can close your eyes to something. And you just turn your head, and you choose to look at something and you choose to not look at something.

The ears—they don't love. The eyes—they fall in love. Well, the ears, too, love certain sounds, music and all that, but the ears are not very keen lovers. They will let in whatever comes to them. The eyes are quite choosy, to the extent of being finicky.

They may not know what they are looking for, but they for certain know what they are *not* looking for.

So, they will just turn away. If nothing else, then… *(closes his eyes)* What does this mean? This means: I am not open to you; I am now literally not open to you. *(Closes his eyes)* I am closed, see? Ears don't have earlids. Or some people have a lot of hair in the ears, so you can say they have earlashes, but they don't have lids.

So, watch your eyes and learn to read the eyes of others.

---

"There is the freedom of Brahm to forget itself. That is Maya. There is the freedom of Brahm to remind itself of what it has forgotten. That is Guru."

---

*Course in Realization, BodhSthal, 2021*

# 25

# Talk Later of the Truth, First Rebel against the False

*The gods will have to compulsorily answer and reward the ones who don't settle for anything less than godliness. Meeting the gods is a lesser challenge than beating one's mortal self.*

**Listener:** Sir, in the *Katha Upanishad*, the young boy Nachiketa attained the highest wisdom and immortality by virtue of his dispassion and firm resolve. Kindly speak on these virtues.

**Acharya Prashant:** Yes, obviously Nachiketa had determination and dispassion. But those are not the only qualities this boy exhibited in front of Yamaraja (god of death). It is common for readers to say that Nachiketa's fearlessness and glory lie in standing unperturbed before death.

That is not the case.

The story of Nachiketa is more about flesh and blood, like our own story. Since it is more like our own story, we have to keep the encounter with Yamaraja aside for a while and look at the more mortal aspects of Nachiketa's story.

Nachiketa is a mere boy who is dependent on his father. The father is a big man—a king of some standing—and the boy has the honesty and audacity to ask the king, "Of what use is all this demonstration? Who will benefit from these old and sick cows?"

I assure you, facing one's own self-righteous and powerful father this way might be more difficult than facing Yamaraja.

We glorify Nachiketa's encounter with Yamaraja, and that keeps things safe for ourselves: "Glory to the boy Nachiketa, who stood unflinching in front of Yamaraja!" This kind of thinking works in our favor because we very well know that this encounter is a myth; we will never have the occasion in our own life to stand face-to-face with the god of death, at least not in the way the Upanishad narrates.

We all will die one day; in that sense, we all will face the god of death one day. But not the way Nachiketa did. We won't have a conversation with him in words and sentences. So, just announce glory to the one who can stand unflinching in front of Yamaraja.

I'll put it differently: Glory to the one who is dependent on somebody close to him and yet has the guts to utter the truth and leave home. That's where Nachiketa's glory lies.

Yamaraja is fictitious. What danger is there in facing fiction? Nachiketa's father is not fictitious. There is great danger in facing someone real, especially when you are dependent on that real person.

A big ceremony is taking place, and the father is busy pompously overseeing the rites. He is doling out thousands of cows to Brahmins while the boy is nagging the wits out of the king: "Father, what the hell is going on? The cows you are donating to the Brahmins are useless. What is such a donation worth?" The father is telling him off, but the boy is unrelenting.

Can you visualize this? The *Katha Upanishad* does not explicitly tell all this. My narration consists of a lot of my own construction. But this is how it would have happened.

Nachiketa, barely a teenager, is hectoring the king, "Father, you can't be serious! Look, that cow is half dead! If this is what you give to those poor men, to whom would you give me?"

The father has repeatedly made his displeasure evident. It's not the first time the brat is bugging him; he has been this way since long.

But the boy won't relent. His questions are darting straight at the king's self-esteem and puncturing his righteousness. Driven to exasperated indignation, the father yells, "I am giving you away to death!"

Obviously, the father is just uttering typical fatherly nonsense in a moment of rage. The boy has been annoying him and questioning his moral authority. The father does not really want death for the boy. He just wants the boy to behave and leave him alone.

And now comes the moment of real glory.

Nachiketa says, in a tone of resolute calmness too mature for his years, "Fine, if you are giving me away to the god of death, away I go to meet him."

That's dispassion. That's determination. After that, what happens is smooth and natural.

Nachiketa has already cleared the big test. Facing Yamaraja is the smaller test. Having cleared the big test, he will obviously emerge with flying colors in the smaller one. The big test is to leave the home.

*The big test is to give up all dependency. The big test is to keep questioning unremittingly, even if it incurs the wrath of the powerful. The big test is to be prepared to sacrifice comforts for the sake of one's integrity. After passing these tests, one qualifies for the Truth.*

Look at Nachiketa; the first thing he asks Yamaraja is, "Let my father be alright. Please bless my father. Please don't let him stay angry." His father has done the unthinkable, and Nachiketa still has no bitterness.

He asks about Truth only in the end. That's his final query: "Tell me that by which immortality is achieved. What really is immortality?" He doesn't directly ask about death. He asks about immortality.

Yamaraja says, "Boy, you can have the most expensive toys, the best of foods, or even the latest gadgets, if you so please. I could also give you a brand new car with a driving license to boot! It doesn't matter if you are underage. I'm the god of death, you see."

He tried to tempt Nachiketa with all his might but failed.

That's the test.

All the knowledge in the Upanishad is easy to get. Once you have overcome dependency, stayed true to yourself, won over the craving for security, stability, the confines of a comfortable palace and the comfort of a routine; once you have been able to go beyond all this, the Truth is obvious.

All the great and golden verses that you come across in the *Katha Upanishad* will spring up right from your heart. They will not be distant or difficult anymore. Those verses are the easiest part. You start hearing those verses right in your breath.

The difficult part is right in the beginning when you demand Truth from your king, employer or leader, knowing fully well that mighty one is not in the Truth, and that your irreverent demand is going to cost you heavily.

Nachiketa asks, "Dad, isn't this ceremony a sham?"

Dad quips, "So, kid, who provides for your pocket money?"

This was predictable. Then, Nachiketa throws him a surprise. The kid says, "Doesn't matter, dad. Out goes the pocket money. I am prepared to give up all comforts, but tell me first what this cow business is."

The trouble with most of us is that we are too afraid or covetous to cross even the first hurdle. Yamaraja did not chase Nachiketa or barge into his palace. Nachiketa took the decision to go beyond the confines and comforts of his home, and thus an Upanishad was born. To me, the Upanishad was seeded the moment Nachiketa accosted his father.

Even as Nachiketa is leaving the palace, I can see the father calling behind him, "Son, I was just joking. Where are you going? I didn't mean it."

Nachiketa is saying, "It's done, dad. Yours is not a palace of honesty. Yours is not a palace where I will be able to break free and stay free of the false. I quit."

The father must have initially thought that the son is joking. Then he sees that junior is actually walking away. He begins trembling and rushes after him pleading, "Where are you going? What will you do? You have no experience or knowledge. Worse still, you have no money. What will you live on? Don't leave. Son, you can have anything you want. If you want me to stop this ceremony, I'll stop it."

Nachiketa says, "I must find out whether there is something more important than money, knowledge and experience."

Father says, "Alright. The sun is setting. Stay over for the night. You can leave tomorrow morning."

What is he hoping for? That the boy will change his mind overnight. But Nachiketa says, "I won't breathe another breath in this place. Not that I hate this place, dad. You know that I love you. But I have to chart my own course. If I keep living on your bread, I will never attain freedom."

That's the real Upanishad—the unpublished dialog between the father and the son. It is not so much the dialog between Yamaraja and Nachiketa. They say *Katha Upanishad* is the dialog between Yamaraja and Nachiketa. No, *Katha Upanishad* is firstly the dialog between Nachiketa and his father. After that, the dialog between Nachiketa and death is a natural corollary.

The gods will have to compulsorily answer and reward the ones who don't settle for anything less than godliness. Meeting the gods is a lesser challenge than beating one's mortal self.

The world does not want to emphasize the important part. Emphasis has to be put on the first few verses of the Upanishad, on the opening scene. That's where the Upanishad is really born and contained.

Here is someone who despite his raw age, inexperience, dependency, and emotional attachment, is still not prepared to call a truce with the false. Once he has known that he will not get the Truth where he is, he just crosses over. When he does so, he meets death. It's symbolic.

We say, "I *live* in my house." So, where is life? Life is in the safety of the house, within its four walls. This is what we define as life. So, outside the house—the physical and the psychological house—is death.

Yamaraja represents the discomfort and insecurity that a dependent person encounters outside his house. Yamaraja does not actually exist, only Nachiketa does. Unlike Yamaraja, Nachiketa is a boy in flesh and blood. On the other hand, Yamaraja is a symbol of the insecurity that awaits you when you leave your physical and psychological house. You say that life is inside that house. The house you sometimes refer to as a living space. This space gives you physical pleasure and security. The psychological space where we live is called the ego-centered mind space.

So, outside the house is death of the secure life as you have known it all along. You say, "Oh my god! Everything is unknown! Strangers all around! Who will feed me? What will happen to me?" This fear is Yamaraja. Nachiketa leaves his home and encounters that fear. That is his dialog with Yamaraja.

Anybody who is truthful will have to cross over. Rather than living a dead but secure life based on fear, venture out. After all, the one who overcomes fear overcomes death. That's the Upanishad.

---

"The big test is to give up all dependency. The big test is to keep questioning unremittingly, even if it incurs the wrath of the powerful. The big test is to be prepared to sacrifice comforts for the sake of one's integrity."

---

*Advait Shivir, BodhSthal, 2017*

# 26

# How to See Krishna Even in the Evil?

*You must learn to see distinction before you come to see unity. If someone starts talking of unity without first being adept in the art of discretion, then he is just fooling himself.*

अनन्याश्चिन्तयन्तो मां ये जनाः पर्युपासते ।
तेषां नित्याभियुक्तानां योगक्षेमं वहाम्यहम् ॥

Persons who, meditating on Me as non-separate, worship Me in all beings, to them thus ever zealously really engaged, I carry what they lack and preserve what they already have.

~ The Bhagavad Gita, Chapter 9, Verse 22

**Listener:** What does it mean to worship Krishna as non-separate or 'ananya' in all beings? I find it easy to see Krishna in animals, but I notice that I see the opposite of love, compassion, and Truth in fellow human beings. I think this is because my mind is dirty and unclean, so I see the same in others. Is the verse asking us to focus on that which is loving, compassionate and truthful in other humans instead of focusing on that which is not?

**Acharya Prashant:** No, no, no! There is just too much of the pop-spirituality in this question. All these notions that you are coming from have sprung up mostly in the last hundred years since the advent of industrialization, and they all just rally against the one fundamental requirement for spirituality. It is called discretion. Discretion or 'viveka' means to differentiate between the temporal and the non-temporal, the true and the false, the deceptive and the reliable.

But if you do that, then the false is not left with a place to hide. Therefore, the forces of falseness all have penetrated spirituality to create a kind of neo-spirituality these days, in which all falsenesses are acceptable in the name of unconditional love or focusing on the positives and such things.

Real spirituality is about rejecting the false. Real spirituality, therefore, is uncompromising, harsh, ruthless. Just reject the false—that's what real spirituality is about.

But if you are living in an age, in an era, in a society, in an economic system that is dominated by forces of falseness, then it becomes imperative for them to invent a new kind of spirituality that engages, even endorses all falsenesses. So, you have terms like, 'don't judge me' or 'don't judge anybody'. Now, what does that mean? That means, don't call the false as false. Because if you start calling the false as false, how will the false sell itself? And how will the sellers of falsenesses profit from your pocket? Therefore, the new spiritual aphorism is: 'do not judge'.

Similar to this idea and belonging to the same family is the idea, 'love unconditionally'. Where is discretion then? If everything is lovable, then the dirt within is also loveable. Then what is the need to improve at all? If one's dirty condition is lovable, is there a need to take a spiritual bath?

Similarly, there are more such aggregates floating in the spiritual places nowadays, and they have become so commonplace that they have almost gained acceptability as something scriptural. People are surprised when I tell them that no scripture ever talks of such things like looking at the true and the false in the same way. No scripture ever says that the false is as lovable and as respectable as the Truth.

So, that's the backdrop from where this question seems to be coming. Now the question.

You see, you are asking, "How to see Krishna in all beings?" It has to be done in two ways. We will elaborate.

Every human being, every sentient, conscious human being is constantly in a state of inner strife. There is the inertia of the body; there is inertia of Prakriti that wants the status quo to continue, that wants the past to keep rolling on into the future. That's the law of inertia, isn't it? If something is moving, it will just continue to move on. In the absence of a resisting force, the law of inertia states that if something is moving, it will simply continue to move till infinity; it will never stop. And if something is not moving, it will not move even in infinite time in the absence of an external force.

So, there is the force of inertia within us, and it is something that has a lot of weight and momentum behind it. That which is rolling is rolling with a great momentum that is obtained from the millions of years of the past. It is rolling on, it is rolling on, it wants to keep rolling on; it is a juggernaut. It is happening within every human being. Something within us just wants to keep rolling on. It doesn't want to look right or left. It doesn't want to exercise the brakes. It doesn't want to see what was behind and what lies ahead. It just wants to roll on blindly.

There's that, and then there is somebody who is contained, confined within that rolling machine, who sees no sense, no purpose, no gain in just rolling on blindly. He also finds that he is in no position to stop the rolling movement. The rolling machine, the rolling apparatus is simply too big, too heavy, and very unstoppable. So, the only option left to him is to either adjust, succumb—or reconcile in polite language—or to find a way to be liberated, liberated from the confines of the machine. That's what every human being is facing.

This is the internal situation within every human being. And, as we have already said, therefore there are only two choices available to every human being.

The machine will continue to roll on. You cannot do anything to the machine. It is almost as if the machine does not belong to you; you are just an unwilling captive inside the machine. You have been vested with no authority to tamper with the machine, apply the brakes or do anything. Don't you see that the heart keeps beating, the lungs keep breathing, the brain keeps thinking? The machine rolls on—what can you do about it? You cannot do anything about it. Even for the most important event, that of your bodily birth, were you consulted? You are so helpless. It all happened without your consent. You are not even engaged in the process. You were just handed over the body, and you are asking, "But why? Why has this been given to me?" You are handed over the body, and the body has not been given to you as a gift. The body has been given to you as a jail. You have been told, "Here it is, and you have to live within it." And you cannot do much about the body.

Obviously, superficially you can change the body, just as a prisoner can choose to paint the walls of his cell, can he not? Superficially you can choose to do something with the body. So, you can, for example, lose weight or gain weight; you can get a haircut of your choice; you can even get your face modified, some surgery, plastic surgery or something, botox and such things are happening; you can get a dental job done. But does any of it alter the fundamental tendency of the machine to keep rolling on? No.

So, confined within the machine, you can at best keep fiddling with the machine in a very inconsequential way. Really you can change nothing about the machine; really you cannot change your primitive and fundamental biological tendencies. Nobody can.

Now you are left with two choices. Either adjust and say, "But this will continue, so I might just as well reconcile, adjust, and make merry in my confinement. I have come to terms with the reality that this is what is called life, and I don't want to spend this life fighting an impossible war." That's what 99.99999% of the people do. They say, "This is an impossible war. So, I will simply accept my fate and decorate the insides of the juggernaut." You can also imagine a huge cylinder that is rolling on, and somebody is caught inside that cylinder, and he is either painting the insides or doing some other stuff; throwing a wedding party, earning money, building a house—all inside the rolling cylinder. How comfortable would it be, by the way? Your house is inside a rolling cylinder which is rolling without your consent into a future that is unseen, not determinable, and yet you choose to just keep celebrating inside your captivity. That's the choice most people make.

"How do I see Krishna in these people?" That's what the question is.

How do you see Krishna in these people? You see Krishna in these people by seeing that they too somehow want to avoid suffering. It's just that Krishna's Maya is such that in the process of avoiding suffering, in their quest to avoid suffering, they are just bringing more suffering upon themselves. So, here what you see is Maya in operation.

What is the aim of Maya? What does Maya promise you to allure you? Maya promises you freedom from suffering. Does Maya come to you and say that, "I will make you suffer"? No, Maya seduces you by offering you happiness, does it not?

So, when you see such people, you have to see Krishna by realizing that everybody, after all, is working for happiness. And so great is the Yogamaya of Krishna that people, in spite of wanting happiness, work against their own happiness.

And then there is the remaining little fraction, 0.0001% of us, who are directly targeting freedom or Krishna; both are synonymous. Krishna is another name for freedom. There is that minuscule fraction that directly targets freedom. Obviously, when you look at them, there is no need for conjecture left now. Those people are Krishna personified. There you will see the love of consciousness for freedom; there you will see how each being is so desperate to reach the same point it is coming from, how we all cannot exist without that one thing, call it Truth or freedom or whatever. But such direct evidence is available only in one out of a million people. In the others, you will only see indirect evidence.

So, when you look, for example, at an instance of obvious evil, how do you see Krishna there? You see that this person, after all, is seeking freedom from his suffering. He too is seeking Krishna but he is under the spell of Krishna's Maya. Therefore, he is not seeking Krishna directly; he is seeking Krishna indirectly. Therefore, he does deserve your compassion. But because he has chosen an indirect path now, therefore direct compassion will not work with him.

What Krishna displays towards Duryodhana on the battlefield of Kurukshetra is surely compassion but indirect. Towards Arjuna, Krishna is displaying direct compassion. Towards Duryodhana, Krishna is displaying indirect compassion. How? The best way to demonstrate, or rather sometimes the only way to demonstrate to a person who is in the wrong that he is indeed in the wrong, is by defeating him. What is it that supports his wrongness? His confidence that wrongness will win. How do you then liberate him from his wrongness? By demonstrating to him that wrongness will not win. Therefore, by defeating Duryodhana, Krishna is offering his compassion to Duryodhana.

You have mentioned here that when you see the opposite of love, compassion and Truth in others, then you tell yourself that it is because your mind is dirty and unclean; therefore, you are seeing dirt and unclean stuff in others. No, please avoid this attitude. If you see dirt, clean it up. It is stupid to see dirt and say, "Oh, it is appearing like dirt because my mind is dirty!" Such an attitude can be especially dangerous in coronavirus days. You cannot say that the virus too is an embodiment of Krishna, and everybody who is carrying the virus is actually not sick but is appearing sick because your mind is sick. No, sickness is sickness and virus is virus. Clean up and avoid.

Love is a highly exclusive thing. You just cannot love wisdom and nonsense in the same way. You cannot talk of the highest and the lowest in the same breath. You must learn to exclude. You must learn to reserve. You must learn to see distinction before you come to see unity. If someone starts talking of unity without first being adept in the art of discretion, then he is just fooling himself.

It is a process in levels. At the lowest level are people who see no distinction. To them clean and unclean are the same. To them right and wrong are the same. Therefore, in the name of rightness, what they usually do is something wrong. To them dharma, adharma are the same. In the name of dharma, what they usually engage in is adharma. This is the lowest level of people. They just cannot differentiate; they have no discretion.

Now, from this stage, to take you beyond this stage, spiritual practice starts. And spiritual practice is about learning to differentiate. Learn to differentiate first of all; learn to see that Truth and Maya are different; learn to see that wisdom and foolishness are different; learn to see that freedom and bondage are different. And once you have become adept in seeing the differences, you then come to a point when you see that even that which is false is false only because it was approaching Truth in a convoluted way, in a personal way. So, the false too is actually a lover of Truth; therefore, the false too deserves consideration and compassion. That is after stage two. In stage two, first of all, you must practice the art of viveka or discretion, differentiation, and only after that you come to a point where you become capable of ananyatā or unity.

Most people, in the name of unity that belongs rightfully only to stage three, keep themselves on stage one itself. What is common between stage one and three? On both these stages, there is no distinction. But in stage one, there is no distinction because you have no eyes, no senses, no faculty, no wisdom to differentiate. And in stage three, you see no distinction because now you can see the true even in the false.

Don't skip stage two. Stage two is where the work lies. Stage two is where the practice lies. Don't just try to have a shortcut to stage three. Stage two cannot be bypassed.

Be intolerant towards falseness—that's stage two. Most of us require that. That is the only practice. Stage three happens on its own; love comes on its own, great acceptance comes on its own. Rejection has to be practiced. You practice stage two, that's your job. That's sadhana.

---

"Learn to differentiate first of all; learn to see that Truth and Maya are different; learn to see that wisdom and foolishness are different; learn to see that freedom and bondage are different. Once you have become adept in seeing the differences, you then come to a point when you see that even that which is false is false only because it was approaching Truth in a convoluted way, in a personal way."

---

*Course in Realization, BodhSthal, 2020*

# 27

# How Does the Wise One Perceive the World?

*We do not see things. We see meanings. And why do we see meanings? Because we sense a certain meaninglessness about ourselves. We want to fill it up. We do not like the meaninglessness, so we want to fill up the meaninglessness with meanings coming from the entire world.*

निराधारा ग्रहव्यग्रा मूढाः संसारपोषकाः ।
एतस्यानर्थमूलस्य मूलच्छेदः कृतो बुधैः ॥

Without any support and yet eager to attain freedom, the fools only nourish the world. The wise cut at the very root of this world, which is the source of all misery.

~ Ashtavakra Gita, Chapter 18, Verse 38

**Listener:** Can you please explain what Ashtavakra means when he says that the wise cut at the very root of this world?

**Acharya Prashant:** Ashtavakra says the fools are without any support and yet eager to attain freedom, and in this pursuit they only nourish the world. The wise, on the other hand, cut at the very root of this world.

What is this world? The world that you perceive around yourself is very little of a fact. You perceive it, and that's what it mostly is—a perception. A perception raised by the perceiver. It would be a fallacy to think that if you are looking at the green here, or the blue up there, the tree, the building, the motorcar, then you are just seeing the green or the blue or the tree or the motorcar.

*We do not see things. We see meanings. And why do we see meanings? Because we sense a certain meaninglessness about ourselves. We want to fill it up. We do not like the meaninglessness, so we want to fill up the meaninglessness with meanings coming from the entire world.*

Now, the world as such has no meaning whatsoever—the grass is just grass, the sky is just the sky—but we imbue it, load it, superimpose on it a meaning. That meaning is not an inherent property of the object itself; that meaning, as we said, is superimposed on the object by us, the perceiver. But if we admit that, then the object will cease to have any attraction for us, any sense for us, any importance for us, because to admit that the object has no meaning is to admit that the object is useless for us—useless not in the physical sense but in the psychological sense. If the object has no meaning, then how will it fill up our meaninglessness? So, it becomes useless.

So, it becomes critical for us to keep assuming that a meaning is vested in the object itself. It is a self-hatched conspiracy against the self.

Now, the world as such being meaningless, can be a cause of neither pleasure nor pain. But a lot of suffering is created by us when we load objects with meanings. The world is not the cause of misery; our perception of the world is. What we think of the world is the cause of our misery. How we interpret the world is the cause of our misery.

Does that mean that one interpretation is better than the other? No, that's not what Ashtavakra is saying. Ashtavakra is simply saying, *any* interpretation will be self-serving because you would have burdened the object and the world with that interpretation; you would have wanted to supply that meaning, that interpretation to that particular object. So, the very fact that you are interpreting something in a particular way immediately means that your interpretation will be harmful to you.

This has to be understood. We sometimes do admit that our interpretations are off the mark, but that only impels us to look for a better interpretation of events, happenings, world, objects. We never really lose hope in interpretations. If one doesn't suffice, then we look for the other.

Your interpretation arises from your need to seek fulfilment through an object. Why does one interpret at all? Why is one not content just looking around at things as if they can supply no psychological fulfilment? Because we need psychological fulfilment. And why do we need psychological fulfilment? Because at the root of the person lies an assumption, rather a delusion. And what does that assumption or delusion say? "I am incomplete." This statement lies at the root of our personhood. This statement lies at the root of our jīva-nature. "I am incomplete. Something is missing."

So, one looks at something—rather anything—always in a motivated way, always with an intention. And the intention is to seek fulfilment. When your defining statement is that "I am unfulfilled" then what would you use the world for? Fulfilment. So, you look at anything, and your purpose is just one: "How do I get fulfilment using that thing?" So, you supply that thing with a particular meaning.

I re-emphasize that the meaning has very little to do with the object itself. The meaning has much more to do with our inherent emptiness—'emptiness' not in the Buddhist sense but in the sense of misery, an inner vacancy, an inner loneliness.

So, all interpretations arise from there. Now, how does it matter which particular interpretation you come up with? After all, it is your own personal interpretation, is it not? Or at least it is an interpretation that you like. And if you like it, it would surely be serving just one purpose. What is the purpose? "Please fill up my inner vacuum!" That's what the ego is crying out.

Now, Ashtavakra is saying, "The wise cut at the very root of this world." Mark the word 'this'. Ashtavakra is not saying that for the wise the world does not exist at all. The world exists even for the wise, but not *this* world.

What is this world? This is a world of meanings, promises, superimpositions, projections, assumptions, imaginations, hopes, and therefore, despair. This world doesn't exist for the wise. For them, another world exists—naked, simple, and innocent.

Our world is a heavily decorated world. And all decoration, as we know, covers up the essence. In fact, that's the very purpose of decoration: you want to hide something, don't you? We often claim that we decorate to embellish, to express, to bring out. We don't decorate really to bring something out. We rather decorate to conceal, don't we?

Do you need to decorate a flower? No, you use the flower to decorate something else. Do you ever decorate a flower? No, but you use the flower to decorate your hair. That only shows how poor your hair is in front of the rose. Do you ever use your hair to decorate the rose? That's not needed. That would be stupid.

*That which is real and genuine needs no decoration. That around which a lot of inferiority exists, that which is perceived as lacking something, needs to be ornamented, embellished.*

For the wise, the world does exist. The grass is grass, the sky is sky, birth is birth, death is death. They have meanings in a physical sense, but they have no meaning in a psychological sense. Yes, certain gain may happen, you may gain a million dollars, and loss may happen, you may lose a million dollars. All that has only a physical context, a material context. "A thousand dollars came to me, a thousand dollars went away from me." For the wise, this event would have no impact on his psychological being, on his core. He would not say that the arrival of the million dollars made him bigger, and he would not say that the loss of a million dollars turned him smaller. He remains who he is. "Yes, something materially came, then something materially went away. But I neither gained nor lost."

For the wise, there is no inner vacuum to be filled. The wise have no existential agenda which all others have. The wise don't want to use this world to become somebody else; the wise is already alright. So, what is his relationship with the world, then? Playfulness. "That is there, that is there. Nice!" They don't have any meaning; they are just playthings.

For the wise, nothing has any meaning. All things are just playthings. And for the fool, even playthings become very serious. Have you not seen kids, adolescents getting into a brawl over a game of soccer? That's how the worldly mind is. For him, everything is important, everything has a meaning, everything is to be taken seriously, because something big is always at stake for the fool. Pride, prestige, advancement, achievement, security—something is always at stake. He is always in the danger of getting belittled. The foolish one is always under attack in his own perception. The wise one is fully secure; he is not being attacked.

The wise man, therefore, has not really cut at the root of this world; he has firstly cut at his own insecurity. When you have cut down your insecurity, then you are no more a slave of the world, you are no more standing in front of the world in hope of fulfilment.

Do not ask how one must look at the world. Ask, how does one look at himself? Does one look at himself as an impoverished being always in need, or does one look at himself as healthy, alright, inwardly full and secure? That must be asked.

---

"What is this world? This is a world of meanings, promises, superimpositions, projections, assumptions, imaginations, hopes, and therefore, despair. This world doesn't exist for the wise. For them, another world exists—naked, simple, and innocent."

---

*Course in Realization, BodhSthal, 2018*

# 28

# Three States of Consciousness, Death, and Liberation

*When alive, you are found in one of the three rooms. When gone, you are found in the lawn. But even death does not liberate you from the boundaries. Even death does not end your dream. Death is just a continuation of the dream.*

**Listener:** Ramana Maharishi says, "There is no difference between the dream and the waking state except that the dream is short and the waking state is long." Further at another place he says, "Just before waking up from sleep there is a very brief state free from thought. That should be made permanent."

What does Ramana Maharishi mean here? Are these two states, dreaming and being awake, the same or different? What is this brief state mentioned between dreaming and being awake, and how to make that brief state permanent in daily life?

**Acharya Prashant:** If you are someone who is identified with fragmented consciousness, then the two states are indeed different, as they are to most people. Most people, when they see a waking man, will immediately know the difference between the waking man and the sleeping man. Nobody would say that the waking man is in the same state of consciousness as the sleeping or the dreaming man, correct?

So, most people indeed see a clear difference between waking and dreaming. It is almost like being inside a house. When you are inside a house, you clearly see the difference between being in one room and being in another room of the same house, correct? You say, "This fellow is in the living room, and that fellow is in the bedroom." So, there is a difference because you are yourself contained in the house.

Now, shift the frame of reference. Consider someone who is standing outside the house. To the fellow who is standing outside the house, the only possible distinction is whether you are in the house or outside the house.

The house has three rooms and a lawn. The ones who remain confined within the house are surely going to be found either in one of the rooms or the lawn. You cannot simultaneously be found in two rooms, can you? If you are within the house, you will be found in one of the three rooms or in the lawn. That's the situation of the normal mortal being. He is either awake, dreaming, or sleeping without dreaming—these are the three rooms—or he is dead—that is the lawn. All this happens within the boundaries of the house.

So, there are these three states of what you call life, and then there is a fourth thing called death, which again happens within the boundaries. And because this man never manages to break free of the house, because this man never manages to leap out of the boundaries, all that he ever knows is the three rooms and the lawn. If you ever ask him, “Where are you?” he will say either the bedroom, or the living room, or the study. Or if he is gone, then he would be found in the lawn, buried.

When alive, you are found in one of the three rooms. When gone, you are found in the lawn. But even death does not liberate you from the boundaries.

Both life and death of the ordinary, the common being are within the four walls of this house. As long as you are alive, you will be found sauntering between these three places, sometimes here, sometimes there, and when you are gone, you are in the lawn—still not liberated.

Then there are those who stand in the free space outside all boundaries. To them this four-fold distinction holds no good. They do not understand what is this distinction about the three states and death and all that. They know only one distinction: are you in, or are you out? They do not even know what is going on inside the house. They do not bother. They stand outside.

To the one inside there are four distinctions. To the one outside there are only two things: are you in, or are you out? If you are in, it doesn’t matter whether you are in the lawn or in the pantry. Doesn’t matter. If you are in, you are in.

So, the saint who stands outside—somebody like Ramana Maharishi who stands outside—does not really distinguish between the waking state, which is the living room, and the sleeping state, which is the bedroom. He says, “How does it matter whether you are waking or dreaming? Whether you are waking or dreaming, the fact is you are still in bondage. You are within the four boundaries."

Now you will know why the word 'waking' is used so differently by the worldly man and the saint. When the worldly man says, "Wake up! Wake up!" what he means is, "It's 7 a.m.! Get up and go and earn your bread! And drop the kid to school!" That is the meaning conveyed by 'wake up' when exclaimed by a worldly man.

All of you have sometimes, or often, or very regularly, been told to wake up. "Wake up! Wake up!" All that this person wants to say to you is, "Come on, get up and move from bedroom to living room." This fellow does not want to say, "Come on, get up and move out of the four walls." That's what the word 'wake up' means in worldly parlance: move from one room to the other. When the saint tells you, "Wake up!" what does he mean? "Come on! If the gates do not open, break through the walls! Wake up!"

Therefore, the word 'awakening' has very different meanings when used by a saint and when used by a commoner. When a saint says, "Awaken and arise," he doesn't mean that you should now come over to the living room all decked up. You know what he means. He says, "Come on, pole vault! Outside! And if the walls do not allow you to break free, then you break your head against the walls. But under no conditions must you accept to remain confined. Wake up! These three rooms and that lawn should not become your destiny. You do not belong here."

Now, you tell me, are the two states of consciousness, which is the waking state and the dreaming state, the same or different? Seen from the point of view of the worldly man, they are different. Seen from the point of view of the saint, they are the same. The saint will say, “You know, son, when you are dreaming, you are dreaming. And when you say that you are awake, you are still dreaming. So, to me it makes no difference whether you are in sleep or awake, no difference at all. You just keep on moving from one dream to the other. Sometimes you dream with your eyes closed, at other times you dream with your eyes open, but never have you ceased dreaming. You dream all the time. You dream for a hundred years, and then the dream does not end; then you start dreaming that you have died.”

Even your death is a dream. Your entire life was a dream spent in three compartments, and then comes another dream called death, which is spent in the fourth compartment called the lawn. Even death does not end your dream. Death is just a continuation of the dream. And that is why India has said that death will not liberate you.

Death does not mean liberation at all. That which was within the four walls will continue to remain the four walls even after your death. Is the lawn outside the walls? It is not. So, how will death liberate you? So, wake up!

That which happens to us every morning, this perfunctory, biological movement of the eyelids, is a very comical and utterly false indicator of awakening. Just because these little muscles over here *(points to eyes)* start twitching, that does not mean that you have woken up, or does it? Tell me, please. Is awakening such a cheap thing that you can achieve it merely by the ringing of an alarm bell? An alarm bell rings and you are awakened—can that happen?

So, surely that which we call as the waking state of consciousness is just an extension of the dream state of consciousness. It is not different at all. It is utterly ignorant and arrogant of us to call the dream in the night as dream and the stuff in the daytime as real. The stuff in the daytime is as much of dream stuff as the stuff in the night.

*There is a dream in the night, and then there is a dream in the day. All this that you see is the dream in the daytime. Just dream, nothing else.*

Are you with me? This is the palace of dreams. What is life? Palace of dreams. What is life and death? A *grand* palace of dreams!

And that is why, you know, the common man attaches so much importance to his dreams. "You are my dream man!" "This is my dream world!" "You are my dream girl!" Without knowing, he is being honest. Actually, he can be honest only when he does not know that he is being honest. So, the dream girl is really that—a *dream* girl. She does not exist at all!

Is freedom from dreams possible? Obviously. If there is someone who is talking of dreams, it means he has woken up. And there have been the ones who have been able to look at the three rooms and the lawn from a distance. So, freedom from dreams is indeed possible. There is life outside the four walls, provided you choose it, provided you pay the price for it.

Then, "What is the brief state mentioned between dreaming and wakefulness, and how to make that brief state permanent in daily life?"

The way the questioner is posing this query, it appears as if there is a little space between the living room and the bedroom, and that little space is outside the four walls. Is it possible? But that is the way the words of saints have been miscomprehended: that between dreaming and waking up, there comes an interval of about two minutes when you are neither in the dreaming state nor the sleeping state nor in the waking state, and hence you must be in some other state.

If you are neither in the bedroom nor in the living room, does that mean you are outside the house? No, you are just at the juncture, at the threshold, that's all. But these things have been very often said. They are meaningless. You do not so easily get to taste freedom. Freedom is not so cheap that you can taste it merely, as we said, by the ringing of an alarm bell. "The alarm bell rang, and there was a brief period of a few seconds when I was neither asleep nor awake. So, surely I must have been in turiya (the fourth)." This is nonsensical. It doesn't happen that way.

What Ramana Maharishi really means to say is: the house might be very, very confined, but there is no house that can exist without a foundation, and there is no house that can exist outside of space. So, even if the house is as barricaded and as closed as a penitentiary, still it has glimpses of freedom to offer you. Even if you are in a jail, you still do get to look at the sky, don't you? No wall is ever high enough to hide the sky from you, and no structure can ever enclose you so completely that you do not even have a window or a crevice or some kind of a little opening from which to look at the sky, or space.

Some fault line would always be there. Why? Because the world is imperfect. If the world is imperfect, then can the world become a perfect prison? Ah! Therein lies your hope. Because everything in the world is imperfect, even the prison that the world is, is an *imperfect* prison. So, there surely would be some little openings, some little glimpses that would be available to you. Use them. Let them be your inspiration. Let them remind you of something.

There would be occasions when you would not know what state of consciousness you are in. You have been through that experience again and again. You know that experience, right? There are times in your life when something entirely new happens to you, something which has never been in your experience before. Those are the glimpses, those are the little cracks in the wall. Through them you get some little idea of what it means to be free. Those moments are precious, those encounters are precious. Stick to them, and let them really motivate you.

And that's the real meaning of the word 'motivation'. Freedom has to be the *only* motive. Therefore, all motivation must pertain only to freedom. If you say you are motivated, it must mean that your motivation points towards liberation. Otherwise, you are just abusing the word 'motivation'.

Let those little intervals be your motivation. That's what Ramana Maharishi really means. In those moments, would you call yourself awake? No. Would you call yourself asleep? No. Would you call yourself dreaming? No. And it does happen to many of you often. You are sitting with your eyes open but you ask me, "Whatever is happening right now, is it a dream?" It is because you cannot be certain where you are right now. It is neither a dream nor the normal waking state. Within the house itself, you have been demonstrated that which is not within the house.

---

"There are times in your life when something entirely new happens to you, something which has never been in your experience before. Those are the glimpses, those are the little cracks in the wall. Through them you get some little idea of what it means to be free. Those moments are precious, those encounters are precious. Stick to them, and let them really motivate you."

---

*Course in Realization, BodhSthal, 2019*

# 29

# Attributes of the Attributeless

*The moment you attach attributes to even Brahm, Brahm is no more Brahm. Now even Brahm is Maya—though we worship that Brahm by the name of Īśvara.*

स पर्यगाच्छुक्रमकायमव्रणमस्नाविरं शुद्धमपापविद्धम् ।
कविर्मनीषी परिभूः स्वयम्भूर्याथातथ्यतोऽर्थान् व्यदधात् शाश्वतीभ्यः समाभ्यः ॥

He, the all-encompassing, the bright, the bodiless, the unwounded, the sinewless, the pure, the unpierced by evil, the wise seer, conqueror, self-born; He has arranged objects according to their nature through eternal years.

~ Ishavasya Upanishad, Verse 8

**Acharya Prashant:** That transcendental element, that all-inclusive, yet very exclusive Truth is being introduced to us here.

He, That, 'Tat', is being called as the all-encompassing one, bright, bodiless, unwounded, sinewless—meaning muscleless, implying bodilessness—pure, unpierced by evil, wise seer, conqueror, self-born. The way the Truth is being described or referred to here is a mix of things, some of which are said to negate and some are said to affirm or establish.

He is being called bright. He is being called bright because we have a fear of darkness. Being the physically evolved creatures that we are, darkness has always been a threat to us in the course of evolution. A part of our primordial psyche continues to remain afraid of darkness even to this date.

Irrespective of our technological progress, irrespective of the control we exercise over day and night, over energy and power, human beings are still nervous when it comes to darkness. And we are not talking of little babies here; even grown-ups are never very comfortable with absolute darkness. The reason, obviously, is body-identification. The most important physical sense that we have, the sense we are the most identified with, becomes dysfunctional in darkness—the eyes. And if the physical sense becomes dysfunctional, the body-identified creature feels that his very identity has become defunct.

In our ancient mind, our physical well-being is directly related to our ability to defend ourselves against aggression and to be able to look around for opportunities of all kinds and gather food—none of which can happen without the aid of eyes, without the aid of light. That's why, in our vocabulary, 'darkness' continues to remain an unpreferred word. Those of us who would like to venture into the psyche of man might be getting a hint regarding the origin of racism here. The more body-identified you are, the more darkness will threaten you. The more body-identified you are, the more unsettling will be the word 'dark' to you.

As things stand, unfortunately, most of us are not only body-identified—we are *only* body-identified. All our other identifications are actually branches of the root body-identification. You might be identified with a lot of other things as well, but if you will go into those identifications, you will find that fundamentally they come from your feeling that you are the body.

So, if you are the body, then you have reasons to be attached to your wealth, you have reasons to be identified with your achievements and possessions. If you are the body, then you have reasons to be attached to your family and to your kids. But all those identifications, possessions, attachments are fundamentally because of your identity with your body—and the body does not like darkness because the eyes are the body's primary way of communicating with the world.

If you are asked, what would you like to give up—given that you can keep only one of the two—your eyes or your ears, the choice would be straightforward, right? May it not come to that, it is a bad choice to be forced into, but your eyes are something that you would always want to retain.

So, there is fear of darkness, and that is the reason why the Truth is often referred to as light or brightness: because the Truth is the dispeller of fear, because the Truth enables you to see.

In fact, the Truth is a special kind of light because the eyes, in presence of physical light, photonic light, enable you to only see the objects. The electromagnetic radiation that we call light enables your eyes to only perceive objects. Truth is light extraordinaire: it enables you to perceive the object and the subject together. Much more on that will be coming in the subsequent verses, but this verse prepares the ground.

Truth is bodiless, muscleless, sinewless, boneless, bloodless; Truth cannot be pierced or wounded. Here the method of negation is being used. You do not know of anything that is not bodily, nor can you ever know of anything that is not bodily. A thing can only correspond with another thing in its own dimension. If you are the body, all that the body can perceive is bodies, other bodies. In other words, all that within you or outside of you that perceives the body is just an extension of your own body.

So, the mind is nothing but subtle body. Be it the telescope or the microscope, they are just extensions of your eyes. Even the fastest rocket is just an extension of your legs. Whatever we think of, is bodily. Therefore, even the richest kind of imagination is nothing but the body stretching itself far and wide. That's the thing with living in a bodily way. You might progress or achieve a lot in your own eyes, but actually you are just confined to the domain of the body, the physical, the material, that which can be sensed by the material senses. If the tongue can talk of it, it is bodily or material. If the nose can sniff it, it is material.

It is easy to agree when I say, "If the eyes can look at it, it is material." But it becomes difficult when I say, "If you can talk of it, it is material." You start saying, "But we can talk of things we can never see—are they still material?" You just said they are things, right? That closes the deal. They are things, and all things are material. Irrespective of whether you have physically experienced them or not, all imagination is physical.

It becomes even more difficult to accept when we say that not only are your words always referring to something material, but even imagination can only point at something material. So, no point imagining Truth or God or freedom. If you are imagining Truth or God or freedom, you have reduced them to a piece of bread or a freshly baked cake or hot oil. If you can talk of your God or Truth, then you are reducing them to curtains, to pillars, to concrete. God that the tongue can talk of is no bigger than the tongue. How expansive can your God be if he can enter you through these little holes, this little tunnel called the ears?

On one hand, we say he is all-pervasive, all-encompassing, infinite. But then, you mention him in words and you can now measure his size. All he requires is this small tunnel to pass through *(pointing to his ear)*.

Look at your eyes. If you are looking towards the sky, you can't even look at the earth. If you are looking towards the right, you will have to miss the left. But then you think that with these eyes you can look at something that is beyond space. Your eyes can't even look at space fully; how will your eyes look at that which is beyond space?

Your mind and your tongue do not even have the power or the vocabulary to express even that which is finite. A new thing comes to you, and you will be groping for the right word to express it. Often you are found saying, "Oh, but mere words fail to convey this!" or "I am short of words." You are short of words when it comes to conveying a new flavor of food, but you think you will have words to communicate that which is beyond all material.

So, the method used here is of negation. That method is needed to drill some sense and some humility into the receiver. The method of negation starts from where you are, and then shows you your little place. It says, our world is the world of body, wounds, impurity, evil, vulnerability, and susceptibility. Given that these are the defining characteristics of your world, how do I then refer to the Truth? I will refer to the Truth as that which you are not. Simple.

So, you are false. I start from there. And if you are not false, then the Rishi will say, "Get up and go! If you are not false, then why have you come to me to waste your time and mine? If you are not false, then everything is alright with you. If you are not false, then you are the Truth. There is no point discussing these things. You are coming to me because you perceive that you are suffering, that falseness surrounds you from within and without. You have some inkling that things are not right with you, that what you take as existent is not really existent; it deceives you. That which you do not know of suddenly appears from somewhere to torment you."

So, your idea of your world is fanciful, imperfect, false, and the cause of your suffering. That's why you are in front of the teacher. So, this is established. "Not everything is alright with me." This is established, and this is where we start from.

Vedanta proceeds in a very scientifically meticulous way. It does not start from assumptions; it starts from the one thing that is absolutely certain. Why talk of this notion, that dogma, this belief, that imagination? No, one is not to imagine anything, one is not to speculate, one is not to assert, one is not to argue. One is to start from that which is indisputable, and what is that? "I am, and I am not good. I am, because if I am not there, then who is talking? Somebody is talking. And the one who is talking I refer to as 'I'. So, I am the talker—and I am not alright." Now, this is irrefutable.

We are not saying in the beginning that there exists Brahm or Atma or this or that. None of that. The student comes to the teacher, that is the beginning. The student exists—at least in his own eyes. The teacher exists—at least in the student's eyes. The student is suffering—at least in his own perception. Can you doubt this?

So, this is where the thing starts from, and this will tell you the genesis of the method of negation or 'Neti-Neti', which means that if you have to get rid of your suffering, you have to start with disproving or disowning your notions.

So, you are vulnerable; you are vulnerable and you don't like that. Therefore, the Truth has to be someone who can neither be touched nor pierced nor wounded. That's what the shloka says here. You are in trouble because things are able to penetrate you—penetrate you without your consent. Something happens, and you find that you have been pierced—you didn't even want that, some accidental thing—and it has hit you right in the core. You are bleeding from within.

So, now how do I talk of the Truth? I will talk of the Truth very humbly as that which I am not; therefore, I will refer to my own fallible characteristics to point to the Truth. My fallibility lies in my vulnerability; therefore, I will say the Truth is that which is not vulnerable.

Similarly, 'the pure', 'the bodiless'. All I know of is bodies, and that doesn't help me in any way, or does it? I know of myself as the born one, and having taken birth as a body, I really have not enjoyed it, or have I? There have been intermittent episodes of pleasure but those are not worth talking of. They were just like little consolations. They were just like the little break that you get before the next bashing. And even before the wounds have healed or dried, you find that the period of celebratory recuperation is over.

And next time? Life is such that it hits you not in entirely new places. What you find as absolutely insulting is that life hits you again where it had hit you the last time even before the wounds from the last time have healed. And then you cannot look yourself in the mirror and forgive yourself for celebrating the little period of relief sandwiched between these two prolonged spells of humiliation.

Therefore, the Truth simply has to be referred to as that which is very, very far removed from me. I see I am false. My entire life I might not be able to get a whiff of the Truth but of one thing I am dead certain: I am false. This is the way of Vedanta.

Vedanta does not deal in fancies. Vedanta does not enjoy speculations, imaginations. Vedanta does not paint pretty pictures. Vedanta begins with destruction—though Vedanta is surely not only about destruction; there is great creation that happens. But before that creation, there has to be an absolute destruction. Certain things can't happen till the last traces of impurity have been wiped away. If traces of the old falseness remain, the new will remain at bay. Therefore, negation first.

'The wise seer', kavirmanīṣī, 'conqueror', 'self-born'. These words are so alien to us, are they not? We are such pathetically dependent beings that we depend on others even for our birth. Does that sound nice? Forget about living in an independent way—independently you cannot even take birth! Two strangers have to get together and work really hard, really beat the sweat out of each other's bodies for you to be somehow born. And they are strangers, are they not? After you take birth, somebody has to tell you that they are your father, otherwise you will not know. And if you talk of the physical bond that you have with your mother, some other lady could have substituted for it; she could have nursed you and you wouldn't have even known. Sometimes even a goat suffices if, unfortunately, the mother is no more.

So, not everybody will turn to spirituality, you see. Only someone who feels deeply disgraced; in some sense, only someone who has an ego which gets offended will turn to spirituality. And only someone who has some intellect, some wit about him; only someone who does not want to console or entertain himself with hollow notions of self-sufficiency or independence or freedom will turn towards spirituality. There are others who would say, "You see, I earn so much these days—so what do I call myself? Independent." You must have a little more intellect. Only someone who applies some thought and says, "What independence?" will turn towards spirituality.

Just before I was to start this session, I received a message on my online college group. They don't usually refer to me, but tonight somebody was probably in a bad mood or something. So, they posted a photo of some guru, and it was carrying the lines that, "To know yourself, go within; for everything else, there is Google." And specifically he tagged me and said, "Kindly comment." So, I said, "This is an understatement." And I was writing on that group after a period of maybe two years or something. But since I was asked, I replied.

So, I said: This is an understatement. Whatever you are, from top till bottom, can be found on Google. If you say that to find yourself you will need to go within, for everything else there is Google, you are assuming that some part of you will not be found on Google. I think that this is conceit; you think too much of yourself! You think that there is something transcendental or extraordinary about you that Google cannot capture. Not at all.

We are crawlers when it comes to life. And Google has trawlers. Trawlers catch crawlers.

Only someone who feels very offended at this state of affairs is likely to turn spiritual. If you are 'somebody'—as most of my batchmates are—everything about you is there on Google. You just type their name and you will get to know everything about them. A few of them probably even have their own Wikipedia pages and things. Even if they don't have that, there is LinkedIn. So, your degrees, your family, your date of birth, your height, your weight, your affairs, your controversies, everything can be found on Google.

Now, tell me, what are you beyond your height, your weight, your bank balance, your family, your career graph? Are you anything?

Now, rare is a rebel who says, "This is unacceptable! Am I me or am I spread all over the internet?" Some part of you is there on Twitter, some part of you can be found on some website, some part of you is there on LinkedIn. If someone wants to see how your physical being is, he just has to click on Google images.

Tell me, what is it about you that someone cannot learn on Google, assuming that you are reasonably famous? Either you are already fully on Google, or you are potentially on Google. Or you are a loser in life who just keeps desiring to be on Google.

Is there anything about us that words, images, data, others cannot capture or cannot know? And if they can capture all this, then you are a captive in life. "I don't like this. There has to be something about me—hell, why something? The most important part of my essence has to be something that no Google can ever touch, that no words can ever describe." Only someone who has this dimension of dissatisfaction will turn spiritual. Others will continue the way they are.

Are you getting an insight into the Upanishadic method? Upanishads do not have feet of clay. When after the French revolution Europe was passing through the age of enlightenment, then the philosophers of the time used to take great pleasure in quipping that the gods have feet of clay, and that the temples are all in the skies and they don't even have pillars to bind them or root them to the earth. In other sense, your temples are all just wisps of imagination; they have no concrete base.

Vedanta, on the other hand, has a very, very concrete base, and that base is not speculative; that base is not dogmatic or doctrinal; that base is factual. What is the base? The base is: *I am*. My life. *My* life. No esoteric base, nothing subjective, nothing that only you can experience; something that is factual and something that is being experienced by everybody. You exist, or do you not? In your eyes you exist. This is where Vedanta starts from.

First: I exist. Would you want to dispute that? Even to dispute that you will have to exist, so let's not.

Second: I am, and I am not satisfied.

This is where Vedanta starts from.

Vedanta doesn't start off by saying, "Oh, there is a holy God sitting somewhere in the skies and let's all worship him." No, not that. Brahm and Atma come much later. Who comes first? Aham (I am). You start from aham, and you want to treat aham. Aham is you. And in the process of treating aham, you reach, you become, you find that you always were Brahm.

But Brahm is not the objective even though the entire thing is called Brahmavidyā. Brahm is not the objective; the objective is to heal your condition. That's the objective, because you do not know of Brahm. How can Brahm be the objective?

What do you know of in your day-to-day living? You know of your daily miseries, you know of how irritated you are at small things; this is what your daily experience comprises, right? So, that's where Vedanta starts from. Let there be no doubt regarding this.

Vedanta is more scientific than science. Science begins by saying, "This exists *(picks up a handkerchief)*. Now, let me investigate this." How will science begin? "This exists. Now I will investigate this by the method of experimentation and observation."

Vedanta says, "Right, this exists. I am not doubting that. But before this exists, I exist and I am not feeling well. I want to talk about that first. Maybe if I feel well, I will no longer feel the need to talk about this. Or maybe I will. If I still feel the need to talk about this, I will talk about this."

Therefore, Vedanta is not at all opposed to science. Vedanta is just more fundamental than science.

Science will say, "Let's talk about this." Vedanta says, "Let's talk about the seer of this and later on we can go into this. And even if I have to talk about this, I will keep in mind the one who is talking about this because even the urge to talk about this comes from someone's dissatisfaction. Remember that if I am at absolute peace, I will not want to talk about anything randomly, or would I?"

We talk of things because things hold meaning to us. We talk about things because we expect to benefit from things. We expect to benefit from things because internally we are impoverished and demanding and expectant.

"So, before I venture into this thing, I want to go into the one within who is seeking solace in things." That's the way of Vedanta.

So, Vedanta is not at all about some God somewhere. In fact, there is no God in Vedanta. Many Vedantic scholars have used the word 'God' but when they have used the word 'God', it does not carry the same meaning as the God of the West. The God of the West, the God of Abrahamic religions, is a very active God: a God that creates; a God that is sometimes merciful, sometimes wrathful; a God that is sometimes even envious; a God that is sometimes even revengeful. And even if he is not revengeful or wrathful, he is surely interested in the world because he keeps accounts, and on a given day he would call everybody and close the cases; some would be rewarded, others would be flogged.

So, that's God. In Vedanta, there is no God. Īśvara is there, but then, that Īśvara is saguṇa (with attributes, qualified), and guṇa (attribute, quality) comes from Prakriti, and another name for Prakriti is Maya. Īśvara is saguṇa, and all guṇa belong to Prakriti, and Prakriti is Maya. Therefore, Īśvara is Maya.

So, the moment you attach attributes to even Brahm, Brahm is no more Brahm. Now even Brahm is Maya—though we worship that Brahm by the name of Īśvara; people say that Saguṇa Brahm is Īśvara. But the moment Brahm starts carrying guṇa, now Brahm is in the domain of Prakriti. Gone, finished—just like us. We are saguṇa. If Brahm also becomes saguṇa, game over.

Though it is a matter of a more detailed and separate discussion that, just as a method, probably human beings or at least some human beings require Īśvara. But Īśvara can at best be a method, never the Truth. There is a difference between the Truth and the method used to reach Truth. Īśvara can be a method, a temporary method, a bridge that you need to use and cross. Once you have crossed the bridge, you leave it.

Brahm is not something that you use; Brahm is unusable. Nor can you cross over Brahm to reach somewhere else. Brahm is the transcendental; you cannot transcend Brahm. But Īśvara you can and you must transcend.

This was about the Vedantic method of negation.

Similarly, the verse mentions, 'conqueror'. Now, why must That be called as the conqueror? I just said that Brahm is not participative at all. If He is not participative, why is He being called as the conqueror? Tell me. Because we are such silly losers. All our experience, all our life has been of losing, losing, and losing. Only if you are dead stupid will you call yourself a winner. Anybody with any brains will surely know that he has surely been a loser. Only very idiotic beings carry the fantasy of being victorious or being achievers and such things. Those who have ever looked honestly at life or thought clearly about things know fully well that there is no victory here. We move from one loss to another humiliating loss.

Because our experience is of defeat and loss and pain and agony, therefore in contrast the Truth is being called as the conqueror. You are the loser, therefore He is the victor. Otherwise, He is not the victor at all.

So, why is the Truth being called as the victor? To impress upon you, to sensitize you to your condition of perpetual loss. "I have suffered defeats and setbacks in whatever I have done. My plans, my proposals, my endeavors have either remained fruitless or the fruit has been extraordinarily awful. Not getting any fruit from my efforts has often been better than getting a fruit. The fruit has been beyond my fantasies. Such bitter fruits I have received."

But this bitterness would be acknowledged only by someone with some honesty. Because it breaks your heart to acknowledge that you have been a total loser, doesn't it? Only someone with a core of steel can acknowledge this. Most people are just too delicate, too brittle to acknowledge the hollowness and meaninglessness of their lives. It breaks them; they just crumble. Therefore, they put up a façade. Therefore, they keep pretending all their life that all is well with them or things are almost well. "Well, there is hot, there is cold, there is this, there is that"; and they will say, "How's life? Well, gray. A few things are good, a few other things are about to get good." This is the language they use.

It requires a hero, it requires a real man to stand up and admit that everything is dead and defeated.

Now do you see why That is being called a conqueror? Also, when That is called a conqueror, then it encourages you to surrender. "If there can be something—even outside my imagination—something that stands for conquest in this mortal world of loss, then I want to surrender to that thing." That's the awe this word inspires in you.

Similarly, 'wise seer'. Who are we? Blind fools. Since we are blind, He has to be called the seer. We don't see anything, or do we? We do not see even that which is in front of our eyes. Don't we stumble on the roads? Anybody here who has never slipped in the bathroom? So many people who get fractures actually get them in the bathrooms. That's the extent of our seeing. We cannot see that which is right in front of us; we cannot see that which is right below our feet, the water, the wetness.

And look at our wisdom. We think we are so independent. But how independent are you? How did you manage that fall and that fracture? The fellow was trying to put on his underwear, so one leg was raised so that the wearing of the underwear could be initiated. And he thought that he can transcend duality! One leg in the air, trying to stand on one leg, and then comes the mighty slip. The nose hits the commode. The elbow hits the wall. The hip hits the ground. Three fractures in one go. And he thinks he is independent!

This is the height of our wisdom. Forget about exceeding the duality of the world—we cannot even exceed the duality of these two legs. Forget about fighting the slippery slope called Maya—we cannot even stand properly in a slippery bathroom. And some really big achievers have managed to fracture their bones in the process of undressing. That's how we are. Now, do you want to call yourself wise? Really?

There were some tremors in the last few days, including today. Quakes of minor intensity. And then you go to Twitter and within twenty minutes you have something trending—"Quake hits Delhi," or, you know, "Something is shaking." Stuff of this kind.

So, I came out of my room and looked at our rabbits in the lawn. And they knew what to do: when there is an earthquake, move away from everything that is fallible. For the few moments the earth was shaking; they all assembled in the middle of the lawn. And not one of them freaked out; not one of them started yelling and shouting; not one of them had to be taken to the psychiatrist. But you go to social media and you have people, men, women, going berserk. One lady was running in the streets; she knocked two old men down. It was not the earthquake that did them in, it was the quaking lady!

We are not wise. We are just beneficiaries of several centuries of accumulated knowledge and technology. Take that away, and who are we? Did you invent the mobile phone? Look at your brains and your intellect. Do you even deserve to hold the mobile phone in your palm? You are just beneficiaries of a very long accumulative process. Otherwise, the animals are better than most of us, are they not? Look at how the common man lives. He is making use of cutting-edge technology—sometimes bleeding-edge technology—without knowing half a thing about technology.

We are just tapping from, drawing upon what a few illuminated individuals have contributed in the course of history. Our religion comes from a few illuminated beings. Our science and technology, our literature, our arts—all of this comes from a few illuminated beings. Take those few beings away, and who are we? You will be left neither with language nor with clothes, no spectacles, no technology, no car, no washing machine, no fridge. The rabbits don't get educated but they at least have some sense of their own. They don't start running helter-skelter on the streets.

Then the verse says, "He has arranged objects according to their nature through eternal years."

We are objects in Prakriti, and That is beyond Prakriti because whatsoever is in Prakriti passes through the cycle of evolution and gets dissolved as well—takes birth, evolves, dissolves. And then comes the next thing and the next cycle again—arising, remaining, falling. That is beyond Prakriti; this is what is indicated by these words.

Next, the verse says, "He has arranged objects according to their nature through eternal years."

We are objects; He is beyond us. He has not really arranged us; it's just that we are prone to being arranged and therefore there has to be something beyond arrangement if peace is to come to us. Do you get the entire drift?

Who am I? I am the one whose fate is controlled by Prakriti. You didn't decide where to be born, how to be born, what the economic condition of your family would be, what your religion or caste or nationality would be. Do you decide all these things? You didn't decide your gender either. You didn't decide which school to go to, did you? You didn't even decide which college to go to. Seriously! Either it was accidental, or it came from the few limited options available to you.

So, we are things that Prakriti plays around with. I may be quoting inaccurately, but it is from Shakespeare and he says that, "Men are like flies, the gods kill us for their wanton pleasure." The picture being summoned here is that of mischievous boys who are carrying fly swatters and they are killing these flies for their general pleasure.

So, Shakespeare is saying, just as these little boys are killing flies for their random pleasure, so are men killed by gods for their wanton pleasure. That's our situation. That's the human situation—at the mercy of chance, circumstances; at the mercy of randomness.

Therefore, I suffer because I exercise no real control over myself, because that which I call as myself is all coming from sources that are external, alien, not under my control. I exercise no power over these other things and, unfortunately, these other things have all been collated and turned into something that I call as 'me'.

It is like this: This is my arm which is not really mine, it belongs to him, and he is holding the strings. These are my eyes that I call mine, but they don't really belong to me; he holds the strings. Similarly, every part of myself. Now, whatever happens to me is happening not because of my desire, not towards my welfare, but because somebody else has his own mind and fancy. That's the human condition.

So, my suffering is all because I am composed of externals. My suffering is all because I am vulnerable to others; my suffering is all because I am controllable. Therefore, if I am to exceed my suffering, there has to be a state that is not prone to being controlled. That state is being talked of here: something-someone beyond the game of Prakriti.

And that is why in Vedanta there is so much emphasis on transcending Prakriti. As long as you are in Prakriti, you are in control—not in the sense that you are exercising control but in the sense that you are being controlled.

*As long as you are in Prakriti, you are being controlled. And if you are being controlled, there can be no freedom, no joy; there can be only frustration and exasperation.*

So, the seer is talking of That as something-someone beyond Prakriti. And that is why it is very important to never talk of yourself as a piece of Prakriti. Never say that. Never say, "Oh, but this is so prakritik, so if I am doing it, isn't it justified?"

No, if it is prakritik, then it is not justified. Because if it is prakritik, it will lead to slavery.

But this is such an oft-repeated argument, is it not? "Oh, why should I be observing or monitoring my sexual urges? Are they not really prakritik?" And people use the word 'natural' for Prakriti, which is not at alright, but fine.

So, people will say, "Oh, but isn't it natural?" If it is natural in the sense of being prakritik, it is not good for you. "Is it not natural to be a little competitive or envious or jealous?" It is. And therefore, it is not good for you. Your argument must be appended. You are saying, "It is prakritik, therefore it is justified." It is not justified exactly because it is prakritik; because if it is prakritik, it will keep you in bondage.

Never try to support your bodily urges or instincts. Prakriti is just that: arising from your body, your body itself. Never try to support them by saying, "Oh, but they are normal and natural." Never.

'Normal' comes from the society; 'natural' comes from Prakriti. Therefore, these two ends are to be avoided. What you call as normal, that comes from society. What you call as natural comes from Prakriti. Both these condition you and, therefore, control you.

You are neither an element of the society—much as you would like to call yourself a social animal or such things. All that is very superficial. You are not a social element, you are not a unit of the society—that's a very superficial description of the human being—nor are you a product of Prakriti.

Who are you? The Upanishad is in no hurry to answer that. The Upanishad takes a lot of time just dwelling over what you are not. And after long, when you are ripe and ready, then the Upanishad silently whispers to you who you probably are, and doesn't say much. Most of the effort of the Vedantic seers was going towards negation, not affirmation—though affirmation does come but later, later and in a very soft and subtle way.

Negation is hard and brutal. Affirmation is soft and just suggestive.

---

"As long as you are in Prakriti, you are being controlled. And if you are being controlled, there can be no freedom, no joy; there can be only frustration and exasperation."

---

*Course in Realization, BodhSthal, 2020*

# 30

# The King and the Sage

*It is a rare combination: to not be fooled by the world, and also to not be fooled by yourself; to have the sureness that you are powerful enough to defeat the world, and equally have the humility that you are not powerful enough to defeat your inner self, the ego.*

**शौनको ह वै महाशालोऽङ्गिरसं विधिवदुपसन्नः पप्रच्छ ।**
**कस्मिन्नु भगवो विज्ञाते सर्वमिदं विज्ञातं भवतीति ॥**

Śaunaka, the great house-lord, came to Aṅgiras in the due way of the disciple and asked of him, "Lord, by knowing what does all that is become known?"

~ Mundaka Upanishad, Verse 1.1.3

**Acharya Prashant:** Let us first understand a few things about discipleship. Discipleship is a ripening. It is valuable; it cannot arbitrarily come to anybody with any kind of mind or any kind of attitude. The Upanishadic tradition is full of worldly and materially successful and accomplished people going to the sages. We have to see that, firstly, these are talented and industrious people; they are successful kings and lords. They know the ways of the world; they know how to win the world. At least they are not victims of others' shrewdness and their own indolence or dullness.

These are the two things that prevent a person from being successful in the world, or rather make a person the slave of the world. First, if you are so naive or ignorant or greedy that others overwhelm you, oversmart you, overpower you by either tempting you or by defeating you with their efficiency, you will be cheated again and again. This is the likely first reason if you find yourself being enslaved by the world: others are able to deceive you. The second reason is inner. Inwardly, you are so slothful, lazy and a victim to your own tendencies, that no well-directed effort arises from you. So, how will you do anything worthwhile in the world?

Now, it is not very significant that those who often came to the sages were kings. What is very significant is that those who came to the sages did not carry either of the two follies we just discussed, viz., one, they were not so naive that the world could take them for a ride, they knew the ways of Maya when they saw Maya in others; and two, they were not inwardly dull or lazy, they could see Maya in themselves as well.

So, these were people with a certain qualification. And I repeat, their qualification is not that they were kings; their qualification is that they knew Maya and were successful against it, at least to some extent. A bumbling idiot will not manage to stay king for long, would he? So, if somebody is a king, we know that he holds at least a certain degree of mental sharpness. Even if we say that the fellow just happened to have the kingdom in patrimony because his father too was a king, yet he won't be able to carry his inheritance for long if he is an utter idiot.

So, these are sharp people; sharp enough to manage the state, and also sharp enough to see what is cooking within themselves, what is empty and hollow and abegging within themselves.

Do you see this particular combination? We are talking of the disciple. We are trying to go into the mind of the right disciple. First thing, the right disciple cannot be the one who is tempted or scared or defeated easily by the world. And that is why it holds significance that these people, Śaunaka, Janaka and many others, are kings.

And the second thing about the disciple is that he sees this: "Well, I do succeed in the world, and I probably can succeed even more in the world, but it is not all quite adding up; something remains to be fulfilled within. I am not someone who is so incompetent that I cannot even win a small worldly battle; I am not that kind of a fellow. I do win battles, if not all at least many of them, but it is not sufficing. So, it is not about winning battles." That is another kind of a problem.

"I am not succeeding at all in the world"—that is another kind of a man. We are not saying that kind of a man is fit to be a disciple. But it is a different person who says, "I am indeed winning in the world, if not everything then at least a lot of things, but it is not sufficing. At least the outer Maya I am able to defeat, resist." People come to a king with all kinds of shrewdness and inner mechanisms and deviousness, don't they? If you are a king, you know what kind of conspiracies are hatched against you and all the palace intrigues and such things. You have read about them.

So, the king has to be a sharp fellow, and he is a sharp fellow. If he is not sharp, he won't last. But he also sees that for all his sharpness, sound sleep eludes him. He is sharper than probably the rest of the world, yet not sharp enough for himself. Ah, that is the problem. He is sharp enough to beat the mechanisms of the outer world, yet something sits within that he is not quite able to make sense of, read, and defeat.

This is the disciple. This is the kind of mind that is needed.

Why is the first condition important? The first condition is important because if you are not able to even compete with the outer world, it will just pick and carry you away. It can carry you away in two ways: one, you are blown away against your wish, almost kidnapped; two, you are tempted and lured away. There is not much difference between the two. Somebody could forcibly just pick you up and take you away if you are powerless; equally, if you are powerless, you can be dangled a carrot and tempted away. This person is not fit to be a disciple. That is why we see a lot of kings in the Upanishadic narrative. The world will be able to neither overwhelm them nor tempt them.

So, you have to ask yourself, are you smart enough? If the world is sly, you at least need to be smart enough to read the world's slyness. Or would you match slyness with stupidity? You need not match slyness with slyness, but you at least need to be smart enough to know slyness where it exists. And slyness never comes announcing its name, does it? Will shrewdness declare itself? Will the fox come and say, "I am so wily!" to the chicken it intends to pick up? No. You need to have the smarts to see slyness behind its disguise. The disguise is slyness, is it not? If it is not disguised, it has no power. So, that stereotype, if it exists at all in some of us, has to be challenged and broken. Which stereotype? The one that says that the man of scriptures, the spiritual man, is a simpleton. Not possible. Simplicity is a great virtue but it is not what we think it to be.

There is a great difference between innocence and ignorance. The ignorant mind cannot even see Maya, and therefore remains happily blissful. So, you say ignorance is bliss. That bliss is obviously both temporary and dangerous. That is the bliss of the drunkard happily lying on the railway track, thinking it is his bedroom. Happy! The happiness won't last; it is temporary. And this happiness would lead to his destruction. Dangerous.

True simplicity exceeds cunningness. It reads cunningness and remains untouched by it.

It is extremely important to be able to read cunningness, and if you can read cunningness, you won't be a victim to it. True simplicity reads cunningness, smiles at it, and does not feel obliged to reciprocate in cunningness. There is no reactionary cunningness that arises from simplicity and innocence. That is a very different thing from, I repeat, not reading or sensing or detecting cunningness at all. That is very different.

Usually, we have only two kinds of people. One, those who cannot even see Maya where it exists and therefore remain happy like our drunkard. "There is no Maya, I am happy. My life is cool. I have a nice life, nice neighbors, nice everything. The sunlight is so nice, my job is so nice, my family is so nice, my bed is so nice. Oh, what is that? Whistle? No, no, that is probably some videogame my little Johnny is playing. No, no, that is not the train approaching on the tracks. No, no, I am on my bed. What kind of train are you dreaming of? There is no train! I am happy."

These are particular kinds of people. You know them, you meet them. They just don't see any evil anywhere. For them evil is fiction; for them evil is in the movies. That done-up and made-up caricature of a villain, they think he is evil. So, ask them, "Who is evil?" and they will say, "Well, that demon with ten heads." Because they live very gross lives, therefore they cannot see the subtle evil where it exists. Evil to them has to be a gross entity—so gross that it announces itself by carrying ten heads.

Now, come on. Will the evil one ever announce himself so loudly that he will declare, show, proclaim his ten heads to you and laugh as the villains do? "Ho ho ho ho!" And because there is no such person they can see around, they declare, "There is no evil, because the evil is supposed to carry ten heads, and has to be loud, and must laugh in a very sinister way." They don't see any such person around, so they say, "There is no evil. Life is cool!" Such people are not fit to be disciples.

And then there is the next category of people who see evil and are taken in by evil. 'Taken in by evil' not necessarily in the sense that they become evil; 'taken in by evil' in the sense that they become reactionaries. Evil manages to induce shrewdness in them. Now, even these people are not fit to be disciples.

Evil can consume you in two ways. One is, you look at evil and you find it beautiful. Some people do; they are captivated by the sheer charm of evil. Aren't the dons in the movies sometimes very charming? In fact, the most charming characters in the movies in the last few decades have all been underworld dons. Scan your memory—many of them at least, if not all. I am entitled to exaggerate a bit, am I not? Can you recall some of those charming dons? We don't call them black; we say, "You know, those are characters in gray." So, evil can be very charming. Or you can be so put off by evil, so incited by evil that you decide to turn evil to avenge evil. That is another way in which evil overpowers you. "The world has done so much wrong to me; evil has done so much wrong to me. Therefore, I will turn evil to avenge myself." This person is also not entitled to be a disciple.

Those who cannot see evil are the first ones to be disqualified.

Those who see evil and find it cute or worth idolizing, they are the next to be disqualified.

And then, the ones who resist evil by turning evil are the next in the queue.

Simplicity is about seeing evil, seeing Maya, and walking past it. "How do you do, lady? Have a nice day! I have work to do; can't just stand and gossip with you. And I know you, aunty. Don't feign a face, drop that mask. I know you. To keep you in good humor, I will say you are cute. That doesn't mean I will fall for your charms. Good day, lady! Take care of yourself. I don't value you so much that I will stop in my tracks to hug you. I won't stop even to abuse you. I know you."

Get this. "Won't embrace you, won't abuse you; I just know you. Just *know* you." That is simplicity. That is innocence. That knowing element is paramount.

Unfortunately, most of us just don't know Maya. You are sitting ducks then. If you don't know Maya, that gives you no protection; that only gives you a certain righteousness. With a sense of uprightness you manage to claim to others that you are not one of her victims or stooges, but that doesn't save you. You may not have consciously embraced her, but subconsciously you have fallen for her because you do not know her.

In fact, so pathetic is your defeat that you do not even know that you have been defeated. She has overpowered you, and you do not even know you have been captivated.

So, it is no excuse. All it can give you is some moral kind of ego boost. "Well, you know, in my knowledge, I have never done any wrong—in *my* knowledge."

Now, your knowledge itself is so narrow, so blind. Outside your knowledge, you have *always* been wrong. In your subconscious ignorance, you have been doing all kinds of stupid things and partaking in evil. How will you be saved from the consequences? Just by offering this kind of a lame excuse, "I didn't do it consciously!" So what? You did it.

Now, and only now, only when the external world does not hold much power over you, you truly come to realize that there is something amiss within. You cannot have an inner focus if the external is taking away all your energy and attention.

Only when the external world becomes irrelevant to you will you be able to hear the murmurs from within.

I said irrelevant; I did not say you have to be an outright winner. What do I mean by irrelevance? Walking past. When you walk past something, you have made it irrelevant to yourself. Only when you come to that condition, when you know evil and walk past evil, you have made the evil irrelevant. It does not hold any meaning or significance to you anymore. Now is the time when you can listen to the internal noises. Now is the time you can go to the sage.

Again, a disclaimer here, listening to the internal voices, if you respond with an assertion that you will be able to defeat these internal problems just as you are able to defeat the external enemies, again, you are not fit to be a disciple.

So many conditions, you see. Very few people first of all come to see that there is a problem within; for them most problems exist without. And the problems that exist externally can be of many kinds; we talked of them. We said one problem is that you do not see any evil; the other problem is that you are charmed by evil; the other problem is that you become evil to face evil. And there can be many other sub-variants of these things. The one who is able to somehow walk past the external chaos manages to hear the squabbling voices within.

Again, there is something to be avoided: the confidence that the same faculty that enabled you to be a winner externally will be able to help you prevail over the internal problems. "I am a great man. I have wealth, I have power, I have success in business and so many other things. If I can manage all that, surely I can also manage myself. I know the world, I know my mind. I am a self-made person. If I could win it all without any help—and there were so many others to be won, I prevailed over all of them without much help from anybody—why do I require any help in winning the one person who sits within?" If you lend your weight to this argument, then, again, you cannot be a disciple.

It is a very peculiar combination. A great fighter externally and very humble internally; knowing fully well that no problem outside is insurmountable, and realizing that the problem within requires transcendental guidance.

This is the disciple; these two things have to coexist. One, no problem outside is insurmountable—insurmountable in the sense that there is no problem in the external world that cannot be exceeded. In the external world, many a times beyondness is victory. By the way, that does not mean that you will be able to declare victory every time by walking past the problem; many a times you have to face the problem head on. But whatever, whether you walk past it or face it head-on, one thing is certain: you do not get bogged down. Because what can bog you down with its hostility will surely manage to tempt you greatly when it sheds its hostility.

Why did something bog you down? Because you found its power irresistible, right? Only when you find the power of something irresistible does it manage to pin you down. Now, the same thing: when it turns favorable to you, would it not just pick and carry you away? Won't you just happily concede to your kidnapping? Tell me, please.

Whether something or somebody just pins you down to the earth or carries you away in his arms, one thing is common in the two situations. What? That person has great power over you. Power is a commonality. If you have a great enemy and he makes you shiver, it is quite likely that you will feel fortunate if that great enemy proposes to you as a friend. You will say, "How fortunate am I to win such a friend! I have a great man as my friend now. When this man was an enemy, he was a great enemy. Now that he is a friend, I must say he is a great friend." That is the problem.

These are the ways in which you are taken away. Not always against your will, not always by shattering your resistance; very often by offering you a temptation that your weak self cannot resist. One way is to attack you frontally and just shatter your resistance; you wanted to resist but the force was so overwhelming. The other way is to tempt and charm you so greatly that your weak self stands no chance.

Such a person cannot be a disciple. He still has a lot to learn and fight in the external sense. His basic lower order faculties need to be awakened. He first of all needs to be taught the virtues of things like discipline, industriousness, order, etc. He does not have even these basic things; he is a loser even in the world. And if you are a loser in the world, the world will not allow you to stay with the sage even if you in a moment of honesty manage to go to the sage. You may go to the sage, but you won't stay for long; the world will carry you away. You have no power to resist the world.

And that is the reason why the sages used to be so selective. They won't allow just anybody to enter their circle; there used to be strict qualifying conditions. If you go to the sage without having the right merit, then de facto you are an agent of the world in proximity to the sage. The sage in principle has no vulnerability, but the system he runs can be vulnerable. Therefore, the presence of such a person in proximity to the sage can be threatening to the project he might have undertaken. Therefore, there were very strict conditions. And people were tested again and again. It is not that you pass one kind of entrance test and you are in forever. The sage would suddenly test you anytime without any pre-intimation, and if you are not found up to the test, you are gone, you are deservedly gone.

So, it is not just some kind of a romantic setting—the king of the world going to meet the sage of the jungle. You read of it in the books and you look at the picturizations on the screen, and it all appears so nice. The king with the flowing golden robe going to the sage with the flowing white beard, and then the conversation flows. You go, "Wow! Both of them are so photogenic, aren't they?"

That is how we tend to look at things—king of one kind meeting king of another kind. No, it is not quite that way. There is a lot of blood, sweat, and thought behind the setting. Just because the king is a king he does not become worthy of meeting the sage. The king is worthy of meeting the sage because he knows and beats Maya every day in the shape of his enemies and adversaries. Do you understand this? Think of the courtiers, think of the palace intrigues, think of the army commander and two ministers plotting against the king, think of the king's own sons and two of his wives conspiring against the king—and the king still manages to remain the king. Why? Because he is sharp enough to see all this, see all this and beat all this. And therefore he deserves to go to the sage.

He is not someone the queens can easily tempt—and let's say he has three queens, five queens, as was the norm those days, and each of these women want supremacy, as every human being does. Don't we want to be the numero uno, all of us, each one of us that is? So, the queens are all vying to have the top position, and so are their sons, and so are the ministers, and so are the neighboring countries, and the king manages to keep all of them in check. Not only does he manage to keep all of them in check, he actually manages to keep them in positions that enable his system to run continuously and smoothly.

He knows Maya. When he sees trouble brewing, he manages it in a way that the trouble actually becomes something beneficial to him. The king has that kind of a mind. Two other kings send over a proposal to him. They say, "Let us enter into an alliance and wage a war against that fourth one," and that fourth one happens to be a bigger king. But our king, the one in question, is discreet enough to reject such offers. He won't be easily tempted; he knows Maya. And if he is easily tempted, he will not be king for long. Now he can go to the sage.

That does not mean that you really have to be a king to go to the sage; it merely means that if you are foolish even in everyday matters of the world, what kind of spirituality can you learn? If any Tom-Dick-Harry manages to come to you and fool you, what kind of a disciple are you?

That is one loud mark of the undeserving disciple: he would be fooled very easily by the world.

Now, ask yourself, do you deserve to be a disciple? You interact with the world and the world fools you at every step. You can't properly talk to the world. You get convinced where you should not, and you fail to convince the world where you should. You abandon your duty and you accept as your duty something very trivial. Your real duty you know not, and when the world calls you with some kind of a duplicate duty, you respond with a sense of morality and say yes. Sometimes you are threatened, sometimes you are tempted, sometimes you just feel attracted, and sometimes you stay attached. If this is your position with respect to the world, how will you manage to even go to a sage, let alone stay with him? You need not be sly, we said that, but at least be smart.

When this fellow who still does not know the world, if he perchance goes to the sage, he is not able to value the sage much. Because what is it that he values? The world. It is just that his interactions with the world have not been beneficial to him of late. So, just as another thing to be tried, he has visited the sage. He has not gone to the sage; he has just visited the sage as some kind of a tourist. But the prime position in his mind still belongs to the world. So, he may stay with the sage for a while, but when the world calls him back, he will quickly hop over, very quickly hop over. And he is not a winner, you know.

When you have won over the world, then you have some kind of contempt for the world. Then you say, "Even if that thing is calling to me, why should I even respond? It is a small thing that is calling, it can wait." But for most people who turn spiritual the world is not a small thing. The world is a thing large enough to defeat them, and that defeat has pushed them to the sage.

Most people who go to spirituality are the ones defeated by the world. And if you are defeated by the world, the world is still something big for you. And if the world is something big for you, then would you be able to resist the invitation of the world when that big thing calls? No, the moment the big thing calls, you are gone because the very reason you came to spirituality was that the world had badly defeated you.

So, ask yourself, are you able to penetrate into the insides of the world? How penetrative are you? How insightful are you? Do you really manage to know the world? How does the world run all over you daily, like trucks run over dogs on these highways? What is left behind is a mauled self—only to rise again the next day and be mauled again.

It is a rare combination: to not be fooled by the world, and also to not be fooled by yourself; to have the sureness that you are powerful enough to defeat the world, and equally have the humility that you are not powerful enough to defeat your inner self, the ego.

And then, the question. You see, if a man still grappling with worldly issues goes to a sage, what kind of a question would he offer? A worldly question. "You know, my wives quarrel with each other. What do I do? One of my sons is hatching a plot against me. Should I just hang him? Which minister to promote? Who should be the next chief of the army? There is discontent in the public. How should I handle it?" So, you can know whether somebody is fit to approach a sage—just look at his questions. What does he want to know?

And here is Śaunaka, and what is Śaunaka saying? "What is the one thing knowing which everything else is known?" Look at this question. He is not asking about food or shelter or kingdom or money or wars or sons and daughters and queens and ministers. All those things he can handle on his own.

That is the kind of person needed. Not the kind of person who cannot manage his own trousers and goes to the sage and asks, "What do I do? I have two quarters of trousers, I want to make it three and a half. What do I do? Oh, great sage, please, show some magic so that my shorts grow long!"

Look at this question. These are the heights of the Upanishads. No gossip, no trivia, no nonsense. Shooting straight at the stars, aiming directly at the sky:

"Lord, by knowing what does all this that is become known?"

"By knowing what does all become known?" Does one need to ask a followup question? Does anything remain to be asked after this? That is what I mean when I say you must be smart. You are given one opportunity; you must know what to ask. And he has asked everything. Aṅgiras would have smiled; he would have smiled in approval, "Yes, the right one."

Just let the question stay within; let the beauty of the question and the deftness of the questioner stay with you. In fact, the questioner is saying, "Tell me everything. Tell me the one thing that tells of everything." One liner. Shortest than the best shorts.

And we thought being brief is a thing of this age. No, if you want to know what brevity is, go to the Upanishads. Or go to the *Brahm Sutras*. They will tell you what it means to be short.

In one word, tell us everything. In one word, can you capture everything? Alright.

AUM.

Done. Finished. Full stop. You need to know nothing more. Stop. No unending narratives, no fairy tales, no this and that. You cannot get more succinct than this.

And now the sage is happy to answer.

---

"If you don't know Maya, that gives you no protection from her; that only gives you a certain righteousness. With a sense of uprightness you manage to claim to others that you are not one of her victims or stooges, but that doesn't save you. You may not have consciously embraced her, but subconsciously you have fallen for her because you do not know her."

---

*Course in Realization, BodhSthal, 2021*

# 31

# Two Ways to Quieten the Mind

*Just as Prakriti allures you, your nature too beckons you. When Prakriti allures you, it is called Maya. When your nature allures you, what you get is Krishna.*

**असंशयं महाबाहो मनो दुर्निग्रहं चलम् ।**
**अभ्यासेन तु कौन्तेय वैराग्येण च गृह्यते ॥**

The Blessed Lord said: O mighty armed one, undoubtedly the mind is intractable and restless, but O son of Kunti, it is brought under control through practice and detachment.

~ The Bhagavad Gita, Verse 6.35

**Listener:** What is meant by bringing the mind under control? Also, please explain how practice and detachment help in achieving the above.

**Acharya Prashant:** In the very same chapter, Shri Krishna has very lucidly explained what mind control is. Mind control is not about suppressing the mind. It is about supporting the mind to take the right route and reach the right destination.

The word 'control' does not have very friendly vibes or connotations. One controls a disease. One controls something that must not be there. The mind does not really need control; the authority in the Gita makes it amply clear. The mind needs to be brought to Atma. That is the central message of chapter six: bring the mind to Atma.

What is Atma? Atma is the highest potential of the mind; Atma is the destination of the mind. It is for the Atma that the mind exists, and it is due to the Atma that the mind exists. Therefore, the Atma is the beginning and the end of mind. Therefore, the Atma is the point from where the mind emerges and the point into which the mind submerges. That is what mind control is.

The mind really wants peace. Peace is Atma. But the mind is a little foolish. Why do I say so? Had the mind not been foolish, why would it have left its Atma state and become the mind? Does the mind not have the choice to exist in the Atma state, which is the topmost state, which is the peaceful state, which is the natural state, all the time? And when you exist in a state all the time, then there is no time; then there is timelessness.

Time is only when time is bounded, right? Time is a concept that demands boundaries. Something has to begin at a certain time and something has to end at a certain time. Where there is a beginning and an end, there is time.

The mind does have the option to always remain in its top potential, at its maxima. And anything that is always is timeless, beyond the scope of birth and death, rise and fall, coming and going. But the mind didn't take that option. What has the mind chosen to do? The mind has chosen to be itself. The mind has chosen to be the mind. Therefore, I am calling the mind a little foolish.

Even though this foolish mind always has the option to go for the top state, the natural state, the peaceful state, the restful state, it being what it is, it takes other options. It wants peace, but will not directly take peace; it will want peace through this and that. It wants rest, but won't directly take rest. It wants security, but won't directly settle into security.

That's the prakriti of mind. The prakriti of mind is not in alignment with the nature of the mind. The prakriti of mind is to go about in cycles. All Prakriti (physical nature) is cyclical—like sea waves. Aren't sea waves cyclical? Like birth and death, like day and night, everything in Prakriti is cyclical. That's the prakriti of mind.

But nature is not cyclical. Nature is submergence, a final settlement, a closure, a peacefulness; no more running around. In Prakriti, there is always movement, a lot of running around.

So, the mind is sandwiched between these two: its prakriti and its nature.

Nature says, "Settle down." Prakriti says, "Run around."

Nature says, "Be simple." Prakriti says, "No, no, no! If you are simple, you will be killed!"

Mind is always in this conflict. What helps the mind in this phase of conflict? Its very nature. Just as Prakriti allures you, your nature too beckons you.

*When Prakriti allures you, it is called Maya. When your nature allures you, what you get is Krishna.*

So, the two sides of the mind, rather the two forces of the mind, both work on the mind in their own ways. Prakriti works on the mind by appearing very convincingly, very enchantingly, very compellingly, very colorfully as Maya. Does that not happen? You open your eyes and all that you see around you is Prakriti—whether Prakriti of the existential kind, which Shri Krishna calls as Apara-Prakriti, or whether Prakriti of the man-made kind, which Shri Krishna calls as Para-Prakriti.

So, through your senses, through your brain, Prakriti always keeps luring you; you could even say trapping you. 'Trap' is not a very suitable word, because Prakriti by itself is not conscious. It only does what its own constitution, what its own predestined dynamics command it to do. Remember that it is called Prakriti. Prakriti means that which comes before any other kind of existence. It is at the root of all existence.

So, there is the mind, the mind of the man. On one hand, this mind, this man is being enticed by Prakriti, Maya. On the other hand, there is someone like Shri Krishna. Now, someone like Shri Krishna does not belong to the usual scheme of Prakriti; therefore, he is called an avatar. That's the difference between an avatar and an animal, an avatar and a normal human being, an avatar and anything else. Everything else on the earth, everything else in the universe belongs to the usual scheme of Prakriti. They are meant to be there. They are like the waves of the sea. If the sea is there, the waves will be there. Nothing unusual, nothing surprising.

So, a man is born, a woman is born; there is the child, there is the animal; there is the rock, there are stars, there is stardust. All this is just run-of-the-mill Prakriti. Nothing astonishing in it. But a Shri Krishna is not called Prakriti; he is an avatar. He is an avatar because he is appearing to the mind, to the man not as Maya but as the dispeller of Maya. Any ordinary man, any ordinary woman would come in contact with you, and that contact will be the contact of Maya, rest assured. But when a Shri Krishna comes in contact with you, something extremely unusual happens. It is not that now Maya will take you further in its fold; rather that contact with Shri Krishna will come to liberate you from Maya.

Therefore, I am saying, even your nature works upon you. It is almost as if your nature, your destination is very interested in you coming to the destination.

The Upanishads say the one who takes a few steps in the direction of Truth finds that the Truth has taken multiple steps to reach him. That will tell you of a crucial difference between Maya and Truth.

The more you move towards Maya, the more distant it seems. Keep running after her all your life. She's unattainable. Charming, but unattainable.

Truth—you move towards Truth, and you find that the Truth is assisting your movement. You grow a little in wisdom, and you will find that the very beginning of your movement towards the Truth was due to the blessings of the Truth, not due to your own internal inspiration.

You go to a bookstore, you pick up a particular book—what do you think? If the book is the *Bhagavad Gita*, it is not you who has picked up the book; it is the book that has picked you up. On the other hand, if you go to the bookstore and pick some usual nonsense, then it is again not you who has picked up the book; the book has picked you up.

Both are working on you. Who will win? The one you fall in love with. So, be very, very alert about the quality of your love. Who is it that you have fallen in love with? There are only two, and both of these are present to be chosen. Always. Which of these are you falling in love with? That's your fate.

*What does it, then, mean to bring the mind under control? Fall in love with the right one. That is what bringing the mind under control means.*

There is no need to probe too much into a man's life. Just ask him, "Show me the picture of your beloved," and that's all. You have known the man, and you have known the man's fate. Whose photo are you carrying in that wallet held to your chest?

That's what is meant by mind control. Therefore, mind control is not about suppressing the mind or killing the mind or taming the mind. It's about giving the mind the one and only befitting lover.

What is the normal tendency of the mind? Remember that it is foolish. Do not consciously give the mind what it needs to have, and the mind will, for certain, in its own primitive unconsciousness, choose the wrong one. Therefore, you cannot leave things to chance. If you are not making the right decision with total determination, the wrong decision is the default. You don't have to *make* the wrong decision. That's man's problem. Do you see this? Do you now see why mankind is usually in turmoil and suffering? Because the right decision has to be made with determination and discipline, and the wrong decision is the default.

Now, what would occur more frequently, determination and discipline, or default? The default is obviously more common.

*Man's default state is of foolishness. Liberation comes through determination. Liberation is not your default destiny.*

Don't leave things as they are. Don't say that you go with the flow. Don't say that life will take care of things or that experience will correct things on its own. No, life will not at all take care of things. No, age and experience will not make corrections in you by themselves. You require a steely resolve. Otherwise, you can live for forty thousand years—nothing will change.

Your default state is foolishness. We are all born like that; what to do? Nobody's fault. We are born like that; our physical configuration is of foolishness. All wisdom, all spiritual practice, therefore, is about going against oneself. Don't go against yourself, and your course is well-set, your life is pre-scripted.

Don't believe in the natural ones. There are many naturals, no? They say, "No, we have had no wisdom education, but we understand things on our own." No, sir. On your own you only have your own foolishness. That's what you have on your own.

Any kind of ascension, any kind of wisdom or liberation will require concerted effort. Want to know the real status of a person? Interested in knowing his stature in life? Just ask him how much has he invested in his self-development, inner development. How many years has he given? How much of his resources has he put into his own liberation? If he says, "No, I have never put time nor effort into liberation," and still claims that he has understanding or wisdom, then he is just bragging. Don't take him seriously.

Wisdom and all higher order things in life will never come on their own. What is it that you experience on your own? You only experience hunger, sleep, lust. The moment you turn thirteen or fourteen, lust arises on its own. That's what you experience without any effort or discipline. You don't require to be disciplined or determined for your pubic hair to grow or your menstruation to start. Stuff just flows on its own. So, don't say that wisdom too will start flowing in your mind on its own. That won't happen. You are not recognizing the nature of things when you make such claims.

This is the most ignored aspect of human life, especially in the contemporary world. We want to acquire all kinds of skills. We would enroll into a three-month course to learn a new language, a new technology, a new skill. But wisdom, we suppose, will come on its own. Never sir, never! It won't come on its own.

I know this admission, this assertion from my side hurts the ego badly. We hate to hear that we are foolish by default. But then, that's what we are. Why and how should I hide it? It is so glaringly obvious.

---

"Even though this foolish mind always has the option to go for the top state, the natural state, the peaceful state, the restful state, it being what it is, it takes other options. It wants peace, but will not directly take peace; it will want peace through this and that. It wants rest, but won't directly take rest. It wants security, but won't directly settle into security."

---

*Course in Realization, BodhSthal, 2020*

# 32

# Resolve for Riches Is Bondage

*Ask yourself: Do your resources exist for you, or do you exist for your resources? Good, simple, fun, but creepily unsettling question to ask. Do they exist for you? Do you exist for them? Are you the owner of your house or the guard of your house? Are you inside your shirt, or is your shirt all over you?*

**अणिमाद्यष्टैश्व-र्याशासिद्धसङ्कल्पो बन्धः ।**

Bondage is the imagination prompted by the desire for the eight powers, anima, etc.

~ Niralamba Upanishad, Verse 21

**Acharya Prashant:** "Bondage is the imagination prompted by the desire for the eight powers, anima, etc."

The various aiśvaryas have been loosely translated here as 'powers'. Aiśvarya is not really power; aiśvarya is richness. I will read out their names: Anima, Mahima, Garima, Laghima, Prapti, Prakamya, Ishitva, Vashitva. The verse says, the desire or resolve to obtain these richnesses or glories, even that is bondage.

The full cannot attain anything, physical or mental. The limitless cannot add to itself anymore. Only the one with boundaries can aspire to attain. When there are boundaries, there is scope for addition. When there is a limit, when there is finiteness, there is a possibility of enhancement or increment. What can you add to infinity? What will infinity further grow into? There is no possibility.

This verse talks of mental attainments—honor, glory, fulfilment of desire—and says even the desire or resolve to have these things is bondage. Why is it a bondage? For the very same reason that physical attainment or the desire for physical attainment is a bondage. You are starting off from a point of incompletion. You are adding layers and layers to your core of incompletion, right? How do you think that the addition or superimposition of these layers can change the very core? It can hide the core, not change it.

You can take a stone, and you can put layer upon layer of gold and silver and tungsten and platinum on it. Ultimately, the piles and layers can combine and show up as a great mass of precious and glittering metal. The mass has increased, the glitter has increased. Has the core changed? What is it that lies still at the core? The stone. And why did the stone attempt to put on these layers in the first place? Because of its stoneness. The stone's success in managing to cover itself up with layers of precious stuff does not rid it of its stoneness; rather, it reaffirms its stoneness.

*When you are feeling little or incomplete or hollow, then any attempt to cover up that hollowness just reinforces the power of that hollowness.*

In such cases, what must be the direction of the right action?

Usually, the direction of action is external. Remaining as we are, we want to obtain, attain, put on things that will make us appear different from others and to ourselves. No, the right direction of action must be internal. If I am not alright with my stoneness or ugliness or worthlessness, then what do I work on? My stoneness, my worthlessness. No amount of fancy stuff that I conceal my reality with will succeed in changing my reality to myself. The world might be deceived for a while because the world looks at you from the outside. And outside, what is it the world might see? Gold and silver and such things. You might manage in fooling the world. But where do you look at yourself from? From the inside.

And if it is the stone looking at gold, will the stone change into gold? Even if you have gathered a lot of gold, who is the one looking at gold? The stone. How could the gold change the stone? In fact, the more the stone looks at gold, the more it develops in inferiority, and the more it gets servile towards the gold. "I am stone, I am looking at gold. Will I allow the gold to be lost? I will remain so insecure. Gold obtained now has to be protected, because who am I? I remain the stone. What is it that gives value and worth to my existence? Gold. I will have to dedicate myself to the gold. The gold is not a resource that I have, the gold is not there to serve me; I am at the service of gold. The gold has to sit, and I have to work for gold." Because, honestly, you do know which of these two is more valuable, stone or gold. It is gold. If gold is more valuable, then obviously the stone has to work for gold. Why will gold work for the stone?

Now you know why people work for money and riches: because they know that money and riches are more precious than their own being.

So, it is a logical thing to do. The worthless one has to work for the stuff that is worthy. You know inside of yourself that you are a worthless being; therefore, you keep serving gold. Wherever you find gold, you bow down to it. Wherever you find gold, you want to add it to your life. Why? Because internally you are just a worthless piece of stone.

It would have been alright had all of this added up to something worthwhile. It doesn't add up to anything. If you have a little gold, then you are a servant to a little gold. If you somehow manage to accumulate a lot of gold, then you are a servant to a lot of gold. Which means, the more you accumulate, the bigger a servant you are. You are working hard to deepen your servility. You are working hard to fetch more masters to rule over you. How intelligent is that?

Ask yourself: Do your resources exist for you, or do you exist for your resources? Good, simple, fun, but creepily unsettling question to ask. Do they exist for you? Do you exist for them? Are you the owner of your house or the guard of your house? Are you inside your shirt, or is your shirt all over you? Technically, these two are the same questions. In reality, not at all. Are you inside that shirt, or is the shirt upon you?

You have all heard that story, right? Sufi story, Junaid and the cow.

So, Junaid is going somewhere with a few of his disciples. In front of Junaid is a man walking with a cow, and the man is holding the leash and the cow is behind him. So, Junaid says, "Wait, this is a moment to learn something."

He asks his disciples, "Who owns whom? Does the man own the cow? Does the man lead the cow? Or does the cow own and lead the man?"

The disciples say, "Sir, it is evident the man owns and leads the cow."

Junaid says, "Had the answer been so simple, why would I ask the question?" Then he says, "Fine. Are any of you carrying a knife or scissors?" He gets one. Insolent as fakirs are, he jumps to the man and cuts the cord. The leash has now been cut, and cows are expert at utilizing such moments: she just sprints away.

It is already quite comical—a sprinting cow. She sprints away and the man is running behind.

And Junaid asks his chaps, "Now, you tell me, who leads whom?"

The bondage of the cow was at least material. For the cow to be kept in bondage, a material leash was required. But the bondage of the man is so subtle: the cow is leading the man with nothing to leash the man with except the man's own mind, self, ego.

That's the question you must ask: "Do I own my things, or do my things own me? What am I without these things? Who is on leash?"

In some sense, spirituality is all about unleashing yourself, which is freedom from bondage. The leash is the bondage.

---

"The full cannot attain anything, physical or mental. The limitless cannot add to itself anymore. Only the one with boundaries can aspire to attain. When there are boundaries, there is scope for addition."

---

*Course in Realization, BodhSthal, 2020*

# 33

# The Desire to Be Close Is Bondage

*Most of our relationships are bondages because they do not exist from the reason of our fullness. They exist because of our incompleteness.*

देवमनुष्याद्युपासना -कामसङ्कल्पो बन्धः ।

Bondage is the resolve to be close to gods or human beings for the fulfilment of desires.

~ Niralamba Upanishad, Verse 22

**Acharya Prashant:** Upāsanā means sitting close, being close. Āsana means position, your position, the place where you are. It is related to asti. 'Asti' means existence; 'upa' means close, so being close is upāsanā, upa-asanā.

Usually, in the name of worship, we make the worshipped one even more distant. That is a distortion of the spirit of upāsanā.

When you are worshipping someone, do you get close to them or do you turn them even more distant? Real upāsanā is intimacy. Up-āsanā, being close.

So, resolving to gain closeness to gods or human beings for the sake of desire fulfilment is bondage. Amply clear, is it not?

"If I can be close to that influential person, my desires will be fulfilled."

When the word 'deva' is used here, obviously that does not pertain to godliness. 'Gods' here pertain to any entity with richness, power, influence. And that's what most people want, right? Don't you want to be very well-networked? Don't you want to be well-connected? Don't you want to hobnob with the who's-who in the elite circles? So, that is bondage.

How is that bondage? In the same way that the tendency to accumulate stuff is bondage. You want to be with someone in the wish that this closeness will grant you some inner completeness or joy. But you are going to that person with the clear belief that you are worthless or of a limited worth, are you not? Had you not felt that you are worthless compared to that person, why would you have gone to him or her in the first place?

*So, most of our relationships are bondages because they do not exist from the reason of our fullness. They exist because of our incompleteness.*

Mostly when we form a relationship, it is coming neither from the realization that one is already full, nor is it coming from the intention to gain fullness. Both these are alright. If you relate to someone without any particular reason, without any particular purpose, without any particular motive, nothing is more wonderful than that. You are already full, and therefore you do not have a particular motive in connecting to the other. Why are you connecting to the other? Just for fun, no particular reason. What is the relationship all about? Nothing in particular, it just is. This is the best way to relate.

However, if you feel internally incomplete, then too there is a great way to relate, which is, "I relate not to hide my incompleteness but to treat my incompleteness." Even this is alright.

What was the best way? "I am already alright and I am relating with no motive, no intention." The next best is, "I know I am not alright, I feel I am not alright, therefore I relate with the intention to be alright." Even this is alright.

But mostly we relate in a third way. What is the third way? "I am not alright, and I relate with the other to hide my incompleteness, sickness, disease, hollowness, all that."

That is what the Upanishad is referring to here. Trying to gain closeness with people of high attainments hoping that the association would grant you your desires is bondage. This happens in our social relationships, this happens in our families, our friend circles. Unfortunately, this happens also in our most intimate relationships, our so-called love affairs. You do not go to the other to heal yourself or to heal the other, right? The intention is neither to heal yourself nor is it to heal the other. The intention is to use the other to forget your problems and sicknesses for a while.

Remember, the intention is not to heal your sickness; the intention is to hide or conceal or forget your sickness for a while.

"Trying to gain closeness with people of high attainments hoping that the association would grant you your desires is bondage. This happens in our social relationships, this happens in our families, our friend circles. The intention is neither to heal yourself nor is it to heal the other. The intention is to use the other to forget your problems and sicknesses for a while."

*Course in Realization, BodhSthal, 2020*

# 34

# Your Liberation Depends on You, Just as Your Bondages Do

*Maya is only as powerful as you want it to be. You are not being puppeted by Maya; Maya depends totally on you for her sustenance. If you ever find her dominating you, you must know that this is what you wanted.*

निर्वासनं हरिं दृष्ट्वा तूष्णीं विषयदन्तिनः ।
पलायन्ते न शक्तास्ते सेवन्ते कृतचाटवः ॥

Seeing the desireless lion, the elephants of the senses silently run away, and if that is impossible, serve him like courtiers.

~ Ashtavakra Gita, Verse 18.46

**Listener:** Sir, I feel distracted, and these distractions are not always pleasurable. What is it that makes it impossible for the elephants of the senses to run away?

**Acharya Prashant:** These two are in relation to each other, the lion and the elephant. They really do not have any objective strength. Their respective strengths are decided by their seer, by their experiencer. It is the experiencer who breathes life into them; it is the experiencer who, one could say, conjures them up. Otherwise, they don't really exist.

Whenever these two are being talked of—take this as a sutra (rule)—neither of the two really exists because the two would always be in relation to each other. This is the classical dualistic paradigm.

If you favor the lion, the lion is a lion. If you do not favor the lion, the lion is a squeaking puppy. Your proximity to the lion renders it its 'lion-ness'. Your proximity to the elephant gives the elephant its magnitude and power. You tilt towards the lion, you abandon the elephant, and the elephant would be reduced to a mere calf or a deer. What resilience would it then have in front of a roaring lion?

If you find that the elephants of the senses are really too big upon you—they are trampling your resistance under their feet—then just see who is riding those elephants. It is you who is the mahout, the trainer, the controller, the rider.

Do you remember the Trojan horse? It looked so big, but was its power rendered to it by its bigness? The deadliness of the Trojan horse did not come from its size but from the ones who were inside it. Similarly, the deadliness of the sense-elephant does not come from its size but from the one who is at its center, in its interior. And in the interior of both the elephant and the lion it is you who sit. Who is the lion? You choosing to be a lion. Who is the elephant? You deserting the lion and favoring the elephant. These are not two distinct entities.

We talked about the dualistic paradigm. The two poles of duality, are they ever distinct? No. They are just the two faces of Maya, and Maya emanates from the Truth. You go this side, this side becomes powerful; you go that side, that side becomes powerful.

It is like a seesaw. Even the kids know the secret. You sit at one end of the seesaw and then you wonder, "Why the hell is this end so heavy? Why the hell is this end dominating the other one? Why is this end gravitating? Why is the other one levitating?" Does the answer lie outside of your intention? It is your intention that is determining the shape of the seesaw. It is your intention that is determining the geometry and the winner. You sit on this side, and the other side would be hanging in the sky helplessly.

Just get up, but get up carefully. If you are not careful, it would hurt your butt. Get up carefully and go to the other side, and the entire scenario would change, in fact, reverse. The one who appeared so confident in his weight and victory would now be hanging listlessly in space, and his erstwhile position would have been usurped by the one who looked equally helpless just a moment back. You are the king; you are the decision-maker.

In mathematical terms you could say, $L + E = K$ or $L \times E = K$, where 'K' is a constant, 'L' is the strength of the lion, and 'E' is the strength of the elephant. Forget 'K' because we are talking of something that is constant; why not call it 'I'? $L + E = I$. 'L' and 'E' represent the respective strengths of the lion and the elephant, and 'I' is a constant.

So, where does the strength of the lion come from? No, it does not really come from the 'I'; it comes from the reduced strength of the elephant. 'I' is the decision-maker; 'I' can decide to invest itself fully in the lion. Then what happens to the elephant? It gets totally enfeebled. The elephant is now starved; it is now merely hollow bones and loose skin. Or the 'I' can invest itself fully in the elephant, or the 'I' may decide to split itself 50-50. Then there would be a war raging between the lion and the elephant, and you would say, "Oh my God! Maya is as powerful as the Truth!"

*No, Maya is only as powerful as you want it to be. You are not being puppeted by Maya; Maya depends totally on you for her sustenance. If you ever find her dominating you, you must know that this is what you wanted.*

Never forget your essential reality beyond your immediate fact. You are really all-powerful, though that is not testified by the way you live, eat, breathe, act, decide, think.

We live lives of helpless compulsiveness. Looking at the way we exist, it becomes impossible to believe that we are omnipotent. But that indeed is our essential reality, which means we really can never be puppets; which means whatever is happening to us is with our due consent. Unless you acknowledge this, there can be no remembrance of your True Self.

*If you will remain insistent that you are struggling, defeated, limited, forced, then your belief will become your false destiny.*

Spirituality consists of no instrument for your welfare other than your own realization. Does spirituality involve the use of muscles or machines? Even the use of intellect is useful only till a point in the spiritual process. Finally, the only instrument that helps and works is your acknowledgment, your own power.

The fellow is sitting in the car in the driver's seat having pulled the handbrake with the maximum power that he has, and he is begging all and sundry to push the car from behind. So, one fellow comes and he is asked, "Sir, who are you?"

He says, "My name is Yoga."

"Sir, my car is stuck. Can you push it a little?" So, Yoga goes and starts trying.

A lady arrives. She appears quite devoted—beautiful and athletic. "Ma'am, who are you?"

"I am Bhakti."

"Can you assist a little? Just lend a hand."

A wrestler comes over, having built himself through sustained action over maybe many decades. All muscles—100 kg, 6'5". "What's your name, sir?"

"I am Karma."

"Sir, you are most well-placed to help me out. Kindly push this car."

Then a somber-looking meditative fellow comes over. "What's your name?"

"I'm Jñāna Prasad."

"Prasad sir, can you join the other three?"

One fellow comes madly dancing. "What's your name?"

"I am Tantra Singh."

"Sir, can you just put your clothes together for a while and help those gentle souls in the behind? Remember, you have to push the car." He too joins them.

All this while, our man in the driver's seat is doing just one thing—what? Ensuring that the handbrake remains firm and tight.

Spirituality, therefore, is about addressing your intention. At least that's how I have always looked at spirituality. Bhakti, Karma, Jñāna, Yoga, Tantra, Mantra, Japa—who will help you when you are in the driver's seat? When the handbrake is in your hand, who will help you? Do you want to be helped? They all may together keep pushing but the vehicle won't move an inch. Not only that, if one of them starts to succeed, you may get anxious and angry and decide to run the vehicle in reverse gear. You will find all four-five of them running helter-skelter. They were pushing you forward, and you actually decided to run in the reverse.

Who can help you? Who can save you? Who can push you? You are the driver. You are the master. You hold the gear. You hold the break. You hold the key. You *are* the key. Bhakti is of great help, so is Jñāna, so is Karma—provided you really want to be helped.

What is 'lion-ness', then? 'Lion-ness' is your decision to be helped.

What is 'elephantness', then? 'Elephantness' is your decision to stay as you are.

---

"Who can help you? Who can save you? Who can push you? You are the driver. You are the master. You hold the gear. You hold the break. You hold the key. You *are* the key."

---

# 35

# Two Birds, Beautiful of Wing

*When will you make the right choice? Only you know it. No method can dictate your choice. Your own sovereign will is the chooser. One can only be pleaded to. The rest is your decision.*

द्वा सुपर्णा सयुजा सखाया समानं वृक्षं परिषस्वजाते ।
तयोरन्यः पिप्पलं स्वाद्वत्त्यनश्नन्न्यो अभिचाकशीति ॥
समाने वृक्षे पुरुषो निमग्नोऽनिशया शोचति मुह्यमानः ।
जुष्टं यदा पश्यत्यन्यमीशमस्य महिमानमिति वीतशोकः ॥

Two birds, beautiful of wing, close companions, cling to one common tree: of the two one eats the sweet fruit of the tree, the other eats not but watches his fellow.

The soul is the bird that sits immersed on the one common tree; but because he is not lord he is bewildered and has sorrow. But when he sees that other who is the Lord and beloved, he knows that all is His greatness and his sorrow passes away from him.

~ Mundaka Upanishad, Verse 3.1.1- 3.1.2

**Acharya Prashant:** Two birds, both of beautiful feather, sit next to each other, and both are related to each other. Out of these two, one bird eats the fruits of the tree. These two birds have been the subject of great deliberation. Who are these two? They are close companions, they carry the same name. What is the name that they carry? 'I'.

So, there are two 'I's. These two birds represent those two 'I's. They carry the same name, they belong to the same family, yet there is a great difference. There is one 'I' that is lost in the world, absorbed in the world, and is busy consuming in the world; the fruit is sweet to this bird. And then there is another 'I' that has no inclination towards consumption; it just watches.

When you talk of the birds, the consumption is physiological. When you talk of 'I', the consumption is psychological. The 'I' consumes the world to have an identity. It cannot exist without an identity, right?

The incomplete 'I', the first bird, keeps nibbling at the world because it is forever hungry. And then there is another 'I' that is psychologically complete. Physiologically, even this bird might need to poke at the fruits—only physiologically. Psychologically, this bird is complete. Psychologically, there is an 'I' that is totally complete and does not need the world for its sustenance. Therefore, it would neither get attached to the world nor would it destroy the world.

The analogy of the two birds in *Mundaka Upanishad* is extremely beautiful, very deep and meaningful, and very popular as well. People read this, and as much as they are baffled by this, they still enjoy this because there is something in this metaphor that appeals very intuitively to us. Even if we do not know the two 'I's, we still sense that something very important is being spoken of.

"The soul is the bird that sits immersed on the one common tree"—immersed in the sense that he is absorbed in the world, attached to the world. "But because he is not complete"—the word here used is 'aniśa' meaning 'not iśa'.

"But because this soul is not complete"—what is referred to as the soul in English here is the Puruṣa in the verse, 'nimagna puruṣa', and that has been very loosely translated as the 'immersed soul'.

"Because he is not lord he is bewildered and has sorrow. But when he sees that other who is the Lord and beloved, he knows that all is His greatness and his sorrow passes away from him."

So, the bird that is busy consuming the world is the Puruṣa, Puruṣa bewitched by Prakriti, Puruṣa captivated by Prakriti. The fruit, the tree, the branches, the entire scenario, the whole jungle in the setting, what do they collectively represent? Prakriti. And in the middle of this Prakriti sits the Puruṣa bird—and this Puruṣa can also be called as aham (I am)—and this Puruṣa has been totally enamored by Prakriti. And he is going towards Prakriti this way, that way, and so on. And in his bewilderment, he suffers, says the verse.

And how does he lose his suffering? It is beautiful, very instructive here. It says: By looking at the one who does not tend to consume. By looking at the one who is complete, and therefore lovable, and therefore the Lord. Looking at that one, this bewildered one, enchanted one, realizes greatness—the greatness of the other one and his own potential greatness—and therefore gains freedom from suffering.

Now, it is quite instructive. You see, we often say that the Lord must look at us. "Oh Lord, why are you looking the other way? Why don't you look at me and relieve me of my sufferings?"

But the verse says, you get freedom from your sufferings when *you* look at the Lord.

The Lord is sitting beside you. The Lord is always watching you; the Lord is the Sākṣī. The Lord is the 'I' you call as Atma. These two have the same name, right? 'I'. One is aham, one is Atma. The Lord is always looking at you because it is in the nature of the Lord to know. But when will *you* look at the Lord?

When you look at the Lord instead of looking so much at Prakriti, that is when you gain freedom from suffering. Beautiful.

So, these two birds are there. Take it as a picture board. One is busy consuming, enjoying the fruit; the other one is just watching. But the first one, irrespective of how much fruit he consumes, is still suffering and bewildered. And when does he lose his suffering? When he looks at the one who is not consuming at all. So, when you come to see that the satisfaction that you want to derive from the fruit is actually a pre-existing thing already available to the one who does not go after the fruit at all, that is when you lose the fruit and gain freedom.

So many lessons are contained here, including the importance of the right company. If you want to be liberated of your existing ways, then you will have to seek the company of someone whose ways are different. Looking at him will give you the strength and the trust to drop your ways. Otherwise, there is too much fruit around to let you really know the Truth. If one type of fruit disappoints you, there is another one to attract you, and then the next one, and then the next one.

*No fruit is ever going to reveal to you that all the fruits taken together can never give you what you really want. But the company of the right bird can deliver you liberation.*

The world is not to be used for existential contentment. The world can give you food, clothes, shelter, money, and pleasures of the body. All these things the world can give, to a limited extent the world is obviously useful. But the world cannot give you yourself; the world cannot give you an identity. If the world is giving you your identity, then you don't exist, right? You are the world then. Where is your independence? Where is your independent existence?

So, being independent of the world, look at the world. Even if at the bodily level there has to be consumption, you consume the world as an entity independent of the world. That is the import of these two beautiful verses.

**Listener (L):** So, the bird that is consuming the fruit, the hungry 'I', will leave its ways when it sees the witnessing bird. How does the bird come to a point where it looks at the other bird?

**AP:** No, there is no method to it really. We cannot make this into an order or a system. When will the first bird look at the other bird? We do not know. What is the process, what is the method? We do not know. How to make the first bird look at the witnessing bird? We do not know. Of that we have no idea. But what we know is, when the first bird will look at the Lord bird, the witnessing bird, then a great change will happen; that much we know. Now, how to make it happen? We do not know.

People keep speculating. Somebody says that when the first bird would get diarrhea from eating so much fruit, he would look at the second bird. Somebody says when the first bird would be tired of eating a lot, he would look at the second bird. Somebody else says when the first bird would have his stomach totally full and bloated, he would look at the second bird. We do not know. All these are just theories.

What we know is, if the first bird is hungry for liberation from his gnawing frustration, then he will *have* to look at the second bird. And the second bird is very easily available to be looked at, not far away. You just have to attend to the right one. There is the fruit, and there is the bird in your neighborhood. It is as easy to look at the other bird as it is to look at the fruit.

You have to decide when you will stop looking at the fruit and turn your attention towards the witnessing bird. It is a matter of choice, not a matter of circumstance. What you are asking for is a template that defines the circumstances that makes the first bird look at the second. We do not know that. Why? Because it is the sovereign choice of the first bird. Only the first bird knows when it will look at the second bird.

That's how easy it is. All that you have to do is make a choice. You have to choose to look at the second bird. Looking at the second bird, sometimes you will say that the circumstances facilitated your looking, at other times you will say that the circumstances opposed, resisted. But the fact is, it is not a matter of circumstances; it is actually a matter of choice.

*When will you make a choice? When will you make the right choice? Only you know it. No method can dictate your choice. Your own sovereign will is the chooser. One can only be pleaded to. The rest is your decision.*

If it becomes a matter of a system or a formula, then it is like the overhead watertank overflowing. We know that after a particular volume of water, it starts overflowing. So, we can say that after the bird has eaten 2.2 kgs of food, it will start overflowing and will look at the adjacent bird. It is not that way, because then there is no space for your choice; then it is a very mechanical thing. We know when the tank will start overflowing, don't we? We know all the variables. We know the flow rate of water, we know the capacity of the tank, so we know when it will start overflowing. Now, there is no space for conscious choice in this. Life does not operate like that.

There are people who don't choose to look at the brother bird even after devouring the entire forest. They have consumed and burned down the entire forest—they still don't want to look at the beautiful bird sitting next to them; they don't want to. And there are those who consume only a little, and they know that this won't do. They start looking at the beloved Lord bird.

You decide.

**L:** Does this mean that the first bird who is hungry is incomplete, but this incompleteness is his choice? The bird is complete, but he chooses to be incomplete?

**AP:** Wonderful. Yes.

**L:** So, incompleteness can be removed by choosing completeness? Would it not, then, become just an idea?

**AP:** All kinds of incompletenesses are ideas. Completeness is not an idea. If completeness is an idea, it is another kind of incompleteness. If completeness is merely an idea, then it won't penetrate into your life; then you won't look at the other dimension, the other bird. Then you will just keep thinking of completeness.

When completeness is more than an idea, it becomes real action, pure action; then you drop the fruit and embrace the real one.

The two birds are one. They are not two birds. Do we see this?

You know, this is what I mean when I say that when you are a lover of Truth, when you are in the Truth, the entire world becomes just the Truth to you. Can you visualize the sage just standing close to this tree one early morning and looking at these two birds? And these are just two ordinary birds. They are chirping, twittering. One of them is busy eating fruit, the other is just silently watching. And these are just two birds. But the sage is so deeply rooted in Truth, so much in love with the Truth, that he looks at these two birds and he immediately realizes something of a very high order.

Now, these two birds have not really been planted by existence to teach the sage a lesson. Their occurrence on the tree that morning is just accidental; they happen to be there on the tree. There are so many birds on so many trees on so many mornings. But who looks at them and comes upon a great truth? Well, hardly anybody. But the sage does.

That is what starts happening to you when Truth is your first priority. Irrespective of the direction you are looking at, there is something to teach you a lesson, to take you to the Truth.

Can you visualize that sage? There is that tree, an ordinary neem tree. One of the birds is busy nibbling at the neem fruit, the other is just watching. And there is a subtle and beautiful smile dancing on the sage's face, and from that smile arises these two verses. Timeless!

The world is Brahm, is it not? But the birds are so ordinary! Still, the world is Brahm.

Depends on you.

Two ordinary birds will become the ambassadors of Truth, provided you love the Truth.

"If you want to be liberated of your existing ways, then you will have to seek the company of someone whose ways are different. Looking at him will give you the strength and the trust to drop your ways. Otherwise, there is too much fruit around to let you really know the Truth."

*Course in Realization, BodhSthal, 2021*

# PRASHANTADVAIT FOUNDATION

PrashantAdvait Foundation (PAF) is a non-profit socio-spiritual organization founded and led by Acharya Prashant. It was established with an objective to demolish falseness—both within the human being and in the society in general—and promote a scientific and spiritual attitude towards self and life.

## How does the Foundation operate?

The Foundation facilitates Acharya Prashant's discourses across various platforms and organizes spiritual retreats, online courses, lectures and conferences. Over the years, Acharya Prashant has spoken on more than fifty Vedantic scriptures. Beyond the Upanishads and Gitas, Acharya Prashant has spoken on saints, sages, and topics of timeless essence.

These discourses are recorded and turned into educational courses, so that they reach as many as possible in the most organized form.

**Where is the content available?**

**Mobile App:** Even as Acharya Prashant continues to generate his literature and commentaries at a prolific rate, the Foundation's role lies in collating, documenting, and publishing everything in a form that preserves the original nature of the works for the centuries ahead. In the most organized form, Acharya Prashant's courses and books have been stored for public use on the Foundation's official mobile app. This app has been created as a timeless source of pure knowledge for all those who will ever seek the Truth.

**Website:** Acharya Prashant's courses and books are also available at the Foundation's website: www.solutions.acharyaprashant.org

**Social Media:** Acharya Prashant's channels on YouTube, Facebook, Instagram, Twitter, etc. all carry huge volumes of educational content for all, and are managed by the Foundation.

## Sections most benefitted by the Foundation's work:

**Non-human life forms** including animals and plants: Given that the overwhelmingly biggest threat to flora and fauna of all kind comes from the ignorance of man about his own body and self, reforming man's mind is the best way to save nature. It is estimated that millions of animals especially animals used for food—chicken, goat, sheep, cows, buffaloes, fish have been saved due to Acharya Prashant's work. Besides, a large number of wild animals too have been saved. With his efforts over the years, it is estimated that lakhs, if not millions of people have adopted vegetarianism or veganism and have chosen an awakened lifestyle involving environmental consciousness and a low carbon footprint. Many see him as the spiritual face of the vegan movement.

**Youth**: Youth, especially in India, face multi-directional challenges because of conditioning acquired from family, society, education, media, career challenges, dilemmas about physicality, love and relationships and deep existential questions about the meaning and purpose of life. They are in a delicate situation where the chances of making suboptimal decisions and life taking unhealthy turns are quite high. Acharya Prashant has been unique in addressing the energy and conflicts of the youth. There are so may who remain indebted to him for having received lifesaving clarity at critical junctures of decision- making.

**Women**: Women throughout the world, and especially in India, continue to be recognized as the largely disempowered half of mankind. While there have been concerted efforts in social, political, economic ways to instil women with due agency and power, nothing is really effective without the inner dimension of clarity and freedom. Acharya Prashant's work has been to awaken women to their true identity beyond the compulsions of the body and the conditioning of the mind. Countless women today—from the teenage schoolgirl to the septuagenarian homemaker—owe their sense of liberty, clarity, and the courage to rise against external oppression and internal debilitation, to the teachings of the master.

**Spiritual seekers**: There is a large class of spiritual seekers for whom spirituality is mere entertainment. Then there are those for whom spirituality is a respectable name for medieval superstition. There are also those who come to spirituality to escape the bare realities of life or those who suppose that spirituality consists of esoteric rituals, methods, and exercises or those who want only superficial treatments to life's deep underlying problems. Acharya Prashant has been well known to vigorously shake all such seekers out of their self-deceptive psychological stupor. And then there is the odd genuine seeker. The one who has already tried hard to go into the recesses of his mind, and the reality of life—the one who is prepared to work hard for his liberation. One who is fed up of self-imposed bondages, and is prepared to pay the price for freedom. Acharya Prashant comes as a rare and real friend to such seekers.

Over the years, more and more volunteers from various fields of life have joined the Foundation, working relentlessly to help spread Acharya Prashant's teachings. Today, the Foundation has touched and affected the lives of more than ten million individuals, and these numbers are only going to multiply in the coming times.

*To know more about the Foundation, visit acharyaprashant.org. Information about the Foundation's courses is available at solutions.acharyaprashant.org.*

*Contact the Foundation at requests@advait.org.in.*